THE OFFICIAL
Rent-A-Husband®
GUIDE
to a safe,
problem-free home

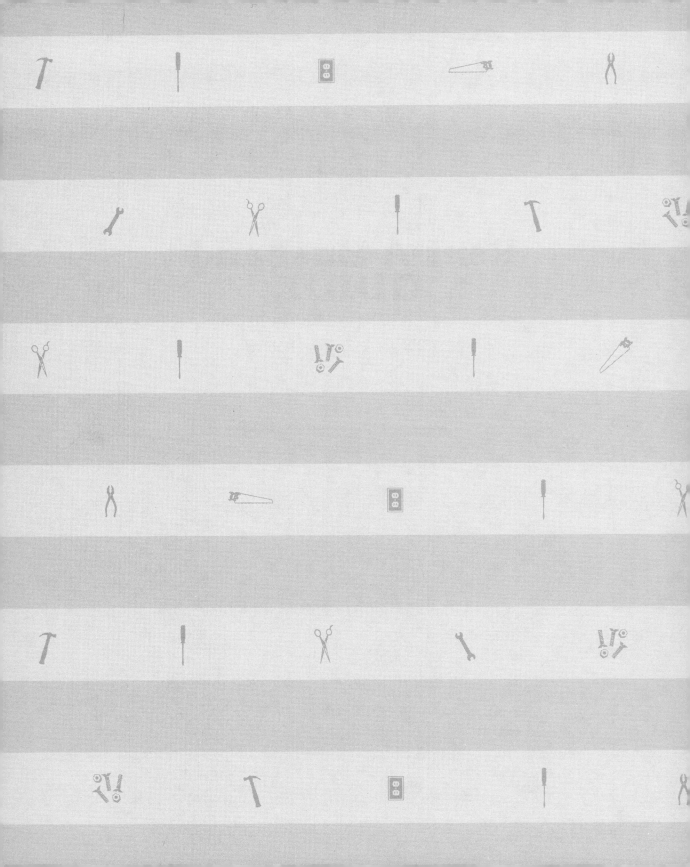

THE OFFICIAL

Rent-A-Husband® GUIDE

to a safe, problem-free home

Quick, Easy, and Effective Solutions
for Everything in Need of Repair or Improvement

Kaile R. Warren, Jr.,
and **Jane MacLean Craig**

BROADWAY BOOKS

New York

BROADWAY

Broadway Books may be purchased for business or promotional use or for special sales. For information, please write to: Special Markets Department, Random House, Inc., 1540 Broadway, New York, NY 10036.

BROADWAY BOOKS and its logo, a letter B bisected on the diagonal, are trademarks of Broadway Books, a division of Random House, Inc.

RENT-A-HUSBAND is a registered trademark of Rent-A-Husband®, LLC.

The intention of this book is to provide the reader with a general introduction to common household repair and maintenance projects. And while every effort has been made to ensure the accuracy of this information, success in executing these repairs does depend on such factors as correct interpretation of the directions, individual accuracy, and good judgment. The publisher and authors, therefore, disclaim all liability for any damage or injury related to the use of this book.

Remember that certain projects (particularly those involving some mechanical devices and electricity) do pose an element of potential risk. If you are unsure as to how to proceed in any area, always consult a licensed professional.

BOOK DESIGN BY LISA SLOANE

ILLUSTRATED BY MICHAEL GELLATELY

Library of Congress Cataloging-in-Publication Data
Warren, Kaile R., 1959–
The official Rent-A-Husband guide to a safe, problem-free home: quick, easy,
and effective solutions for everything in need of repair or improvement / Kaile R. Warren, Jr., and
Jane MacLean Craig.—1st ed.
p.   cm.
1. Dwellings—Maintenance and repair—Amateurs' manuals.
I. Craig, Jane MacLean, 1954–   II. Title.
TH4817.3 .W37 2001
643'.7—dc21   99-051303

ISBN 0-7679-0696-9

First Edition
01 02 03 04 05 10 9 8 7 6 5 4 3 2 1

*For my beloved, late parents, Shirley and Kaile Warren, Sr.,
who taught me everything I know about home repair, as well as
the importance of integrity in an industry not traditionally
known for it; and who, in so doing, laid the foundation on
which Rent-A-Husband, LLC, is built.*

—KRW

*For my amazing sons, T.J. and Mac, who fill me with
boundless pride and joy and forever light my way.
Thank you for being just the way you are.*

—JMC

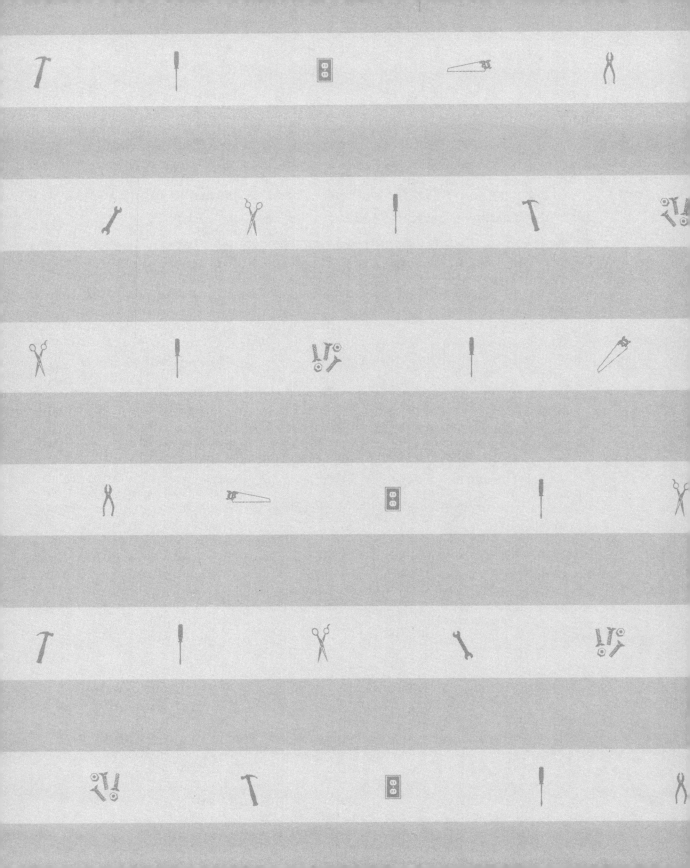

WE WOULD LIKE TO EXPRESS our sincerest appreciation to several individuals whose creative vision and unflagging support were so crucial in bringing this book to life: first and foremost, Broadway's extraordinary and brilliant editorial director, Gerry Howard, the true "godfather" of this project, who championed it from the start; the divine Judy Kern, who waved her purple editing pencil over the manuscript like a magic wand; Frances Jones, who so spectacularly assumed the reins; and Trish Medved, who wrapped it all up with such aplomb. Additionally, a debt of gratitude goes to Stedman Mays of Clausen, Mays & Tahan Literary Agency, who, as an agent and a friend, is in a class by himself. Kudos to his wonderful partner, Mary Tahan, and superb assistant, Michael Mezzo, as well.

—KRW and JMC

I WOULD ALSO LIKE TO PERSONALLY THANK my attorneys at the law firm of Preti, Flaherty, Beliveau, Pachios, and Haley, with special praise to associate Tim Bryant for the legal expertise.

—KRW

IN ADDITION, I WOULD LIKE TO EXTEND my heartfelt appreciation to my mother, Helen Carter MacLean, a wonderful writer, who, as my first editor, showed me the ropes of the craft; my father, Nelson MacLean, whose confident reassurance and generosity of spirit have never waned; and the many other family members and friends—especially my uncle, Raymond MacLean, and my dear friends, Tricia Greaves and Co.—who have so freely provided much-needed emotional sustenance. I also owe a debt of gratitude to Neal H. Rosenberg, a remarkable attorney, who never fails to provide me with the answers I need.

—JMC

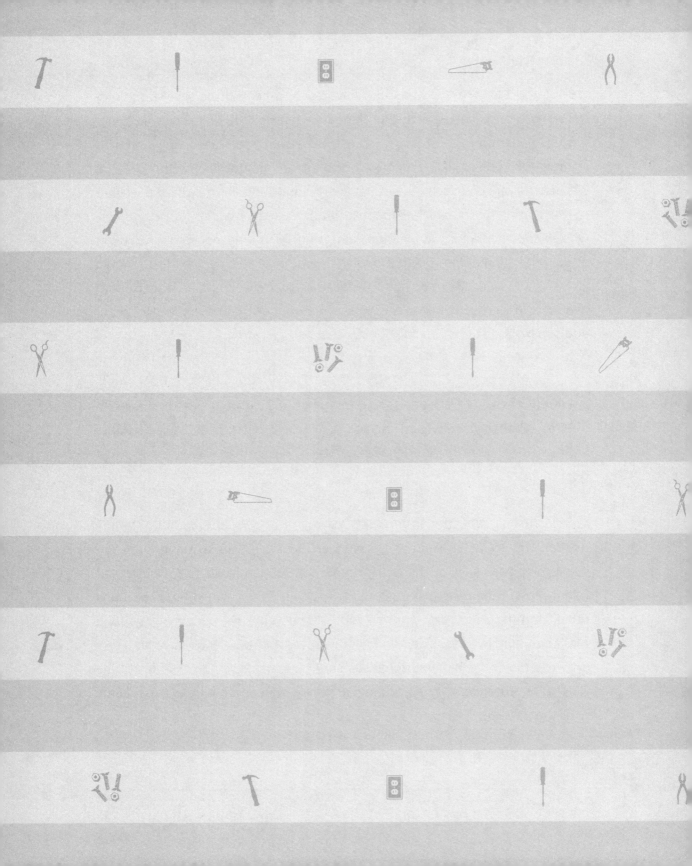

Contents

Introduction:

IN THE BEGINNING . . .
Tracing the Roots of Rent-A-Husband xv

PART I

HELP HAS ARRIVED! 1

Chapter 1

TOOL TIME GALS:
Getting Down to Brass Tacks 3

All Your Ducks in a Row 4

But First . . . 4

Down to the Nuts and Bolts 5

Also Useful 10

Tier Two 11

Chapter 2

BRIDGE OVER TROUBLED WATERS:
Handling Your Plumbing Needs 21

Flooded with Emotion 22

Reversing the Flow 24

When Your Toilet Refuses to Flush 27

You Can Run,
but You Can't Hide . . . 29

Shut-Off Valve Replacement 30

The Endless Drip: Faucet Repair 31

Compression Faucets 31

Resurfacing/Replacing
Compression Valve Seats 33

Get Packing:
How to Stop Handle Leaks 35

Washerless Faucets 36

Cartridge Faucets 36

Replacing a Toilet Seat 37

Chapter 3

ELECTRIFYING:

Light Up Your Life! 41

That Tingling Feeling 42

Playing the Circuit 42

Before You Blow a Fuse 44

Troubleshooting 45

Down to the Wire 46

Wire's Three Sisters:
Hot, Neutral, and Ground 46

Getting Plugged In 48

Making a Switch 48

Replacing a Three-Way Switch 50

Replacing a Dimmer Switch 52

Replacing an Outlet 54

Replacing Plugs 55

Repairing a Faulty Lamp 56

Replacing a Lamp Cord 57

Repairing a Broken Doorbell 58

Chapter 4

SCRAPE, SPACKLE AND ROLL:

These Four Walls 63

Change Your Surroundings
with Color 64

Getting the Lead Out 64

Readying to Prepare 65

Fix It First 65

Is It Paint Yet? 68

Prime Time 68

Primary Colors 69

What You'll Need to Be Covered 71

The Tools of the Trade 71

Technique 73

Cleaning Up 74

Wall Coverings 75

How It Measures Up 78

Preparing for Change 80

Take It Off 82

Hanging in There 85

Making the Cut 88

Chapter 5

SOMETHING'S AFOOT:
Flooring 105

Walk All Over Me 106

Laying Vinyl 106

Out with the Old 106

Installing Tile Squares 108

Replacing a Damaged Tile Square 112

Installing Sheet Vinyl 114

Repairing Sheet Vinyl 118

Laying Ceramic Tile 119

Regrouting Tile 125

Replacing a Cracked
or Broken Tile 125

Carpet Care 126

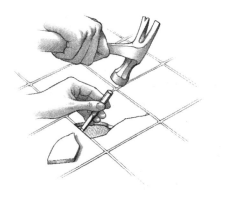

Chapter 6

**BRINGING ON THE
REINFORCEMENTS:**
Hiring a Contractor 131

Starting the Search 131

Getting Down to Business 132

Gentlemen, Start Your Engines 134

Working Out a Three-Payment
Schedule 136

PART II

ROOM FOR IMPROVEMENT 141

Chapter 7

DOWNSIZING:
A Storehouse of Ideas 143

Space: Maximizing What
You've Got 143

Storage Units 144

Shelving It 146

Quick Storage Fixes 152

Chapter 8

KITCHENS 155

Divide and Conquer 156

The Big Three 156

Chapter 9

BATHROOMS 161

Sizing Up the Situation 161

Clutter Containment 163

Supplemental Storage 164

Chapter 10

LIVING ROOMS 167

Sizing Up the Situation 167

Storage Solutions
You Can Live With 168

Chapter 11

BEDROOMS 171

Sizing Up the Situation 172

Organizational Tips to Sleep On 172

Closet Organization 173

Chapter 12

CHILDREN'S ROOMS 177

Room to Grow 178

The Child's Bedroom 179

Teen Central 180

Chapter 13

UNEXPECTED SPACES:
Finding Them in Places You've Never
Thought to Look 183

Exploring Space 183

Personal Hideaways 184

Chapter 14

MINDING YOUR OWN BUSINESS:
The Home Office 187

Sizing Up the Situation 187

File It 189

Shelve It 190

Made to Order 191

PART III

**HOME SAFETY FROM THE
INSIDE OUT** 193

Chapter 15

INDOOR SECURITY 195

Safe Air 195

Fire 202

Creating a Healthy Work
Environment 207

Testing the Waters 208

BYOB 211

Chapter 16

FAMILY SAFETY 213

Child-Proofing Your Home 213

Bathroom Safety 215

Safeguards for Seniors
and the Disabled 216

Kitchen Safety 217

Chapter 17

OUTDOOR HOME SECURITY 221

Safety Specifics 221

Home Security Alarm Systems 222

Afterword

RESTORING A HOUSE DIVIDED 227

Index 229

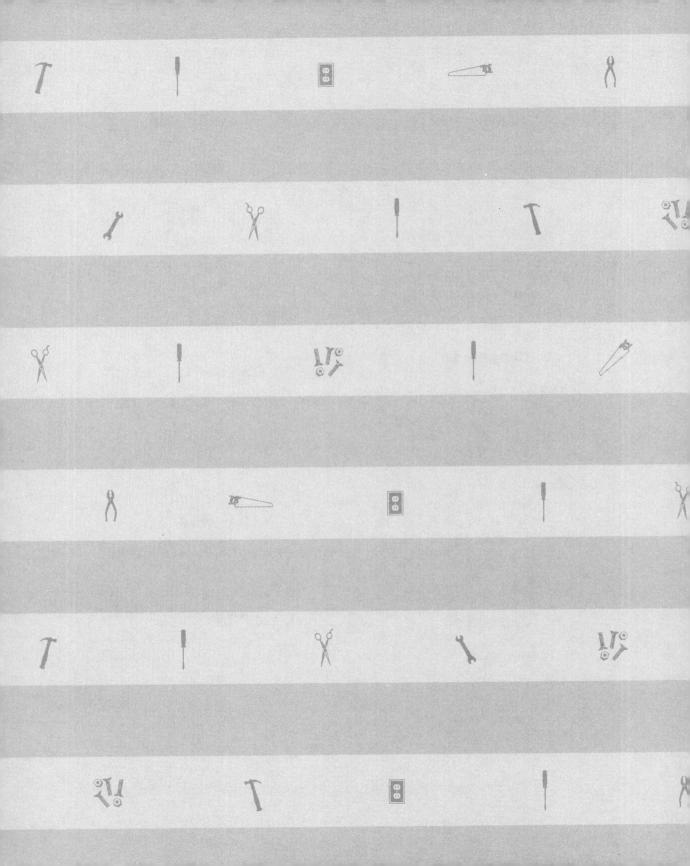

In the Beginning . . .

Tracing the Roots of Rent-A-Husband

Today, if anyone asks me how I'm doing, my immediate response is—thankfully—I'm on top of the world! And why not? I've had the remarkably good fortune to see Rent-A-Husband (the handyman business I founded just over four years ago "for those jobs that never get done") enjoy a meteoric rise in success. But life was not always so rosy.

The Rent-A-Husband story began on a May night in 1996; a night not unlike so many others that had preceded it. Living in one room of a run-down warehouse, I was well into the latest in a string of fitful slumbers. Having spent eighteen of the prior twenty-four months recovering from a debilitating automobile accident (which had rendered me unable to keep my small but relatively successful construction business afloat), I was trying to figure out what to do next.

Feeling hopeless and completely helpless in my—to date—failed attempts to improve the situation, I prayed for a break. And at 3 A.M. on that spring night, my prayers were answered. It came in the form of three little words I suddenly awoke to find dancing in my head: Rent-A-Husband. While initially overcome by the sheer and startling drama of it all, the idea—once it sank in—made perfect sense. To me, if you separate the words—*Rent-A-Husband*—they indicate a short-term, trustworthy, and ultimately satisfying relationship, which is exactly what I envisioned the company providing for its customers. And, after all, I had grown up in the construction industry, working part-time by my father's side from the age of eight on, assuming the lion's share of the load at the age of fourteen, when he suffered a massive heart attack.

As my father's condition continued to deteriorate and it became apparent he would never be able to return to work, my mother assumed the reins of the company. It was during this period I witnessed the terrible advantage taken of women in this male-dominated industry, and vowed someday to find a way to empower them. In the process, I had to forgo my long-held dream of becoming an architect and work full-time for my mother's struggling business. We never had much money, even though we both worked around the clock.

But one thing I did have plenty of was experience working in homes, where I observed—firsthand—the frustration that results from those pesky household chores that never seem to get done. The drips, drops, squeaks, and cracks of daily life; seemingly benign problems that, left untended, cumulatively conspire to drive a person mad. Yes, I decided, there was definitely a need out there just waiting to be

filled . . . and I was going to be the one to fill it.

Equipped with what was to become a very lucrative idea, I invested my last bit of money in paint and flyers. The former was used to inscribe the new moniker on the side of my beat-up old van, while the latter were turned into a company "birth announcement" of sorts. I distributed them on cars parked in a churchyard where a divorced women's support group was holding its meetings. The flyers read: NEED A HUSBAND? OBVIOUSLY. THEN WHY NOT RENT ME? Amazingly, the response was so overwhelming that I was forced to hire three more "tall, dark, and handy" *husbands* to merely keep up with the demand. Soon even they weren't enough.

Ironically, one of our first customers was the local correspondent for the Associated Press. So intrigued was she by the concept, she wrote a story about Rent-A-Husband that appeared in newspapers all around the country. And the rest—as they say—is history.

In *The Official Rent-A-Husband Guide to a Safe, Problem-Free Home*, you'll find answers to the questions I've been most frequently asked "in the line of duty," as well as secrets for handling household tasks in the simple, quick, and pain-free manner I've developed over the years. We've made sure they're presented in the user-friendly, easy-to-understand style that, I'm proud to say, has become a Rent-A-Husband trademark.

As for the moral of my story, I'd first have to stress the importance of keeping the faith. No matter how dire the situation may seem, never forget the endless possibilities that await all those who refuse to stop searching for them. And remember, it truly *is* often darkest before the dawn—I'm living proof of that fact.

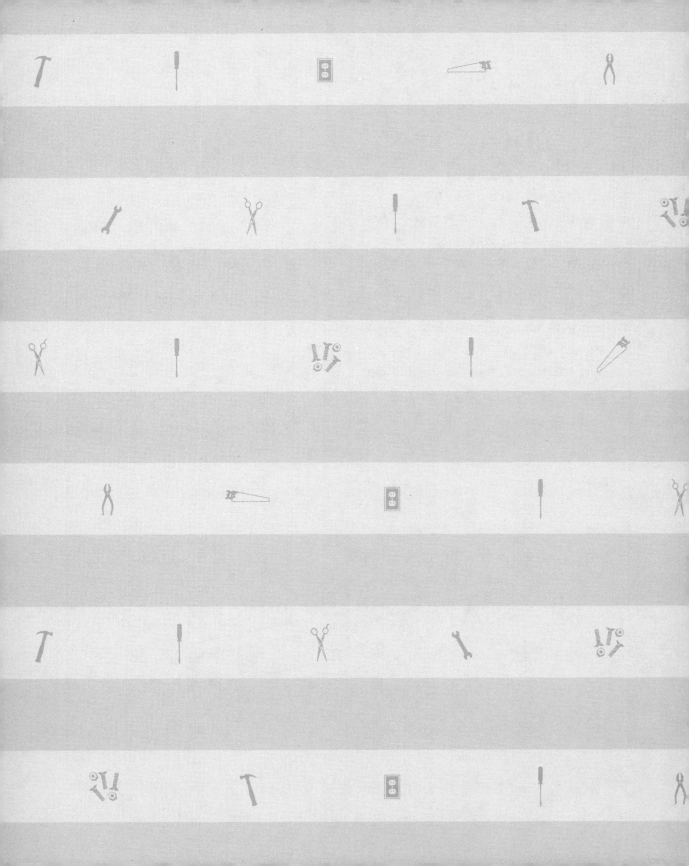

PART 1

Help
Has Arrived!

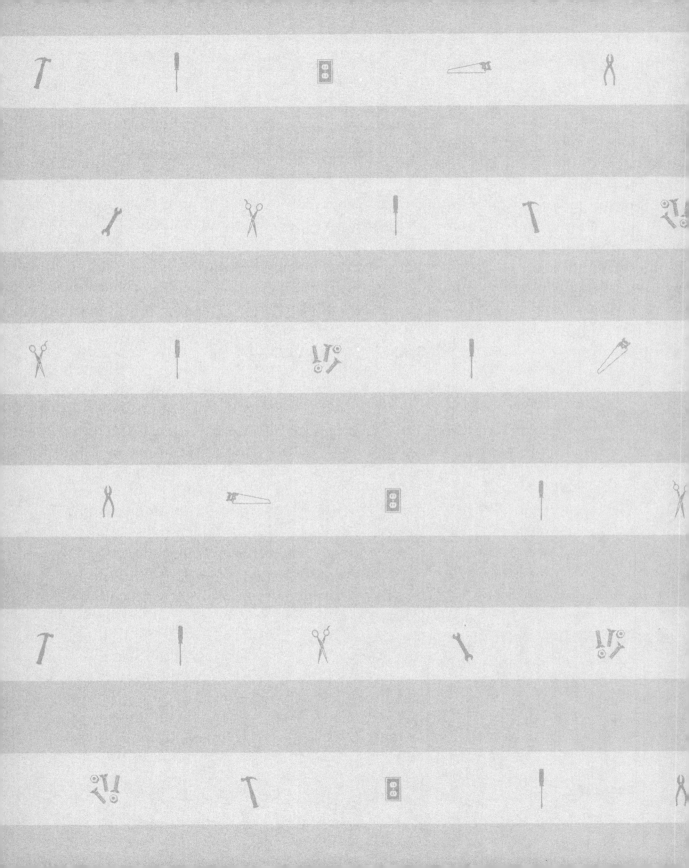

Tool Time Gals:
Getting Down to Brass Tacks

Indisputably, Shakespeare was right about a name . . . as far as the rose goes, anyway. For time and space have not altered the fact that such a flower by any *other* name would indeed smell as sweet. But the "name game" tends to take on much higher stakes—often to the point of being a downright occupational hazard—when it comes to naming tools of the Rent-A-Husband trade. Take a recent case in point.

Arriving at the home of a family of four early one morning, Rent-A-Husband was greeted at the door by the lady of the house and her two young sons, aged five and six. His assignment for the day called for repairs to the upstairs bathroom, so he began to unload the necessary tools. It was then that he felt the piercing stares of two little sets of eyes.

Both boys were completely amazed to discover that their toy tools not only came in such big sizes but really worked (without batteries, even!). Why, there were hammers that actually pounded in nails and wrenches that could turn any size screw. Most fascinating, in their minds, however, was an item known as a caulking gun, which became the tool to have.

Extensive questioning resulted in the knowledge that the true purpose for this handy little device is to shoot a filler known as caulk (rhymes with "chalk") into bathroom cracks and crevices. But at this point, the boys' only concern was the acquisition of said item, for which they had far greater plans. The young lads threw caution to the wind and seized the first opportunity to make it their own. (Fortunately, their mother managed—after just two short rounds—to wrestle the tool from their tiny but firm clutches.)

While she was busy pointing out areas of particular concern around the sink and tub, her real husband called. In response to the question "Where's your mother?" Dad was informed, with all of the honesty and innocence a five-year-old could muster, that "Mom's upstairs with the Rent-A-Husband, showing him where to shoot his caulk."

ALL YOUR DUCKS IN A ROW

While most forays into the land of home repair do not pose imminent danger, ironically, the real stumbling block seems to lie neither in the tools, per se, nor in the average person's ability to work with them effectively. Rather, the problem appears to stem from the language barrier that separates those conversant with "all things handy" from the rest of the population. But now that you've decided to plunge into this "brave new world," here's a little inside information to cheer you on: *Half of any repair problem is already solved when you know the right tool to use.*

(Naturally, knowing *how* to use it is the other half of the equation!)

Therefore, the importance of equipping yourself with a working knowledge of the local dialect prior to storming the fortress (i.e., the local hardware store) cannot be overstated.

BUT FIRST . . .

To make sure you get off to a smooth start, here are Rent-A-Husband's tips on how to prepare for the new "additions":

DESIGNATE A SPECIAL AREA IN WHICH TO STORE YOUR TOOLS. Although this doesn't have to be a very large space—whether in the basement, garage, or another part of your home—make sure to keep everything neat and orderly, with easy access. You'll really appreciate it if a pipe bursts some night at 3 A.M. (which has been known to happen!).

BUY THE BEST YOU CAN AFFORD. As with most other long-term material investments, it doesn't pay to cut corners when shopping for tools. So, if you think the "good wrench fairy" is smiling down on you because you've come across six for the price of one, you're probably just blinded by the glare of half a dozen shiny yet inferior wrenches that are destined to lose both their glitter and their usefulness practically before you get them home.

SHOP WISELY. Although you can conceivably get all you need at a variety of electrical supply, plumbing supply, and building supply megastores, the advantage to shopping at your local hardware store (especially for the beginner) is that the employees are usually well versed in just about everything related to your needs and can be extremely helpful.

BE SURE TO SAVE ALL SERVICE MANUALS AND RECEIPTS. In addition to making returns, such records are very handy when it comes to establishing the length of a warranty and the date of a purchase, as well as for ordering specific replacement parts.

KEEP SHARP AND WELL ADJUSTED. The tools, that is.

And always remember to inquire at the time and place of purchase where maintenance services can be had.

DOWN TO THE NUTS AND BOLTS

Even the most minor repair is going to require a starter kit of basic tools. While chances are you won't be bringing them home all at once, bear in mind that any investment you do make in this regard will undoubtedly be one of the very few to pay tangible dividends so quickly! But buyer beware: Success in home repairs has been likened to eating peanuts—it's hard to stop with just one! So, to assist in prioritizing your purchases, here are Rent-A-Husband's choices for the tools that are the most consistently reliable, valuable, and useful for long-term service. In other words, those that are worthy of a spot in anyone's Toolbox Hall of Fame.

CLAW HAMMER

A 16-ounce hammer with a fiberglass handle (that will assist in cushioning the blow to your hand) is the best bet here. The curved claw gives extra leverage, whether it's used to remove nails or as a prying tool, and the weight won't wear your arm out before the task is completed.

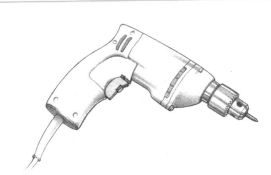

ELECTRIC DRILL

A ⅜-inch reversible model with an assortment of drill bits will give you all the power you need. Although the cordless model does offer flexibility where no electricity is available, unless you're planning a big project in a remote location, opt for the plug-in variety. Because you don't run the risk of dead batteries, it's generally better for the long haul.

WRENCHES

The main purpose of a wrench is to improve your ability to grip something firmly and to apply leverage. A 10-inch, adjustable model should enable you to keep a grip on things right now. Also, look for wrenches made of drop forged steel, as they're the strongest competitors in this league.

INSIDER'S TIP: Size does count when it comes to drilling holes, so try to get the bit to fit the screw the first time around, or at least early on in the drilling process. And remember, it's always easier to enlarge a hole than to reduce one, so think "less is more" when you start to drill.

SCREWDRIVERS

Screwdrivers come in two basic types: the flat head (or single slot) and the Phillips head. Which one you should use is determined by the design of the screw you're working with (the single slot is self-explanatory, while the Phillips head

looks like a cross). By starting out with a large and small version of each style, you should be able to screw anything that comes your way.

☞ **INSIDER'S TERM:** A variety package screwdriver comes with an exchangeable head, which is very handy, since you can go back and forth from the flat head to the Phillips head just by popping one off and screwing the other back on. Since the heads are stored in the handle of the screwdriver, this is one convenient little item to have on hand.

NAILS, SCREWS, AND ANCHORS

Because these will vary according to the project, the following is an overview of the nails, screws, and anchors most commonly used:

▶ **COMMON AND BOX NAILS** have broad flat heads that won't pull through and are designed for general use. Coated ones have more holding power than uncoated ones.

▶ **CASTING AND FINISHING NAILS** are small-headed and suitable for finishing work on cabinets and trim. Although casting nails hold better, finishing nails leave a smaller hole.

▶ **BRADS** are tiny finishing nails used for narrow moldings and paneling.

▶ **MASONRY NAILS** are used for nailing into concrete walls or mortar contained in brick or block walls.

▶ **WOOD SCREWS** come in three kinds (with either single-slot or Phillips heads): **FLAT-HEAD SCREWS** that can be driven flush with the surface or concealed; **ROUND-HEAD SCREWS** that sit atop the surface; **OVAL-HEAD SCREWS** for decorative applications.

▶ **LAG SCREWS**, due to their coarser thread (which causes more wood to be absorbed and—hence—a stronger "bite"), provide extra holding power.

▶ **PLASTIC OR NYLON SCREW ANCHORS** are tapered in shape and—much like an umbrella—open when screwed into a wall. This action provides extra pressure and holding power when hanging pictures or wall displays. They are, however, reserved for use in solid walls (brick, for example), as plaster and sheet rock are not strong enough to hold them.

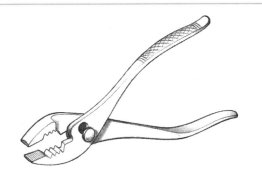

> 💡 **INSIDER'S TIP:** Is a long screw really better? Most professionals agree it is, since a longer screw holds better than a wider one. So, when it comes to screws, choose length over width every time for greatest satisfaction.

PLIERS

SLIP-JOINT PLIERS are equipped with something known as "toothed jaws," which allow you to grip objects of various sizes—everything from a water pipe to items your toddler accidentally drops in the toilet and you need to retrieve. As such, slip-joint pliers are the most versatile and should be your first acquired pair. Also, for working within a narrow space, **NEEDLE-** or **LONGNOSE PLIERS** are an addition you'll welcome.

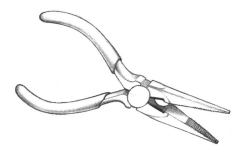

> 💡 **INSIDER'S TIP:** For especially tough turns, try tightening a wrench onto the handles of your pliers and using it to turn them. It will substantially increase your leverage.

CARPENTER'S LEVEL

One of the few tools whose function is spelled out in its name, this straight-edged wood or metal tool has glass insets that contain a bubble and are marked with two black lines. Essentially, when the bubble falls between the two lines, whatever you're leveling is level—or precisely horizontal or vertical.

> **INSIDER'S TIP:** When you're cutting wood, take extra care not to cut through a knot. These areas are extremely dense and can cause the blade to bounce back.

METAL FILE
Useful for sharpening the edges of everything from putty knives to shovels and gardening tools.

HACKSAW
This nonelectric, handheld saw has a small, thin, replaceable blade and is very useful for working in tight quarters. However, to ensure that you finish the job with all your fingers intact, always remember to move your hand as far away from the blade as possible, while still maintaining a hold on whatever you are cutting.

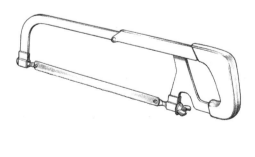

UTILITY KNIFE
A compact model with replaceable blades that's strong enough to open

heavy cardboard and exact enough for trimming wallpaper is the preferred choice. And be sure to opt for one with a retractable blade . . . you'll be glad you did if you have any plans to squat down with this item in your pocket!

STEEL TAPE MEASURE

Since so many projects require accurate measurements, a steel tape measure can prove invaluable. And while professionals wouldn't think of leaving their vans without the 25-foot version strapped on, a 12-foot tape should provide you with a more than adequate measure of success.

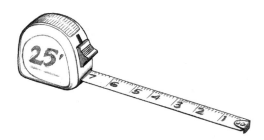

> 💡 **INSIDER'S TIP:** It's worth paying a little more to get a steel tape measure with a tape-locking device that will hold it in position while you make your mark.

AWL

The purpose of this small, sharp, pointed tool is to start holes for driving in nails or screws. Because you can ruin a good piece of wood if you try to drive a nail or screw into a spot that has not been properly prepared, the awl is used to "pave the way" by puncturing the spot where the nail or screw is supposed to go.

ALSO USEFUL

Intended to complement your primary tool arsenal, these "extras" will prove indispensable when it comes to the safe and successful execution of any project you choose to undertake.

SCISSORS—For snipping and cutting.

DUCT TAPE—Equally useful for wrapping a pipe and repairing running shoes.

SANDPAPER—For any number of smoothing tasks, sandpaper comes in coarse, medium, and light grains.

PUTTY KNIFE—Used to apply paste or perform light scraping jobs on peeling surfaces.

HEAVY-DUTY STAPLER—For a variety of attachments.

ADHESIVES—A wood glue that provides extra reinforcement for items joined with screws or nails.

WD-40—For taking the "squeak" out . . . also useful for loosening things, like drawers, that are stuck. (A clear or white candle rubbed on stuck drawers will free them as well.)

And for your personal safety and comfort, don't forget to include:

WORK GLOVES—For needed protection, have at least one pair of gloves made of rubber and another made of leather or canvas.

KNEE PADS—To cushion your knees.

EYE GOGGLES—To save your sight.

DUST MASK—To protect your respiratory system.

TIER TWO

The next rung on the ladder to becoming master/mistress of your home repair domain, this section is intended to provide you with an expanded arsenal of tools. With increased experience, your particular interests will surface and dictate the exact choices that will best enhance your personal collection. In the meantime, the following is designed to provide an overall look at what's out there.

ABRASIVES

ALUMINUM OXIDE—Comes in many grades, ranging from extra-coarse 36 to extra-fine 220. Used to sand wood, metal, plastic, and fiberglass.

EMERY—Available in three grades—fine, medium-coarse, and extra-coarse. Used to polish metals.

FLINT—Fine, medium, and coarse grades are useful for light sanding and sanding tacky surfaces.

GARNET—Sold in the same wide range of grades as aluminum oxide (above). Used for woodworking projects.

SILICON CARBIDE—Comes in the most popular grades as well as an extensive range of fine grades from very-fine 180 to ultra-fine 600. Used to sand floors and smooth glass, fiberglass, hard plastics, and soft metals.

STEEL WOOL—Ranges from No. 3 coarse to No. 0000 extremely fine. Used to remove rust or corrosion from metal.

ADHESIVES

CONTACT ADHESIVES—Used to apply plastic laminate and wood veneer, as well as to repair veneer. Good holding power and is water-resistant.

EPOXY ADHESIVES—Will bond almost any material to any other material. Excellent holding power and water resistance.

LATEX-BASED ADHESIVES—Will bond fabric, carpeting, canvas, and paper. Fair holding power and water resistance.

MASTICS—Come in latex and resin-based. The former bonds ceiling tile, floor tile, and paneling. The latter is used for ceramic, plastic, wood, and cork. Good holding power and water resistance.

PASTE ADHESIVES—Used to apply wallpaper and create other thin paper bonds. Good holding power but poor water resistance.

PLASTIC ADHESIVES—Used for wood, glass, plastics, pottery, china, and model work. Fair holding power but poor water resistance.

POLYVINYL RESIN ("WHITE GLUE")—Bonds wood, plywood, hardboard, and paper. Good holding power but poor water resistance.

RESORCINOL AND FORMALDEHYDE—Bond plywood, hardboard, and reclaimed wood products (chipboard). Excellent holding power and water resistance with resorcinol; excellent holding power but poor water resistance with formaldehyde.

RUBBER-BASED ADHESIVES—Bond wood, wood to concrete, paper products, plastic, and cork. Fair-to-good holding power and good water resistance.

CYANOACRYLATES (SO-CALLED INSTANT-BONDING ADHESIVES)—Bond rubber, plastics, metals, hardwoods, ceramics, and glass. Excellent holding power and fair water resistance.

CAULKS AND SEALANTS

ACRYLIC LATEX—A good fast-drying, general-purpose sealant that's ideal for filling small cracks and joints, patching plaster walls, and sealing around baseboards and window trim. It can be painted.

VINYL LATEX—Highly adhesive as well as waterproof and weatherproof, this type is excellent for use around wet areas such as tubs and showers.

SILICONE—A very expensive product that is best saved for small jobs where exceptional adhesion and long-lasting elasticity are necessary. It is ideal for sealing around tubs, showers, and outdoor outlets and fixtures. Paint does not adhere well to most kinds.

CHISELS

WOOD CHISEL—For cutting and smoothing wood joints.

BUTT CHISEL—To remove large quantities of wood; useful in tight spots.

POCKET CHISEL—For use by hand or with a hammer for forceful, sudden impact.

PARING CHISEL—Thin-bladed, for very fine work.

CAPE CHISEL—Normally used to gouge metal.

FLAT CHISEL—Will sheer metal and can cut through bolts and screws.

DIAMOND-POINT CHISEL—Makes V-shaped cuts and grooves in metal.

BRICKLAYER'S CHISEL—Cuts and forms masonry and stone materials.

DRILLS

HAND OR PUSH DRILL—Nonelectric, this is used for such delicate work as drilling small holes in wood, plastic, and metal.

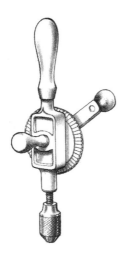

FILES, RASPS, AND PLANES

Files and rasps perform the same job on different materials. Files remove and smooth metal and plastic; rasps finish only wood.

DOUBLE-CUT FILE—Removes lots of material.

SINGLE-CUT FILE—Used for smoothing (general texture finishing).

PERFORATED RASP—Removes as well as smooths wood.

SMOOTHING PLANE—For all-around work that encompasses jointing (where two corners come together) and smoothing.

BLOCK PLANE—Used for end-grain work (finishing edges of wood).

HAMMERS

In addition to the aforementioned claw hammer:

RIPPING CLAW HAMMER—A 20-ounce hammer that is useful for rough work such as removing studs (short, thick nails or rivets with large heads).

SPECIALTY HAMMERS—These include **TACK HAMMERS** with magnetic heads to hold and drive tacks; **BALL PEEN HAMMERS**, with round and flat heads for metalwork; **MALLETS**, which have large wooden, hard rubber, or plastic heads and are used to drive chisels; **MASON'S HAMMERS** and **SLEDGEHAMMERS**, with more substantial heads, which are used for working with brick, concrete, and cinder block (building foundation material).

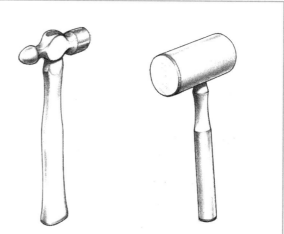

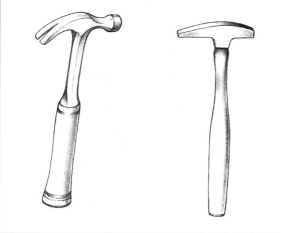

MEASURING TOOLS

In addition to the retractable steel tape measure and carpenter's level already discussed:

STEEL RULER OR STRAIGHTEDGE—For measuring and for cutting against a utility knife.

PLUMB BOB AND LINE—For determining a straight vertical line. (You can also use a weight tied on to a piece of string.)

COMBINATION SQUARE—For establishing right angles.

PATCHING MATERIALS

WOOD PUTTY—Comes in stick or paste form and fills gouges, cracks, and nail holes in wood; can be sanded and painted.

PATCHING PLASTER—For filling large or deep holes and cracks in plaster and drywall.

SPACKLING COMPOUND—For filling narrow cracks, small indentations, and nail holes in walls. (Toothpaste does the same.)

JOINT COMPOUND—Comes premixed to a gooey consistency for filling joints between drywall panels; also good for large and small patching jobs. (Again, toothpaste can be substituted for more minor repairs.)

SAWS

CROSSCUT SAW—Works best across the grain of wood; a **RIPSAW** cuts best with the grain.

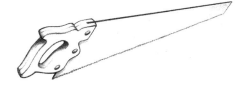

KEYHOLE SAW—Makes tight-radius (or hole in the center) cuts on pieces of large, thick material.

A **COPING SAW** is better for creating outside-edged, more accessible curves.

BACKSAW—A small, fine-toothed crosscut saw used for exacting work.

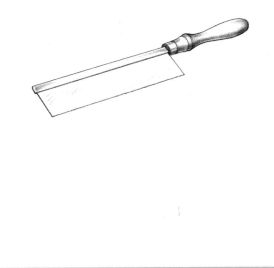

JIGSAW OR SABER SAW—Can crosscut, rip, miter, bevel, and cut holes in almost any material.

CIRCULAR SAW—A power saw with a circular blade that's controlled with a handle on top, the circular saw is capable of making a 45-degree cut in 2-inch-thick material and will rip long boards and paneling quickly. Extra care must be taken when using this, however, as it can "kick back" and cause injury if not properly operated. To minimize this risk, set the blade approximately ¼ inch deeper than the material you are cutting.

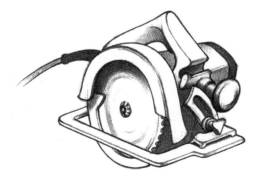

SCREWDRIVERS

In addition to the single-slotted and Phillips head varieties:

CABINET SCREWDRIVERS—These have special straight-sided tips to drive or remove countersunk screws without marring the surrounding material.

SPECIALTY SCREWDRIVERS—Include those for particular jobs, such as electrical and jeweler's screwdrivers.

WRENCHES

In addition to the adjustable-end wrenches:

ALLEN WRENCHES—These are used to tighten setscrews (small headless machine screws with a hex—6- or 8-sided—recess in one end that the wrench fits into). They are generally packaged in sets of assorted sizes.

SPECIALTY WRENCHES—These include **PIPE WRENCHES**, which are ideal for plumbing jobs; **OPEN-END**, **BOX-END**, **COMBINATION**,

and **SOCKET WRENCHES**, which are fixed-jaw relatives of adjustable wrenches.

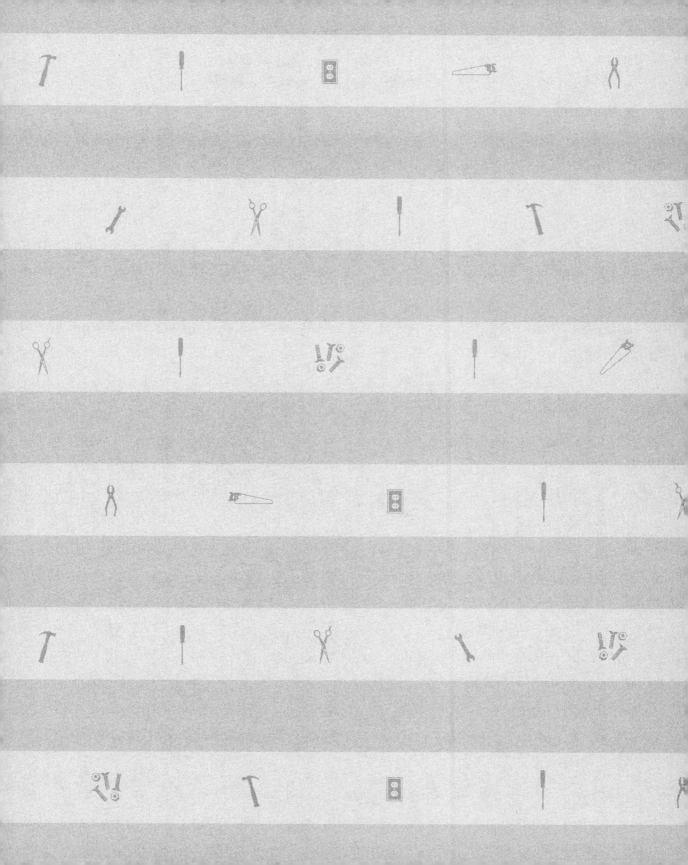

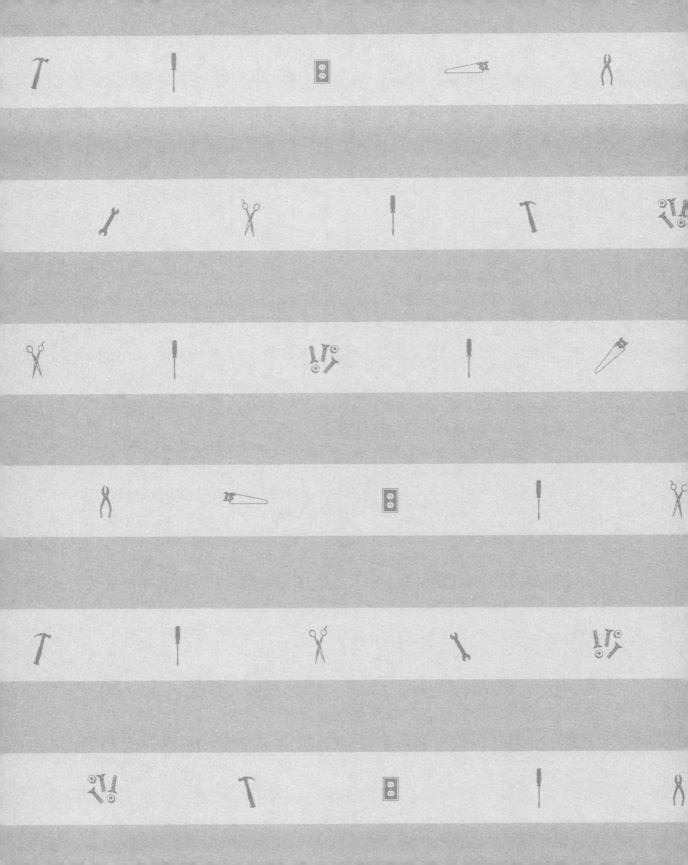

CHAPTER 2

Bridge Over Troubled Waters:

Handling Your Plumbing Needs

On occasion, Rent-A-Husband has been called upon to strike a compromise between the services a customer requests and what he's able (within the bounds of state law) to provide. Such was the case with Carol. The eldest of six children from a large extended family (the majority of whom married young), Carol was—at forty-nine—the oldest living single among them . . . currently considered something of a family relic. But the relentless grilling she'd endured about her marital prospects at every family event had finally come to a head the month before at the double wedding of her two youngest siblings. Tired of feeling like "the cheese stands alone," Carol vowed never again to return to a family gathering *uncoupled*.

This left her precious little time, however, when—just four weeks later—Carol's "little" cousin (the one for whom she had baby-sat *as an adult*) sent her an invitation to her own upcoming nuptials. So when she spotted the Rent-A-Husband van driving around the very next day, she believed her prayers had been answered—at least as far as an escort for the wedding was concerned—and immediately called to schedule a "booking."

After carefully explaining her predicament, Carol was sorely disappointed to learn that her request simply didn't fit any of the criteria for the services Rent-A-Husband provided. (Now, here's where the "bargaining" comes in.) For after going over all of the chores the surrogate spouse *did* take care of, she decided her single greatest need—*home repair–wise*—was in the plumbing department.

Therefore, as planned, five days before the wedding, Carol hired Rent-A-Husband to initiate work on her drains, pipes, faucets, and so on. And while she still arrived at her cousin's ceremony unescorted, Carol was able to honestly say that her "husband" was home finishing work he'd been doing all week on the bathroom!

FLOODED WITH EMOTION

Of all the calls Rent-A-Husband receives, those involving the bathroom are by far the most desperate. Fortunately, they're also among the most manageable. So the next time you think your only alternative is to pack up the family and head for higher ground, read on. You'll be pleasantly surprised to discover the power to stare that "rising tide" right back down the drain was within you all the time. We're just going to show you how to tap into it.

Before you begin, it's important to have a general understanding of the inner workings of your water system. Reassuringly, when stripped to its bare essentials, plumbing is actually a fairly straightforward system. You see, water enters your home (from a public utility or well) through a large pipe. If purchased from a public utility, the water passes through a meter on its way into the house. The supply pipe splits into two lines shortly after entering the house, one of which goes to the water heater. Parallel hot and cold-water supply lines then feed every plumbing fixture in your home (with the exception of toilets, which are supplied only by a cold-water feed). These supply lines move water through the house at a constant pressure of between fifty and sixty pounds per square inch.

Another major component of a plumbing system is a waste system, made up of a series of pipes that carry waste from your home to a city sewer or your septic tank. Rather than using water pressure, these pipes employ gravity to do their work.

A third set of pipes vents gases and odors to the outside of the house. In addition to these vent pipes, drain traps located under your sinks prevent a buildup of sewer gases from going back into your home. Because they are U-shaped, these pipes allow running

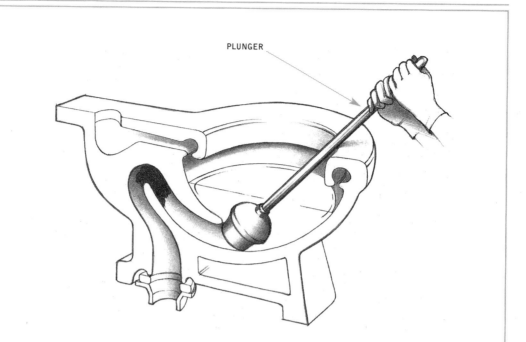

PLUNGER

💡 **INSIDER'S TIP:** An ounce of prevention truly is worth a pound of cure when it comes to plumbing concerns. So, if you notice that your toilet fills almost to the top of the tank and drains slowly, be warned: A clog is forming. It is much easier to deal with the problem when these symptoms first develop than after the clog has fully formed. At this early stage, a plunger will most likely solve the problem, therefore be sure to add one to your tool collection if you haven't already done so.

water to flow down through them, but as soon as the faucet is turned off, the water that lies "trapped" at the bottom of the pipe blocks the gases from reentering your home.

While most houses are equipped with water shut-off valves under each of the plumbing fixtures, this is not true 100 percent of the time. So if the toilet, sink, or shower you are planning to work on does not have a shut-off valve, before attempting any plumbing repair, you must turn off *all* the water in the house at the main shut-off valve. (This valve is located near the water meter or in close proximity to the wall where the main water line enters your home.) **AND NOTE:** If you need to turn off the main shut-off valve, it is vitally important that you also turn off the power to your water heater. This is due to the fact that with no water entering the heater, the internal elements will burn and could start a fire. To accomplish this, simply turn off the circuit breaker switch that regulates the operation of the water heater.

REVERSING THE FLOW

If your toilet does happen to stop up and overflow, rest assured that all is not lost (except, perhaps, the bathroom carpeting). In fact, reversing the flow in such instances is really quite a simple procedure. All you need is a little know-how, a plunger, and a closet auger (an inexpensive device available at your local hardware or plumbing store). Here's what to do:

▶ Put on a pair of rubber gloves.

▶ Cover the area of the floor around the toilet with newspaper.

▶ Turn off the water at the shut-off valve near the base of the toilet (or if there isn't one, turn off your home's main shut-off valve).

▶ Position the plunger over the hole in the bottom of the toilet and push up and down, with force. Because this action creates a partial vacuum, it should dislodge the clog.

▶ Repeat procedure several times and your "free flow" should be restored.

If the obstruction still remains, however, you will need to move on to a bit of "advanced surgery," using the closet auger (a hollow cylindrical tube with a handle on the top and a "snake" that proceeds from the bottom as the handle is turned). The lower end of the auger curves in a J-like shape. To use it:

▶ Slide the tip of the closet auger down into the drain opening.

▶ Now, turn the handle clockwise until the auger tightens. When this happens, turn the handle counterclockwise.

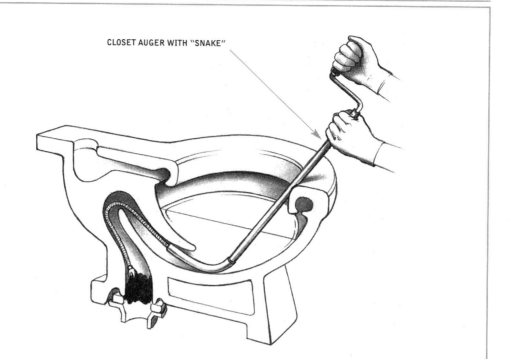

CLOSET AUGER WITH "SNAKE"

▶ Once the auger tightens again, simply crank it clockwise one more time until it is completely extended. Hopefully, whatever is clogging the toilet will be hooked on the end of the cable or broken up at this point.

▶ To remove, slowly pull the handle of the closet auger up and out. If it doesn't pull out freely, gently push it back in, and then pull it out again.

▶ Repeat the steps until toilet flushes normally.

If, after using the closet auger, the blockage still remains, call in the "back-up" (i.e., a licensed plumber), as the only solution now is to disassemble the toilet, which is a very difficult job.

☞ **INSIDER'S TERM:** The overflow tube is located in the toilet tank and prevents the water from rising too high and—hence—overflowing.

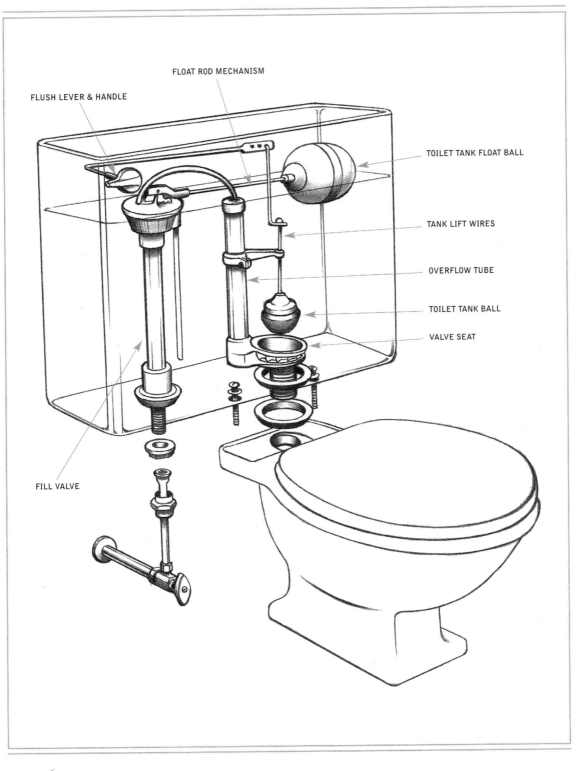

FLOAT ROD MECHANISM

FLUSH LEVER & HANDLE

TOILET TANK FLOAT BALL

TANK LIFT WIRES

OVERFLOW TUBE

TOILET TANK BALL

VALVE SEAT

FILL VALVE

WHEN YOUR TOILET REFUSES TO FLUSH

If your toilet tank doesn't fill with a sufficient amount of water, the toilet doesn't flush completely. It's as simple as that. Therefore, the logical solution is to raise the water level in the tank. To accomplish this task:

► Remove the toilet tank cover and locate the float mechanism (newer models come in plastic, while the older, stronger—and still available versions—are a brass rod and ball).

► If your toilet has a plastic float mechanism, start by turning the knob at the base of the regulator clockwise. For those with the brass rod and ball, lengthen the distance between the ball and the shut-off valve by unscrewing the ball on the connecting arm just a little. If, however, the ball is unscrewed as far as it will go, then gently bend the connecting arm up.

► Check the new water level by flushing the toilet. Ideally, the water should sit about ¾ inch from the top of the *overflow tube*.

If the toilet does not flush at all, it's probably because the water in the tank is leaking out as fast as it's running in. At the bottom of the tank, there's a rubber ball that sits on an opening. When the toilet is flushed, the ball is forced up by the toilet handle, which allows water to flow out of the tank. Once the tank empties, the ball falls back over the hole and forms a seal against the opening as the tank again fills with water.

However, as the ball becomes worn, it allows water to leak out of the tank. It is, therefore, necessary to replace the ball so that you will have a proper seal. To accomplish this:

▶ Shut off the water to the toilet by turning off either the valve underneath the toilet tank or (if one doesn't exist) the house's main shut-off valve.

▶ Remove the old ball. It may be connected by a collar slipped over the valve seat or by a hook connected to two hooks on the side of the overflow tube. (In older models, you may find a chain linked to a lever that is attached to the flush handle.)

▶ Bring the old ball to the hardware or plumbing supply store to replace it.

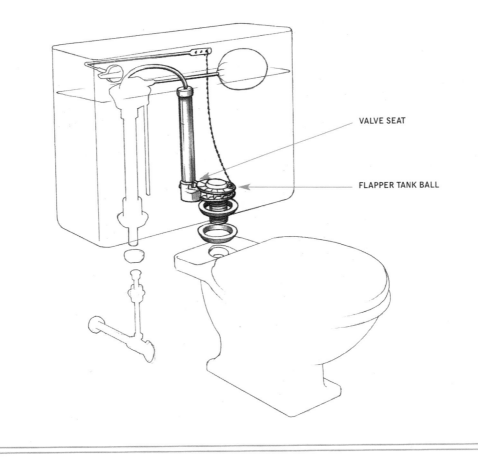

VALVE SEAT

FLAPPER TANK BALL

NOTE: A ball with a chain is difficult to duplicate, so you can purchase a new "flapper" mechanism, instead. The flapper slips onto the overflow tube and comes with a chain that connects to the flush handle. You must adjust the chain so that the flapper rises and then lowers, to sit snugly over the hole in the tank.

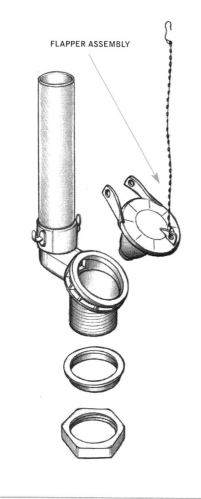

FLAPPER ASSEMBLY

YOU CAN RUN, BUT YOU CAN'T HIDE . . .

From the auditory torture of a running toilet! Like old man river, it just keeps rolling on and on until you're prepared to do almost anything to *make it stop!* Well, fear not; for help has arrived.

The fact is, water only should be circulating from the tank to the bowl when the toilet is flushing. Otherwise, water is entering the bowl when it's not supposed to and you're wasting *a lot of it!* If your toilet is using water between flushes, you can tell by the sound in the tank and the ripples of running water in the bowl. If that's the case, it's time to lift the lid and take a look at what's going on. Inside the tank, you'll find water and an overflow tube. When the water level is too high, the water rises above the overflow tube and flows into the toilet. Hence, the source of the problem.

You will, therefore, need to adjust the water level to just *below* the opening at the top of the overflow tube. The water level is regulated by the large floating ball in the tank that's connected to the shut-off valve by a brass arm. The ball floats upward as the water in the tank rises, creating downward pressure on the shut-off valve, which eventually closes. In order to make the shut-off valve close faster, you must *increase* the downward angle of the brass arm. Here's how:

▶ The distance between the shut-off valve and the ball needs to be reduced by screwing the ball in a little on the connecting arm.

▶ If the ball is totally screwed in, lightly bend the connecting arm down to lower the ball in the water.

▶ Now flush the toilet to observe how high the water rises in the tank. If it still rises above the top of the overflow tube, gently bend the float arm slightly more so that the ball is lowered further in the water.

SHUT-OFF VALVE REPLACEMENT

Sometimes a defective shut-off valve causes the aforementioned problem. If the water doesn't shut off as you pull up

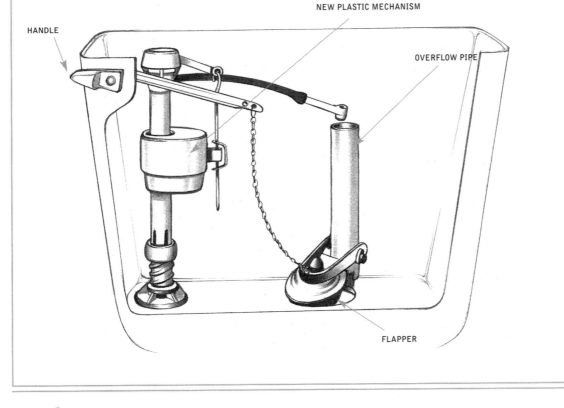

HANDLE

NEW PLASTIC MECHANISM

OVERFLOW PIPE

FLAPPER

on the ball, the old valve mechanism will need to be replaced with a self-contained plastic mechanism. These new and improved versions are available at any plumbing supply or hardware store. To make the change:

▶ Close the water intake valve under the toilet tank (or the main one, if none exists) and then flush the toilet. Remove lid.

▶ After placing a pan under the tank (to catch any remaining water), loosen the nut under the tank that holds the old mechanism in place with an adjustable wrench. Unscrew and remove old mechanism.

▶ Follow the package directions to install the new plastic mechanism, which regulates the water level according to the pressure in the tank. Turning the knob at the base of the regulator mechanism clockwise will increase the water level, while turning it counterclockwise will decrease it. Begin with one turn at a time. Flush the toilet and then check the water level.

THE ENDLESS DRIP: FAUCET REPAIR

Faucets fall into one of two categories: *compression* and *washerless*. The older *compression faucets* have separate handles for hot and cold water; while the newer *washerless* varieties rely on just one handle to control both flows, most commonly with a cartridge. Regardless of which type of faucet you have, always begin your repair by turning off the water at the shut-off valve (either under the sink or the main one). Next, open the faucet(s) to drain any water left standing and then stop up the sink and line it with a cloth to prevent loss of parts as well as scratches. Now, on to drip control.

COMPRESSION FAUCETS

Compression faucets work by pushing a *washer* against a valve seat. Most failures to perform are due to a worn-out washer, often caused by a rough valve seat that actually tears it up. As a first line of defense, try replacing the washer. Here's how to do it:

▶ After the water has been turned off, the faucet(s) drained, and the sink

INSIDER'S TERM: A washer is a small, round, flat piece of rubber with a hole in the middle that matches the diameter of the bolt being fastened through it.

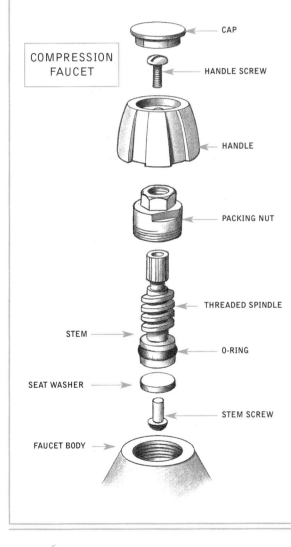

COMPRESSION FAUCET

CAP

HANDLE SCREW

HANDLE

PACKING NUT

THREADED SPINDLE

STEM

O-RING

SEAT WASHER

STEM SCREW

FAUCET BODY

stopped up and lined, remove the faucet handle by prying off the decorative cap on the top of handle (if it has one) with a small screwdriver and removing the handle screw.

► Using an adjustable wrench, remove the stem assembly by turning the packing nut counterclockwise and then pulling up the stem assembly by hand.

► Remove worn seat washer (located at the bottom end of the stem) by unscrewing the brass screw that holds it in place. (Make certain that the screw is brass and not steel-colored to look like brass. Steel can corrode; brass won't.) Since there is such a wide variety of washers, be sure to take the worn one with you to the plumbing supply or hardware store for replacement. Repeat the process with the other handle.

► Replace duplicate washers and retighten screws.

► Insert stem assembly into faucet body. Using an adjustable wrench, tighten packing nut.

▶ Reinstall faucet handles.

▶ Turn on the water supply valves and turn off faucets. If the faucet(s) continue to drip, tighten the packing nut further. If that still doesn't do the trick, the problem may be a worn valve seat, so read on.

> :bulb: **INSIDER'S TIP:** As you remove faucet parts, lay them out in order of disassembly so that you can reassemble them properly.

RESURFACING/REPLACING COMPRESSION VALVE SEATS

If the valve seat becomes rough (as often happens over time), it will "eat" as many new washers as you "feed" it. Therefore, it must be resurfaced or replaced. To determine which, begin by following the first two steps in the prior section.

Once you're back on the "inside," insert and twist your forefinger in the faucet body. If the surface feels uneven, a change is definitely in order. Now, shine a flashlight on the valve seat. If you see a round hole (as is found in a laundry sink, for example), you will have to try resurfacing or grinding it, as these valve seats are nonremovable. If, on the other hand, you see a square or hexagonal opening, these seats can be removed and replaced with new ones. Let's start with the nonremovable varieties.

You will need to acquire something known as a seat-grinding tool, which is another rather inexpensive but very useful device.

▶ Insert the seat-grinding tool into the faucet so that its cutting edges sit squarely on the valve seat.

▶ Now, holding the tool perpendicular to the seat, turn the handle back and forth several times while applying light, downward pressure. You want to smooth the seat, not grind it down "to the bone."

► Wash away the loose pieces of metal, install a new washer, and then reassemble the faucet.

For valve seats that can be replaced, proceed as follows:

► A seat-removing tool, available at plumbing supply and hardware stores, is necessary to remove the seat (makes sense, doesn't it?).

► Slip the tool into the valve seat, tap it into place, and unscrew.

► Take the seat back to the plumbing supply or hardware store to buy an exact replacement.

► Install with same tool. Coat the threads of each new seat with a thin layer of Vaseline or pipe joint compound so they'll come out easily the next time (hopefully in the very distant future!).

► Install new washer and insert the stem assembly into the faucet body and tighten the packing nut with the adjustable wrench.

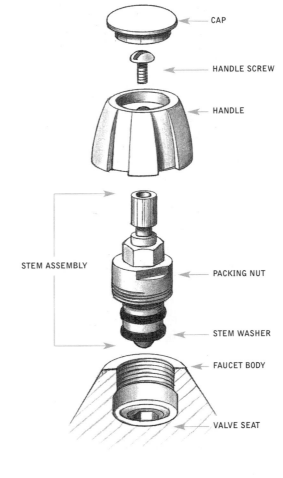

CAP

HANDLE SCREW

HANDLE

STEM ASSEMBLY

PACKING NUT

STEM WASHER

FAUCET BODY

VALVE SEAT

ALLEN WRENCH

VALVE SEAT

FAUCET BODY

► Turn the water supply valves back on and turn off the faucet.

Whether the seat was repaired or replaced, you should now find yourself sitting pretty and, best of all, *dripless*.

GET PACKING: HOW TO STOP HANDLE LEAKS

Many compression faucet problems occur at the seal between the packing nut and the stem. "Packing" of various kinds is used to keep water from seeping up the stem around the handle. In older faucets, this seal comes from something known as packing material; while in newer models, special washers called *O-rings* seal the deal.

Packing leaks are fairly easy to recognize because they happen only when the valve is open, since there is no water pressure on the packing when the valve is closed. So, if your faucet handle drips when the water is on, rather than (more usually) after it's been turned off, the source of the problem is likely to be defective packing material, O-ring, or packing washer. If tightening the packing nut a little fails to provide the desired result, follow these steps:

☞ **INSIDER'S TERM:** An O-ring is a round rubber ring that seats inside a premolded metal groove, located inside a faucet. Its purpose is to keep the water from leaking outside the faucet.

► Once again, start by turning off the water supply valves under the sink or at the main shut-off valve. Open the faucets to drain any water left standing, stop up the sink, and line with a cloth.

► Unscrew the packing nut with an adjustable wrench and check to see the type of packing material contained therein. If you find a globlike matter pressed into place, you will need to replace the packing material and retighten. If you discover a solid washer or an O-ring, a replacement of either is the order of the day.

Just remember to take the carcass of whatever you do unearth to your plumbing supply or hardware store so you'll be sure to get an exact duplicate.

► Install and reassemble faucet.

WASHERLESS FAUCETS

The majority of washerless faucets use one handle to control the flow of both hot and cold water, most frequently with a cartridge. When the handle is moved, the cartridge shifts, thus opening a channel for water to flow.

CARTRIDGE FAUCETS

Cartridge faucets use a replaceable, cylindrical, metal or plastic cartridge located inside the faucet body to control the flow of hot and cold water. So if your sink has a cartridge faucet and it's leaking, the solution is to replace it. Since, however, there are literally dozens of cartridge styles, don't try to rely on memory alone when you go shopping for a replacement. Take the old cartridge with you to the plumbing supply or hardware store to ensure you come home with an exact

duplicate. Now, here's how to make the switch:

► Of course, start by turning off the water at the shut-off valve. Open the faucet to drain any remaining water, and stop up and line the sink with a cloth.

► If your handle has a cap covering it, pry it off with a small screwdriver

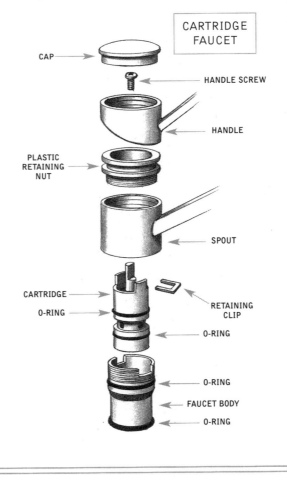

CARTRIDGE FAUCET

CAP

HANDLE SCREW

HANDLE

PLASTIC RETAINING NUT

SPOUT

CARTRIDGE

O-RING

RETAINING CLIP

O-RING

O-RING

FAUCET BODY

O-RING

and remove the handle screw. Remove the faucet handle by lifting it straight up and off.

▶ With an adjustable wrench, remove the plastic retaining nut.

▶ If there's a retaining clip holding the cartridge in place, remove it with needle-nose pliers.

▶ Remove the spout by pulling up and twisting.

▶ Grip the cartridge stem with slip-joint pliers and pull straight up to remove the cartridge.

▶ Cut off the old O-rings with a utility knife.

▶ Take the worn-out cartridge and O-rings to a plumbing supply or hardware store to purchase exact replacements.

▶ Coat new O-rings with heatproof grease and seat them in their grooves in the body.

▶ Replace remaining parts.

▶ Install replacement cartridge in same position as the old one.

Now, turn the faucet on and slowly open shut-off valves to restore the flow of water. If you spot any leaks, tighten connections, as necessary.

NOTE: If cartridge has either a tab or a flat surface, make sure it faces forward.

REPLACING A TOILET SEAT

If your toilet seat is chipped, stained, or just generally old and tired-looking, it's time for a change. With replacement seats available for as little as $10 and easy-to-follow instructions for making the switch outlined below, there's no reason to delay! Here's all you have to do:

▶ Since the vast majority of toilet seats are the same size (the only variation to note is whether yours is round or elongated), there's no reason to take the old seat with you to the hardware store or home center when purchasing a new one.

▶ Once you're back at "head" quarters, check to see if the bolts

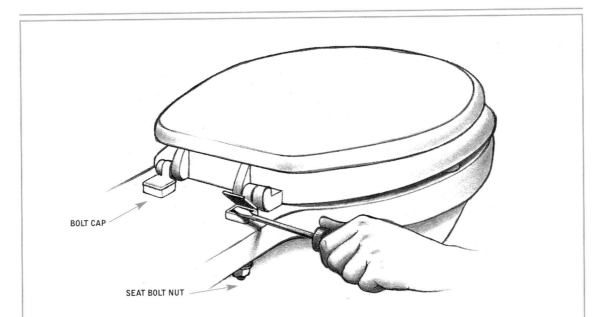

BOLT CAP

SEAT BOLT NUT

securing the old seat are hidden under caps. If they are, pry the bolt caps up with a screwdriver. If you'd prefer, wear rubber gloves for this job.

▶ Hold the seat bolt nut under the toilet rim with an adjustable wrench and use

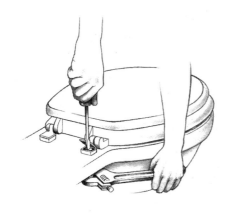

a screwdriver to turn the seat bolts counterclockwise to remove them.

▶ Remove the old seat and clean thoroughly around the mounting holes with a scouring pad.

▶ Position the new seat on top of the bowl. Now, place the new seat bolts in the mounting holes, align the seat, and attach the nuts. Using a screwdriver on the top and your adjustable wrench on the bottom, tighten the seat bolts securely.

▶ Finally, snap the bolt caps closed. That's all there is to it!

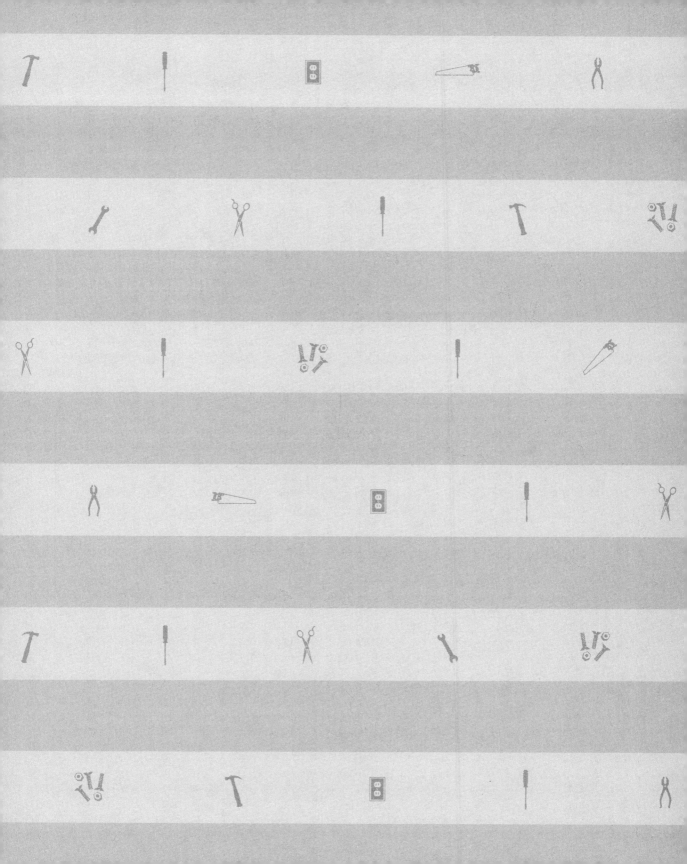

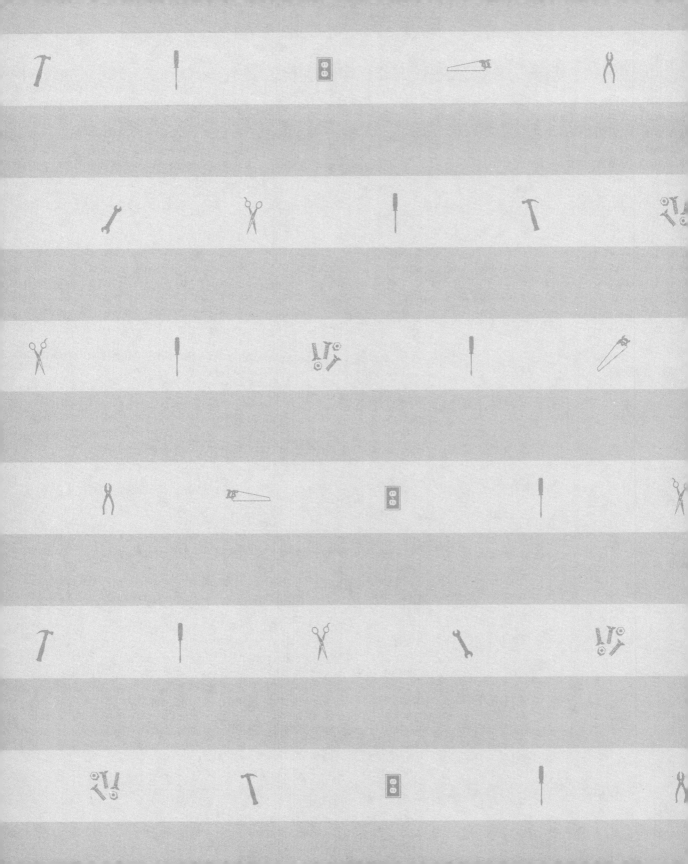

3

Electrifying:

Light Up Your Life!

Sometimes what customers say when they call to request Rent-A-Husband's services and what they actually mean (as revealed when he arrives for the job) are two separate things entirely. Take the case of Sarah. In the midst of a rather premature heat wave last spring, she called to say she needed Rent-A-Husband to install an air conditioner in her bedroom window. She went on to explain (rather resentfully) that ever since her real husband had acquired a new "mistress" (by the name of golf), he never had time to do anything at home, a sore point only further aggravated by the fact he'd spent a small fortune on equipment for the sport.

But while this particular customer claimed she wanted to cool things down, apparently her true intent was to heat them up. For just as Rent-A-Husband had the air conditioner balanced in the window and ready to install, she snuck up from behind and grabbed him on the rear end! The unprovoked action took him by such surprise that he dropped the unit out of the second-floor window and watched (to the seemingly great delight of this woman) as it landed right on top of her husband's new clubs (which were propped up against the side of the house).

Needless to say, the clubs were a fatality of the collision. And to stop her husband's constant crying, Sarah was forced to spend the money she'd been saving for a romantic getaway on a new set of clubs for him, as well as another air conditioner. Always the gentleman, however, Rent-A-Husband offered to install the second unit at no extra charge.

THAT TINGLING FEELING

Ever since a rain-drenched Ben Franklin was shocked to see what could be generated with just a kite and a key, electricity has held a magnetic appeal. After all, it takes only a temporary outage (created by a hurricane, for example) to cause the natives in most huts to get pretty restless. So while we can appreciate the many amenities this invaluable "charge" affords us, we must also maintain a healthy respect for the hazards it can pose. When working with electricity, always remember to start by *turning off the power* at the service panel (circuit breaker or fuse box). And proceed with caution!

PLAYING THE CIRCUIT

While most people tend to dance around an electrical repair like a caveman who has just discovered fire, their "fear of frying" is most frequently unfounded and stems from a simple lack of education about the subject. After all, knowledge is *power!* So before you start to feel the surge brought on by successfully tackling overloads and the like, it's vitally important to understand just how your electrical system works.

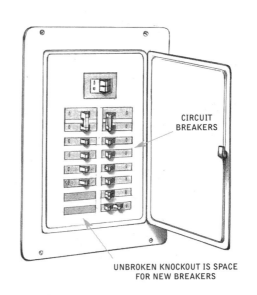

CIRCUIT BREAKERS

UNBROKEN KNOCKOUT IS SPACE FOR NEW BREAKERS

Basically, it's pretty simple. Power enters your home one of two ways: through wires that attach at a pole on the roof or via an underground feed. The voltage is then transferred to your main electrical panel, located inside the house. (The meter box—the utility company's device for measuring the amount of electricity you use—is located outside the house; or in the case of apartment buildings, in the basement.) The electrical panel serves many vitally important functions. First, it distributes power to the different circuits, which in turn provide "juice" to the various outlets, appliances, and light fixtures throughout your home. Additionally, the panel contains the fuses or circuit breakers that "break" the electrical flow to each circuit in case of a *short*, as well as a *main shut-off switch* that disables power to all circuits at once.

So before we go on, why not take a moment to look inside your home's electrical panel? If you're not sure where it's located, check to see where the power lines attach to your roof. The electrical panel is usually found right below the power "drop." If your power arrives through an underground feed, look for a pipe coming up from the ground to a metal box attached to the side of your home (the meter box).

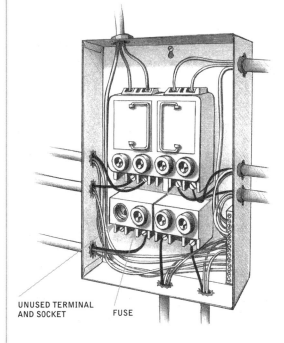

UNUSED TERMINAL
AND SOCKET   FUSE

> **INSIDER'S TERM:** A short (nothing to do with height) can occur when a worn hot wire touches a worn neutral (or another hot) wire.

> **INSIDER'S TIP:** Because the electrical panel is often located in the basement (where floors are usually made from concrete—an efficient electricity conductor—and also tend to be damp), always wear rubber-soled shoes and stand on a dry surface (such as a piece of lumber) when opening the panel box. This will help insulate you from the ground.

Upon opening the panel, you'll notice a series of switches (breakers) *or* a series of round (screw-in) or cylindrical fuses. As previously noted, these "break," or control, the power to the various circuits in the house, a vitally important safety function.

Typically, wires and connecting bars are hidden behind a metal partition located inside the panel. Therefore, only the fuses or circuit breakers should be exposed when you open the panel lid. If that is not the case: *Stop and call an ex-*

pert! Poking around potentially live wires could cause serious injury—even death (or at the very least, give the fillings in your teeth a good rattle).

BEFORE YOU BLOW A FUSE

In most cases, the electrical panel in your home will already be labeled when you move in, indicating which switch or fuse controls what portion of the house's electrical system. Check for a list inside the front cover or labels beside each breaker with things like "kitchen lights" and "bedroom outlets" written on them. If, however, you proved unlucky in that department and your cupboard is bare, it's an easy problem to rectify. The first thing you do is round up a helper, as you'll need to work together. One of you will flip each of the circuit breakers (or unscrew the fuses) while the other (preferably the more fit of the duo) runs around and indicates, via shouting, walkie-talkies, or carrier pigeon, which lights go out when. You'll typically find that the same circuit controls one, two, or even three rooms of light. Be sure to accurately note your findings beside the breaker or inside the panel cover.

The main breaker is usually (but not always) located at the top of the panel and is frequently painted red. It may look like two breakers with the switch bars tied together. And while most fuse boxes have a pullout main or a lever on the outside of the panel, if you are unable to determine which is your "main" breaker, stop until you're able to find someone who can assist you in identifying it.

Certain very old panels may not even have a main breaker. If that's the case, it's probably time to install a new panel. But please, do not attempt this yourself! Hire a licensed electrician for the job!

> **INSIDER'S TIP:** Just as a precaution, it's a good idea to confirm that your main breaker is operating properly. Flip all the individual breakers to "on" and then switch the main breaker to "off." Check to make sure the power is really off—all interior lights, appliances, and outlets should *not* be in operation. When you're finished, flip the main breaker back to "on" (and don't forget to reset your clocks!).

TROUBLESHOOTING

CIRCUIT BREAKERS

If you find that more than one light or outlet is not working, it's a good bet you've simply "tripped" a circuit breaker. When breakers are tripped by an overload in the circuit, the breaker switch moves away from the "on" position, but may or may not make it all the way over to "off." Look for one that is out of alignment with the other breakers in the box, flip the switch firmly all the way to "off," then back to "on."

If there is one circuit breaker that trips repeatedly, it's most likely due to one of the three following problems. First, you may merely have overloaded the circuit by using too many appliances that draw power at once. If you think that might be the case, unplug everything on that circuit (or if it is a lighting circuit, turn all lights off), reset the breaker, and check to see if the problem has been fixed. Now, plug in one appliance at a time to determine the limit. If that's not the source of the difficulty, move on.

A second possible cause of breaker trouble is a short in a particular appliance or an overly taxing draw for the *amperage* of the breaker. So, if the breaker trips every time a certain ap-

pliance is used, it's a pretty good indication you've found your problem. Try plugging the appliance into a different circuit; if the breaker trips on that circuit, as well, you should seek professional appliance repair.

The third possibility is that there could be bare wires touching one another or some other form of short within the household wiring for that circuit. If you've ruled out the first two possibilities, it's definitely time to call in a professional.

> ☞ **INSIDER'S TERM:** Amperage refers to the amount of energy released through an electrical breaker.

FUSES

Fuses differ from breakers in that they must be *replaced* when they have suffered an overload. By looking through the little window in a screw-in-type fuse, you'll be able to see a broken metal tab in the middle, indicating that the filament has melted. Replacing a new fuse usually involves nothing more than simply screwing in a replacement or sliding in a new cartridge-type fuse.

It's very important to use a replacement fuse with the same amperage as the one you are replacing. And again for safety's sake, never try to rectify the problem by using a higher amperage replacement fuse, or by inserting a penny (or any other object) in the fuseholder. This creates an unrestricted conduit allowing a virtually limitless amount of energy and can be deadly. *Remember... if fuses are blowing, there's always a reason*.

> ☀ **INSIDER'S TIP:** Be extra careful with cartridge-type fuses, as their exposed metal ends can conduct electricity from the mounting bracket. You will want to shut down the main breaker before changing a fuse, just as a precaution.

DOWN TO THE WIRE

Electricity is conducted by wire. So why, you may ask, doesn't that electricity burn right through everything the wire comes in contact with? The answer lies in insulation. In fact, all of the wiring in your home is insulated, either with cloth in older homes or plastic coating in newer ones.

Although it's unlikely you will ever need to know the precise size of wire necessary for any one electrical appliance, the general rule of thumb is the larger the diameter of the wire, the more efficiently it conducts electricity from one point to another without a drop in power. This will be evident if you've ever tried to run an appliance on an extremely long extension cord. You'll notice there is always some drop in voltage the farther away from the power source you move. This effect can be offset, to a degree, by employing a bigger-diameter wire.

As far as wire sizes, the two most common ones you are apt to come across are Number 14 (used to wire light fixtures) and Number 12 (a slightly heavier gauge wire used to provide power from the fuse or breaker panel to outlets).

WIRE'S THREE SISTERS: HOT, NEUTRAL, AND GROUND

When trying to visualize how electricity works, it's helpful to think of water, since, in both cases, the element has to *flow* from Point A to Point B. To operate effectively, the wiring in your home needs electricity coming in, as well as a "drain" channel through which it can flow out.

Over the last century or so, some standard electrical terminology and color conventions have evolved that leave most mere mortals completely in the dark when it comes to understanding what it all means. But fear not. We're about to shine a light on the subject and, in the process, decode it all for you. Imagine a "family" of three wires, all working together for a common goal. The wire that brings power *into* a circuit or appliance is usually *black* (sometimes *red*) and is referred to as the "hot" wire; the "drain" wire (or the one that takes the power out) is generally *white* and is known as the "neutral" wire. In most homes built after 1945, there's also a third wire, known as a "ground" wire. You should think of it as a standby exit to channel electrical flow in an emergency. The ground wire is typically uninsulated copper, is most often attached by green screws, and ultimately leads to a rod buried in the ground somewhere in or near your foundation.

> **INSIDER'S TIP:** Never touch wires, connectors, or shiny bars inside your main electrical panel even if it's in the *off* position. Household circuits may be disabled, but there will still be power coming into the box itself.
>
> **NOTE:** To disconnect all power to the box, call your electric company and/or a licensed electrician.

If you have an older home, this color-coding of wiring may not apply. In fact, you may run into situations where the wires are all black, or a red instead of a black one is pressed into service as the hot wire. Depending on the creative nature of the previous homeowner, you may even find yourself facing a house full of rainbow wiring in any combination at all. But those situations are rare. Generally speaking, you'll be fine if you simply remember that black is hot, white is neutral, and green (or uninsulated copper) is ground.

GETTING PLUGGED IN

Now that you're "wired" into the basics of your home's electrical system, you should feel qualified to branch out and tackle some *simple* yet frequently requested repairs. We stress simple because of all of the areas of home repair/improvement, those having to do with electricity remain the most intimidating. Nonetheless, if you follow our instructions exactly, rest assured there will be no unexpected *shocks* or *jolts* awaiting you at the end of the "line"!

> ☞ **INSIDER'S TERM:** An inexpensive, two-probe device, the neon circuit tester is designed to indicate whether or not a wire is safe to touch. Simply hold one probe to the metallic box or bare wire and touch the other probe to the wire in question. If the neon bulb lights, the wire is "hot."

MAKING A SWITCH

If, upon entering a room, you flip the light switch and are still in total darkness, one of the following could be the reason:

▶ **THE CIRCUIT BREAKER MAY BE OFF FOR THAT PART OF THE HOUSE.** To determine if this is the cause, check to see if other electrical units in the room are operating correctly. If the light you switched on is the only thing not working, replacing the bulb will probably serve to illuminate things.

▶ **THE SWITCH MAY BE DEFECTIVE.** If changing the bulb doesn't help, you should test the switch. This is accomplished using a device known as a *neon circuit tester* (available at your local hardware store). Once you've acquired one, remove the switch cover with a screwdriver. Now, take your neon tester and touch its probes to the terminal screws with the

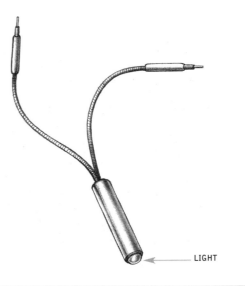

LIGHT

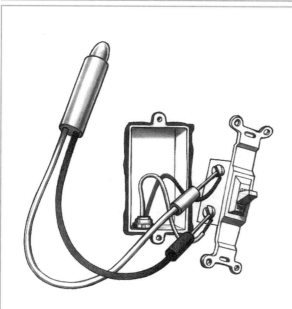

switch in the *on position* (making sure not to let the probes touch the box sides). If the tester lights, the switch needs replacing.

To replace the switch, proceed as follows:

► Turn off the power to the switch at the circuit breaker.

► Remove the switch cover with a screwdriver. You will see two screws holding the switch in place on the wall.

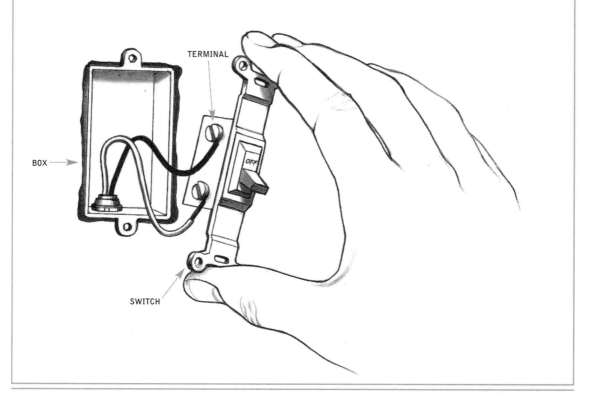

TERMINAL

BOX →

SWITCH

▶ After removing these screws, pull the switch out of the wall. You'll now see two wires connected to the switch (either attached to two screws on the sides of the switch, or inserted into the back of the switch).

▶ Loosen the screws and disconnect the wires, or gently pull the wires out of the back of the switch. To assist you when you reconnect the new switch (and repeat this procedure in reverse order), make a diagram showing where the wires were originally attached. The switch will now be free.

▶ Take this switch to an electrical supply or hardware store and replace it with a similar one.

▶ Reconnect the new switch to the wires in the wall, screw it back onto the wall, replace the cover, and turn the power back on. *Voilà!* Your problem now should be solved.

REPLACING A THREE-WAY SWITCH

Installing a pair of three-way switches allows you to control a light from two different locations (such as at the top and bottom of a staircase or at opposite ends of a hallway). The three-way switch is so named because these switches have three (instead of the usual two) terminal screws. Two of these are known as the *traveler screw terminals,* while the third, which is darker in color, is referred to as the *common screw terminal.* The traveler wires connect the two three-way switches. Just remember to try a new bulb before replacing the switch. If that fails to give you light, proceed as follows:

▶ Turn off the power to the switch circuit at the main panel.

▶ Remove the switch cover and the two screws fastening the switch to the box. Use a neon circuit tester to make sure that the circuit is dead. (See page 48.)

▶ Unscrew the switch from the electrical box and pull it out with the wires still attached.

▶ Label the wire under the darkest of the three terminals COM with masking tape.

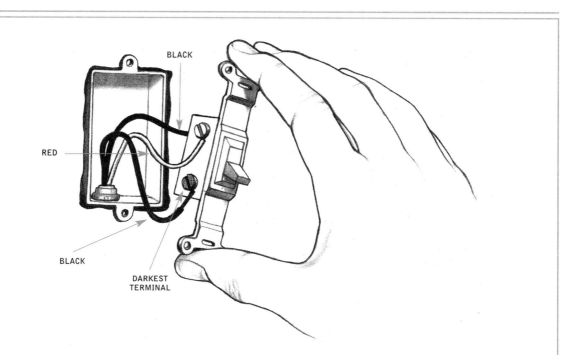

BLACK

RED

BLACK

DARKEST
TERMINAL

▶ Remove the wires from the switch.

▶ Buy a replacement three-way switch
at an electrical supply or hardware
store.

NOTE: If wiring is aluminum (silver
color), be certain the switch is
marked CO/ALR, indicating compat-
ibility with both copper and aluminum wiring.

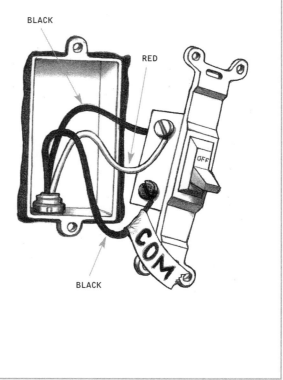

BLACK

RED

BLACK

▶ Ensuring that the wire labeled COM goes to the darkest screw, refasten the wires to the terminals on the new switch.

▶ Fold the wires into the box, fasten the switch, and restore the power. If the light doesn't go on, you probably replaced the wrong switch. Replace the other switch with the one you removed (which is probably still good).

REPLACING A DIMMER SWITCH

To create a more romantic mood or highlight a particular piece of furniture, art, or a specific area of the room, dim is the right setting. While bright lights tend to provide a cheery ambiance, dim lights create a sense of intimacy and relaxation. A dimmer switch enables you to control the amount of illumination, as well as helping to conserve energy. And because a dimmed filament burns at a lower temperature, which slows the burnout process, these switches also help to increase the life of your bulb. It is important to note, however, that dimmer switches can be used only to control lighting—not appliances or the functioning of an electrical outlet.

Now, if you're ready to, once again, "set the tone" or just want to hide the dust, here's how to do it:

▶ Turn off the power to the switch at the circuit breaker.

▶ Remove the switch cover with a screwdriver and you will see two screws holding the switch in place on the wall. See illustration page 53.

▶ Remove these screws and pull the switch out of the wall. You will now see two wires connected to the switch. They will either be attached to two screws on the sides of the switch or they will be inserted into the back of the switch.

▶ Loosen the screws and disconnect the wires. Again, make a diagram showing where the wires were attached so that you can retrace your steps when reconnecting the new switch. The old switch will now be free.

▶ Take this switch to a hardware or electrical supply store and replace it with the same type of dimmer switch.

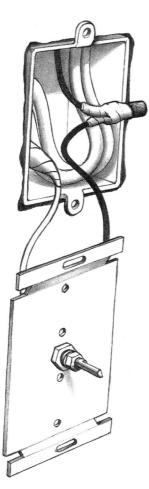

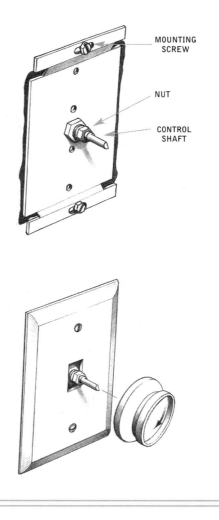

INSIDER'S TIP: Dimmer switches can sometimes cause interference with AM radio channels and television signals, so place your radio or TV far away from the dimmer switch or plug it into another circuit.

MOUNTING SCREW

NUT

CONTROL SHAFT

▶ Reconnect the dimmer switch to the wires in the wall and screw it back into the wall.

▶ Reinstall the cover plate and attach the knob to the protruding shaft.

▶ Turn the power back on.

REPLACING AN OUTLET

Outlet (also known as receptacle) replacement is similar to replacing a switch. The obvious test for an outlet is to plug in an electrical appliance that you are *certain* works. If it doesn't, read on. To correct the problem:

► Turn off the power to the outlet at the circuit breaker box. Use a neon circuit tester to test the circuit so you can be sure the power is off.

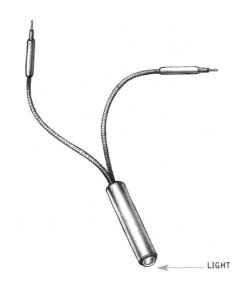

LIGHT

► Next, remove the outlet cover with a screwdriver. Take the two screws out of the outlet to remove it from the wall and note how the wires are con-

nected: either via two screws on the sides of the outlet or fastened on the back of the receptacle.

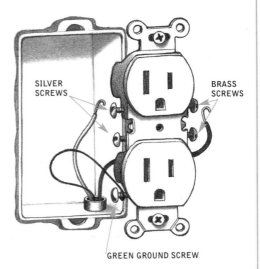

SILVER SCREWS

BRASS SCREWS

GREEN GROUND SCREW

► Loosen the screws and remove the wires, or depress the release slot if the wires are fastened on the back of the receptacle.

► Take the old outlet to an electrical supply or hardware store and buy an exact replacement.

► Install the new outlet by performing the above steps in reverse. Put the cover back on and turn on the power. Retest the appliance . . . it should work now.

REPLACING PLUGS

Thanks to the invention of the "quick-connect" replacement plug, replacing a two-prong plug is an easy task. Just be sure to note the difference between *non-polarized* and *polarized* (see description below) plugs. Don't substitute one for the other.

Here's what to do:

▶ Using diagonal-cutting pliers (or heavy-duty scissors), cut off the old plug.

▶ Take the old plug to the hardware store and buy a "quick-connect" replacement plug with the same prong pattern, as follows:

Both prongs of a nonpolarized plug are the same width.

One prong of a polarized plug is wider than the other.

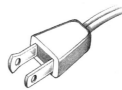

▶ Separate the prong assembly of the new plug from its casing by squeezing the prongs together and pulling the casing off.

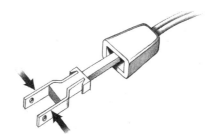

▶ Without removing any insulation, insert the old cord through the casing.

▶ Spread the prongs and push the cord into the prong assembly.

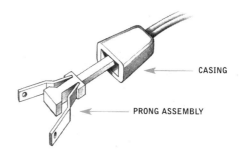

NOTE: If the plug is polarized, position the cord so that the side with the groove goes into the side with the wider prong.

► Now, squeeze the two prongs together and push the closed prong assembly into the plug casing.

REPAIRING A FAULTY LAMP

Fortunately, lamps tend to be among the
more reliable electrical appliances. But
after a while, even they may start to
rebel, as evidenced through such "behav-
iors" as flickering, difficulty in turning
on, or flat-out refusal to light. If such is
the case with one of the lights in your
life, you can easily give it a new lease by
adhering to these easy instructions:

► First check the lamp by switching
   outlets and bulbs. If there's still no
   light, unplug the lamp and disassemble it from the top down, as follows:

1. Most sockets have the word "press"
   marked in two spots on the shell.
   Squeeze the socket shell at those
   points and pull up to remove it.

2. If the shell doesn't move, try pushing
   the end of a screwdriver between the
   base of the socket and the side of the
   shell. Now, pull the shell up and off
   the socket base.

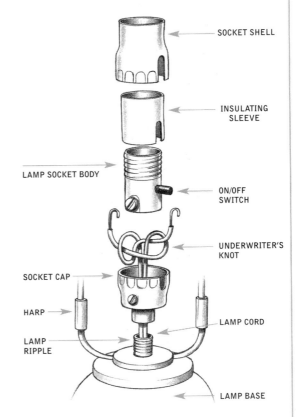

SOCKET SHELL

INSULATING
SLEEVE

LAMP SOCKET BODY

ON/OFF
SWITCH

UNDERWRITER'S
KNOT

SOCKET CAP

HARP

LAMP CORD

LAMP
RIPPLE

LAMP BASE

► Plug the lamp in and carefully touch
   the probes of a neon circuit tester to
   the two exposed terminal screws,
   making sure not to touch the tips
   against any metal. If the neon bulb
   lights, proceed. If not, go to the next
   section, "Replacing a Lamp Cord,"
   page 57.

► Unplug the lamp once more and remove the two terminal screws and
   wires.

- Take the old socket body to an electrical supply or hardware store and purchase a replacement.

- Install the socket by looping the wire ends under the terminal screws of the new socket body and tightening the screws.

- Place the new socket shell over the socket and push the cover down until it snaps into place.

- Replace the bulb and plug in the lamp.

REPLACING A LAMP CORD

Since lamp cords are walked on by two-legged members of the family and chewed on by those with four, they often do require replacement. Fortunately, it's a relatively simple procedure:

- Unplug the lamp and remove the lightbulb(s).

- Take the lamp apart from the top down. (See "Repairing a Faulty Lamp," page 56.)

- Loosen the terminal screws and remove the wire ends.

- Remove felt from the base and cut the plug from the old cord with diagonal-cutting pliers or heavy-duty scissors. Tape it to the end of the new cord with electrical tape. Pull the cord up through the base until the new cord appears. Untape and remove the old cord.

- Using a utility knife, split the top three inches of new cord. Next, strip

> **INSIDER'S TERM:** Known as the electrician's multipurpose tool, the wire stripper strips insulation, cuts wire, and measures the size of wire, among other things. Available at electrical supply and hardware stores.

¾ inch of insulation from the ends with a *wire stripper.*

▶ Now, tie the underwriter's knot (see illustration, page 56).

▶ To pull the strands together, twist the end of each wire. Then attach each wire by looping the end clockwise around its terminal screw and tightening the screw.

▶ Reassemble the lamp in the reverse order in which it was taken apart. Plug it in, and let there be light!

INSIDER'S TIP: Want to truly be seen in your "best light"? Well, your lightbulb can actually help. General Electric's new Enrich bulbs produce a crisp white light that flatters skin tone and makes colors appear more vibrant. You see, in the bulb's glass, neodymium filters out portions of the yellow and green spectrum, enhancing natural hues and boosting color contrast. Now you'll always be "ready for your close-up"!

REPAIRING A BROKEN DOORBELL

If no one's been ringing your chimes lately, perhaps it's a simple matter of a faulty doorbell. The good news about making such repairs is that the voltage for doorbell circuits is very low and so, therefore, is your risk of hearing bells prior to the completion of the task!

By way of a little background, electrical power for your doorbell proceeds from your circuit breaker at 120 volts of current. Since this is substantially stronger than a doorbell can handle, the transformer performs the job of reducing the volts from 120 to between 6 and 30. From the transformer, an open circuit is created. When you press the button, the circuit closes and the doorbell rings. Before you start any repair, go to the main service panel and check for tripped circuit breakers or blown fuses. If none are apparent, the following is all you need to know, part by part, to return the ebb and flow of traffic through your front door:

THE PUSH BUTTON

▶ Start by turning off the power to the circuit breaker that services the doorbell.

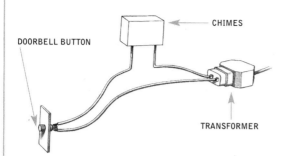

CHIMES

DOORBELL BUTTON

TRANSFORMER

across the terminals (the two prongs revealed on the back of the mechanism). If the bell rings, the button needs to be replaced. Read on to find out how.

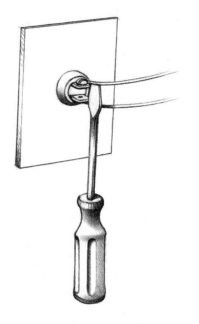

▶ Remove the push-button switch cover from the doorframe with a screwdriver. (It should be easy.)

▶ Since contact points for doorbells located outside the house are often corroded (due to exposure to the elements), try cleaning them by gently rubbing with a piece of fine sandpaper.

▶ Pry up the contact points slightly with a screwdriver. Replace cover, turn on power, and push the button. If the bell rings nonstop, it means the contacts are pried too high. Turn off the power again, remove the push button, and adjust the contact points. If there's no sound at all, read on to find out how to replace the button.

▶ Unscrew the push-button mounting plate from the outside of the door and place a wire or screwdriver

▶ Once again, turn off the power to the circuit that services the doorbell.

▶ Remove the old push button and mounting plate and disconnect the wires. Take to an electrical supply or hardware store for replacement.

▶ Reconnect the wires to the terminal screws of the new mounting plate, making sure all wire connections are tightly fastened. Now, press the button again. The bell should ring. If it doesn't ring when you place the screwdriver across the terminals, read on to find out how to check the transformer.

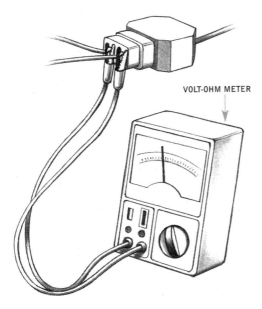

VOLT-OHM METER

THE TRANSFORMER

The transformer is usually located near the circuit breaker box or close to the door itself. The safest and best way to test whether the transformer is working properly is to use a device called a *volt-ohm meter*. To operate, set the voltage range on the volt-ohm meter to 120 volts AC and measure the voltage be-

tween the two low-voltage terminals on the transformer. If the transformer is functioning properly, the meter reading should match the secondary voltage (6 to 24 volts) marked on the transformer or bell. If the meter reads significantly higher than the indicated secondary voltage, the transformer should be replaced. Read on.

► After shutting off the power, unscrew the transformer from the junction box and disconnect the wires.

► Since there are several different kinds of transformers, it is important to take the old one to the electrical supply or hardware store so that it can be replaced exactly.

► To install the new transformer: Feed the two wires through the junction box, twisting one transformer wire to the white wire and the other one to the black wire. Fasten the ends with a wire nut.

► Screw the transformer to the junction box and connect the bell wires to the low-voltage transformer terminal screws.

▸ Turn the power on and test the doorbell again.

If there's still no connection, you will need to check the chimes.

> **INSIDER'S TERM:** A volt-ohm meter measures voltage and resistance. It also tests for grounding and continuity. Although the volt-ohm meter looks like a complicated device, it is really very easy to use.

THE CHIMES

Most doorbell chime assemblies have three terminals marked **FRONT**, **TRANS**, and **REAR**. They are connected to the **FRONT** door push button, the **TRANSFORMER**, and the **REAR** push button. Here's what you do to replace a doorbell chime:

▸ Shut off the power at the circuit breaker box.

▸ With masking tape, label each wire **FRONT**, **TRANS**, and **REAR** before disconnecting them.

▸ Loosen terminal screws, remove wires, and unscrew chime from the wall. Buy an exact replacement unit.

▸ Install replacement unit by threading the wires through the opening in the back of the new unit. Screw it to the wall. Hook each of the labeled wires to their corresponding terminal screw. Tighten the screw and replace face cover on the chime. Restore power and test your system.

If you still get no ring, the problem is probably with the wire that forms the circuit. Since replacing the wire is a difficult task, you will need to call in a professional.

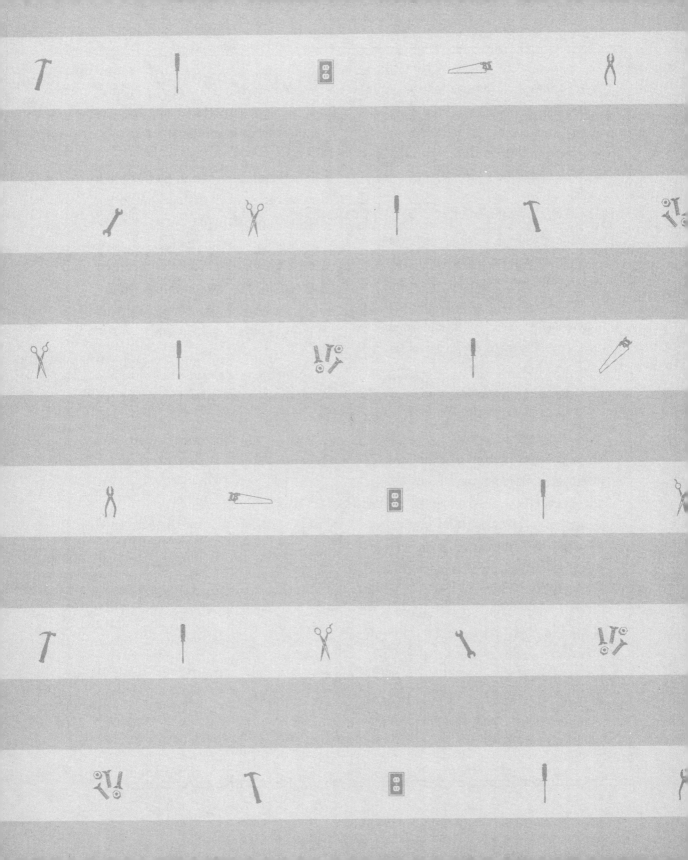

CHAPTER 4

Scrape, Spackle, and Roll:
These Four Walls

Rent-A-Husband tends to occupy a unique position in the families for whom he works. Because he performs his services in the sanctity of their homes—yet is generally not involved in his customers' day-to-day lives—he is frequently viewed as a neutral "sounding board" and finds himself privy to the sort of personal "tidbits" otherwise reserved for hairdressers and therapists. A recent case in point:

It was the afternoon of her husband's birthday, and Karen had hired Rent-A-Husband to hang the portrait she'd had done (as a surprise for him) in the master bedroom. At some point in their conversation, she suddenly confessed she'd never really felt "accepted" by her very conservative mother-in-law. She went on to say that she hoped the

party that night would provide them with an opportunity to somehow get closer. As he would later learn, it most certainly did . . . but not in the way you might expect.

You see, somewhere during the course of the meal, Karen commanded the full and immediate attention of the assembled multitude when—in the process of discussing her afternoon—she was overheard to say, "Jack [her husband] ruined the surprise when he came home early and walked into our bedroom just as Rent-A-Husband was nailing me to the wall." Suffice to say, Rent-A-Husband gained a whole new following that evening, but most ironic of all, he actually provided Karen with the opportunity she'd been seeking. For instead of chastising her for making such seemingly "indiscreet" remarks, her mother-in-law was, instead, the first in a long line of female guests to corner Karen with the same whispered but urgent request: "May I *please* get that number?"

By way of segue into this chapter, it should be noted that prior to the "hanging," Rent-A-Husband had repainted not only the bedroom in which it took place, but two other bedrooms and a den, as well. With that said, let's get down to the business of overhauling the view from inside "these four walls."

CHANGE YOUR SURROUNDINGS WITH COLOR

One of the easiest and most inexpensive ways to transform your "view" and, hence, change your outlook in more ways than one is to apply a fresh coat of paint to your rooms. And if you're a novice in the home repair department, you're in luck! Painting is the perfect project for first-time do-it-yourselfers. You can acquire the necessary skills on the job, and the cost of paint and equipment is minor considering the payback. Plus, painting poses very little threat in the safety or risk department. As you begin, however, bear in mind that Michelangelo didn't start his painting career with the Sistine Chapel . . . so follow his lead. Begin small with an easy project you can complete quickly and without too much preparation. With time, your confidence and abilities will increase, as will the size of the projects you take on.

> **INSIDER'S TIP:** A "goof-proof" project for beginners is to paint the walls and ceilings the same color. This all-for-one method eliminates much of the "cutting in" (painting a straight line at the edge where the two painted areas meet) that's required when you use two colors.

GETTING THE LEAD OUT

Before the health hazards of lead paint became generally recognized, the majority of paint was lead-based. This means that the paint found in most homes built prior to 1950, and in many others built before 1980, is lead-based. This can pose significant risk, particularly to pregnant women and to children. Ingesting lead paint—whether in the form of peeling chips or as fine dust particles—causes lead poisoning, which can lead to brain damage.

If you live in an older home, have the paint tested professionally. You can check your Yellow Pages under "Lead Paint Detection and Removal Services" for help in testing. The U.S. Department of Housing and Urban Development (HUD) recommends that action be taken to reduce exposure when lab tests indicate that the lead in paint is greater than 0.5 percent.

There are six different methods used to reduce lead hazards. Two methods (encapsulation and enclosure) work by isolating lead hazards, and four other methods (chemical stripping, abrasive removal, hand scraping, and component replacement) permanently remove the lead from the dwelling. Before deciding on the best strategy for your home, consult with the experts.

READYING TO PREPARE

Like any other canvas, the surface of your walls must be cleaned, smoothed, and properly primed before you actually begin to apply color. Starting with a dirty or damaged wall can sabotage your efforts before you even begin. If yours have smudges from messy little (and big) fingers, or if you're painting a kitchen that's been subjected to food or chemical splashes, wash the soiled areas with a mild household detergent and allow them to dry thoroughly before proceeding any further. Also, scrub down any walls exposed to dust, smoke, or other contaminants.

Some walls require extra cleaning. To eliminate mildew, for example, wash the affected area with a mixture of 1 cup chlorine bleach per gallon of water. Or, to cut through grease and other tough stains, use trisodium phosphate (available at paint supply stores). Be sure to follow the directions and precautions exactly as printed on the label.

FIX IT FIRST

From wallpaper paste residue to a few nicks and scratches, every blemish will diminish the quality of your finished paint job. Therefore, the following are some suggestions for repairing the scars of wear and tear.

TO REPAIR A CRACK OR SMALL HOLE IN THE WALL

You will need a can of spackling compound (or, if the hole is very small, try substituting toothpaste to fill the "cavity"). Also necessary is a putty knife about 1½ inches in width, and a piece of fine sandpaper.

► Scrape away any loose plaster along the crack. A good way to handle this problem is to gently run a bottle opener along the crack.

► Scoop the spackling compound onto your putty knife and run the knife over the crack.

► Continue applying layers of spackle until the crack is completely filled.

► When the final layer is dry, gently sand the repaired surface with the sandpaper until it is smooth.

TO REPAIR A LARGER HOLE IN A PLASTER WALL

You will need—in addition to the aforementioned supplies—a container of joint compound, a wire screen, a thin shoelace or wire, and a pencil or small stick that is longer than the width of the hole. Also required are a pair of scissors and a small paintbrush.

► Get started by removing all the loose plaster from around the hole.

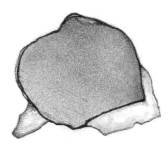

► To construct a supporting device within the hole to hold the joint compound used for the repair, cut a section of wire screen considerably larger than the hole.

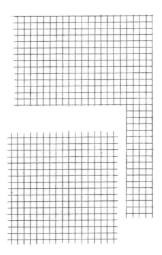

▶ Thread the shoelace through the screen. You will use this to pull the screen tightly against the hole once it is inserted.

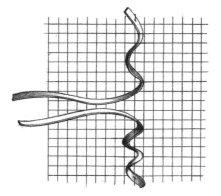

▶ Insert the screen into the hole, pull on the shoelace so that the screen fits tightly against the hole, and tie the shoelace to the small stick or pencil, which you will place across the hole. This will hold the screen in place while you put the first coat of joint compound into the hole.

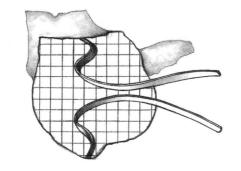

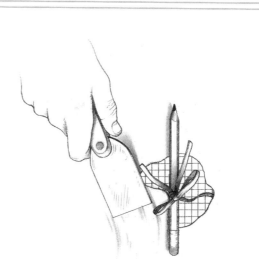

▶ To apply the joint compound, first use your paintbrush to moisten the hole and screen with water. Using your putty knife, insert enough joint compound into the hole so that it oozes onto the screen and covers the sides of the hole.

▶ After the first layer of joint compound is thoroughly dry (24 hours later), remove the stick or pencil and pull out the shoelace. Fill the small hole that remains with joint compound.

▶ Now three more coats of joint compound can be applied to the hole. Allow the joint compound to dry 24 hours between coats.

▶ When the hole is fully covered and dry, sand the area smooth.

> ⋐ **INSIDER'S TIP:** Although some people use a hair dryer to speed the process along, air drying provides the most uniform and thorough result.

IS IT PAINT YET?

Not quite. Before the inside of any can of paint sees the light of day, it is essential that your walls be properly prepared. This will further ensure a result that matches the vision you have in your mind's eye.

Accomplishing this rather simple but important task is much easier than you probably think, but you will need the following equipment:

▶ **A SANDING SPONGE**—Simply by brushing the entire area with the sanding sponge, you will remove any rough spots that would mar your paint job.

▶ **A TACK CLOTH**—This furthers the smoothing process by removing any lint from the wall it is wiped across.

PRIME TIME

First of all, understand that primers are not just cheap versions of white paint. Because drywall and other wall surfaces will absorb paint, the primer prevents an uneven finish and a washed-out look when the color is applied. A primer is a basecoat designed to create a solid foundation on which to apply the color. A quality primer should do its job in one coat. If the wall is already painted, you probably won't have to use a primer. However, if you're painting a lighter shade over a darker one, if you're painting over a pattern, if you've made repairs to the wall, or if you're painting a new surface, look for a primer formulated for your particular situation.

The following is a run-down of the specific functions of the various primers:

▶ **LATEX VS. OIL-BASED PRIMERS**—Match the paint. In other words, if you're painting with an oil-based paint, use an oil-based primer. Likewise for latex.

▶ **UNIVERSAL PRIMERS**—These primer-sealers bond and seal a surface for a consistent finish. Cover new drywall and/or walls that have been patched with a coat of universal primer before you paint.

▶ **SEALING PRIMERS**—These are formulated to prevent stains from seeping through the painted finish. Use sealing primers to spot-cover visible water marks or other stains on your walls before you paint.

> 💡 **INSIDER'S TIP:** If the instructions on the can of primer specify a coverage of 1 gallon per 400 square feet, don't try to stretch the coverage to 450 square feet. Your primer will be too thin, and the finish coat may not adhere properly.

▶ **COVER-UP PRIMERS**—These are created to conceal dark colors and bold patterns beneath a lighter shade. Very dark undercoats may require more than one coat of primer.

PRIMARY COLORS

Once you've followed all the steps above, your walls will finally be ready for the actual application of color.

Before you can start to paint, however, you have to know what kind of paint to buy. All this takes is a little know-how, so pay careful attention to the information you're about to receive.

The first thing you need to understand is the difference between oil-based (alkyd) and water-based (latex) paints. The oil-based variety creates a more durable and washable surface, but it's harder to work with and requires you to clean your rollers and brushes with paint thinner (also known as mineral spirits.) Water-based paint is much easier to handle because it cleans up with just soap and water, dries much faster, and has a less offensive odor than the oil-based variety.

> 👉 **INSIDER'S TERM:** Alkyd paint is modern oil-based paint containing synthetic resins called alkyds. It has replaced oil paints containing linseed and other natural oils.

Hence, water-based paint is clearly the formula of choice for the first-time painter. A good strategy to remember is to use water-based paint on the walls and oil-based paint on windows and door trim where you need a hard finish that stands up to frequent washings. Also, don't leave the store without several standard stirrers, a paint tray (from which you will roll) and painter's masking tape (which sticks to the wall and, because painter's tape is wider than the roller, it will prevent paint from spilling over where you don't want it). Painter's masking tape also has an "easy release" that—unlike regular masking tape (which, by the way, should *never* be used for this purpose)—enables you to peel it off without tearing the paint underneath.

Paints come in a variety of gloss levels—or sheens—that determine the shine and brightness on your walls and ceilings. Here's what you need to be aware of:

> ► **FLAT PAINT** is at the low end of the brightness spectrum, which is why it's frequently used on ceilings and walls. This type of paint also reflects a minimum of light off walls, thus reducing glare and helping to hide small imperfections in the surface.

> ► **EGGSHELL, LO-LUSTER, AND SATIN PAINTS** have a slight sheen, hold up a bit bet-

> 💡 **INSIDER'S TIP:** When deciding which brand of paint to buy, always err on the high end. Better quality paint will end up costing you less in the long run because of its durability and its innate ability to keep its great looks longer. Also, ask the store to mix a small amount of any shade you think you're interested in. The "real thing" looks very different on the walls than the paint chips indicate. So, even if you have to buy a quart (although some stores will mix as little as a pint), you're better off finding out before you invest in gallons of the stuff whether or not it's a color you want to live with.

ter than flat paints, and are easier to wash (which makes them best suited for hallways and other high-traffic areas that require frequent washing).

> ► **SEMIGLOSS** is usually the paint of choice for such areas as kitchens, bathrooms, and kids' rooms. Its slightly greater sheen makes it easier to wash than satin paint.

► **GLOSS AND HIGH-GLOSS PAINTS,** aka enamel, are likely candidates for covering woodwork, furniture, and cabinets because they dry to a very hard and shiny finish. They are also able to withstand heavy use and scrubbing.

WHAT YOU'LL NEED TO BE COVERED

When estimating paint quantities, remember that a gallon of paint generally will cover about 400 square feet. Provide the salesperson with the dimensions of the room you're planning to paint by multiplying the room's height by the length of all walls; and be sure to include the number of openings (alcoves, chimneys, etc.), which will not be painted. Also, let him know whether you plan to use a different type of paint on

---

INSIDER'S TIP: To help air out a freshly painted room, cut an onion into several large pieces and place the pieces in a pail of water in the middle of the floor. Neither odor will make you "cry" because the gases released by the onion will neutralize the paint fumes.

---

woodwork and doors. Include windows and doors as part of the surface unless they are especially large. When it comes to estimating for windows, the general rule is to allow 2½ square yards for a small window, 4¾ square yards for a medium-size, and 6 square yards for a large window.

THE TOOLS OF THE TRADE

Since a painter simply can't paint without an applicator (a brush or roller), the importance of choosing the right one for the job cannot be overemphasized.

BRUSHES

When using latex paint, stick with a synthetic brush. Natural-bristle fibers will absorb the water in the paint, causing the bristles to frizz and perform badly. Either a brush or a roller will work with oil-based paints, but natural or high-quality synthetic brushes are best.

When choosing the size of your brush, use the following as a guide:

► A 3- to 6-inch-wide brush will provide you with speedy coverage on walls and ceilings (if you don't opt for a roller).

▶ A 1- to 3-inch-wide flat sash or trim brush is what you need for cabinets, shelves, doors, and wide moldings. The same size brush but with angled bristles is best in tight spots such as window trim, moldings, and corners.

> 💡 **INSIDER'S TIP:** To ensure you are buying a quality brush, tap the bristles on the edge of a counter (before you leave the store!). If more than a couple of bristles come out, it's not what you're looking for.

ROLLERS

When deciding on a roller, choose one with a heavy wire frame and a comfortable handle that has a threaded end to accept an extension pole (a must for tackling ceilings). Also, opt for a roller that is heavy and stiff, thus enabling you to work with constant pressure and get into corners without bending it. Naps—not the afternoon variety—but rather the sort that slide on over the roller's sleeve are also sized according to function. Here are the specifics:

▶ Use a foam nap for work on wood and polyurethane (which require a thinner coat), as it doesn't retain a lot of fluids and paint.

▶ For a smooth finish on ceilings, a $\frac{3}{16}$-inch nap is best because ceilings almost always have a smoother finish than walls. (The only exception lies in a specially textured ceiling, which requires a $\frac{3}{8}$-inch nap.)

▶ Because walls have a slightly grainier surface than most ceilings, they need a bit more texture and are best served with a $\frac{3}{8}$-inch nap.

▶ The big one—$\frac{1}{2}$-inch nap—is necessary for jobs done on concrete and textured walls because the larger the

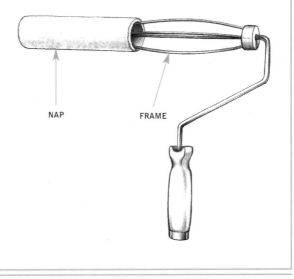

NAP   FRAME

nap, the more paint it holds. It also enables you to get into and around those uneven crevices and bumps very efficiently.

TECHNIQUE

Move all the room's furniture into the middle of the floor, cover both floor and furniture with drop cloths, remove all switchplates, ceiling fixtures, and wall sconces so you don't have to "cut in" around them. Now you're finally ready to paint. If you're using more than one color, begin by applying professional painter's tape (a specialized masking tape available at hardware stores) over the areas you want protected. Also, if your paint has been sitting for more than 2 days, stir it for about 3 minutes to ensure an even, smooth consistency before pouring it into your tray.

You should always paint from top to bottom, starting with the ceiling. And, as much as possible, the light should be natural. This will provide you with the truest picture of how the paint actually will look. Another key to painting like a pro is always to use an adequate amount of paint, so don't hesitate to load it on. As strange as it might sound,

INSIDER'S TIP: If the sunlight is direct and proves to be "too much of a good thing," there's a chance you might notice something called blistering which resembles alligator-like skin. This happens when a layer of paint dries faster than the primer or paint beneath it. Before you try to correct the problem, wait for the entire area to dry completely, then scrape away the blisters, sand and repaint. (And try to do it after the sun goes down!)

this actually lets the paint (rather than you) do the work—lay it on, roll it off.

When the ceiling is done, it's time to tackle the walls. The best approach is to do one workable section (a 3- to 4-foot span) at a time. Tape it off from the ceiling with professional painter's tape, roll the paint on, and move to the next section. Also, for flawless blending, always remember to lighten your stroke as you head toward the completion of each section. As far as painting with the roller goes, the most common mistake people make is to load their roller up with paint and apply it in an up-and-down motion. What this does is to create something known in the paint world as "holidays"—the kind nobody wants to see come around (or in lay terms, an uneven distribution of paint). This is because there is a heavy concentration at the top that fades more and more the farther down you go. Years of experience have taught that the most practical approach (and the one that virtually guarantees even distribution of the paint) is to direct your roller—left to right—in a series of "V" movements (think upside-down teepees). When you reach the end of the area you're working on, roll back over the area in reverse. As final coverage assurance, go over the same space once again, but this time with horizontal strokes.

Trim is done last. You can do the windows and doors, and then the base molding. Here again, don't be afraid to use paint: not so much that it runs, but enough so you don't have to paint and repaint each area. A tried-and-true professional painter's technique is something known as painting "from the dry into the wet." You dip about a third to a half of the brush into the paint, and then skip ahead a couple of feet from the end of the previous brush stroke and paint back into the wet paint.

> ☼ **INSIDER'S TIP:** If you find yourself running out of paint, end at a corner or another natural breaking point. Stopping in the middle of a room can lead to something "insiders" call *lap marks*, which occur when freshly applied paint overlaps the existing dry coat.

CLEANING UP

When you are finished for the day, there are a number of steps to take. First, when cleaning brushes and rollers, remove as much of the paint as you can before using solvents. To clean a brush, lay it on a sheet of newspaper. Then push down on the bristles with a scraper or a joint compound knife (a flat, 6- to 14-inch knife used to apply joint compound), squeezing as much paint as possible out of the bristles. When you've removed as much paint as you can, wash the brush.

If you're using water-based paint, immerse the bristles in a solution of water and mild soap. Knead the bristles with your hand, then rinse them in clear running water. Wrap the brush in newspaper or its original package.

If you're working with oil-based paint, immerse the bristles in a can of mineral spirits and—as before—knead them with your fingers. (Wear rubber gloves for this one.) Next, immerse the brush in another can with paint thinner in it; rinse and repeat this step. When using rollers, apply the same guidelines, but use a stick to first squeeze out the excess paint.

WALL COVERINGS

For those who crave more drama and dimension in their surroundings than mere paint can provide, wallpaper may be the answer. Or, to be more precise, wall coverings, a name that reflects the amazingly diverse array of textures and styles currently available. It isn't just about paper anymore! And to illustrate this point, here is an overview of what you can expect to find "hanging around."

NOTE: Although some wall coverings do require that paste be applied, for the purpose of do-it-yourself paper hanging, it's best to stick with prepasted paper.

CHOICES IN MATERIALS

Frequently, the use a room receives will dictate the best material for the wall covering. For example, although areas such as children's rooms need only washable paper, a scrubbable one will withstand rough treatment and thorough cleaning much better. The material content of a wall covering is a determining factor in its durability and

☞ **INSIDER'S TERM:** Strippable wallpaper is wallpaper that can be removed from the wall by hand, without tearing or leaving any paper residue. It may, however, leave some adhesive.

☞ **INSIDER'S TERM:** Peelable wallpaper is wallpaper that can be removed from the wall by peeling off the top layer. This leaves a thin residue of paper and adhesive, which is removable with water.

☞ **INSIDER'S TERM:** A pattern repeat indicates the vertical distance between one design element on a pattern and the next occurrence of that design element.

ability to be cleaned, as well as in its appearance, cost, installation, and ease of removal.

When shopping for wallpaper, be sure and check the back of all the samples that interest you. You'll find such valuable information as the wallpaper's content, its ability to be washed, whether it's *strippable* or *peelable*, and the size of its *pattern repeat*.

VINYLS

Most do-it-yourselfers prefer wallpaper with some vinyl content, because vinyl's durability and strength make these papers relatively easy to install and maintain. They include:

▶ **VINYL-COATED PAPER**—Since this wall covering is made of paper that's coated with just a thin layer of vinyl, vinyl-coated paper is the least durable of the papers with vinyl content. It is best reserved for areas with less than heavy traffic.

▶ **PAPER-BACKED VINYL**—Paper-backed vinyl has a vinyl top layer with a paper backing. It comes *prepasted* and is often peelable and washable, as well. A special type of paper-backed vinyl, known as *expanded vinyl*, has a three-dimensional effect. Often designed to look like another surface (such as rough plaster, granite, grass cloth, or textured paint), it is especially suitable for walls that are less than perfectly smooth.

▶ **FABRIC-BACKED VINYL**—The sturdiest kind of wallpaper, fabric-backed vinyl has a top layer of vinyl and a backing of fiberglass or cheesecloth. It is washable, frequently scrubbable, and usually strippable. Fabric-backed vinyl is also more moisture-resistant and less likely to tear than most other papers. Because it's too heavy to roll well if prepasted, fabric-backed vinyl usually comes unpasted. It is, therefore, not the best choice for a beginner.

> ☞ **INSIDER'S TERM:** Prepasted wallpaper has been factory-coated with water-soluble adhesive. You can activate the paste by soaking the paper in water for the time recommended by the manufacturer.

TEXTILES

Textile wall coverings are available in an array of colors and textures, ranging from casual to elegantly formal. Usually made of cotton, linen, other natural plant fibers, or polyester, they're frequently bonded to a paper-type backing.

Since many textile wall coverings require *liner paper* underneath, they should be installed only by a professional. Also, be aware that most textiles fray easily and are not washable.

Some popular entries in this category include:

▶ **GRASS CLOTH**—A long-standing favorite in textile wall coverings, grass cloth contains threads that provide great versatility, because they can be arranged horizontally, vertically, or in a woven pattern.

▶ **HEMP**—Similar to grass cloth, but with thinner fibers, hemp is proving to be a more popular choice because it is easier to install than grass cloth.

▶ **PAPER WEAVE**—Although it resembles grass cloth, paper weave is actually made of paper that has been cut into strips and then pulled to make hanks of material or yarn. This yarn is then turned into a paper backing.

> 👉 **INSIDER'S TERM:** Liner paper is blank paper stock hung under wallpaper in order to smooth wall surfaces, absorb excess moisture, and provide a breathable layer between a nonporous (water or water-soluble adhesive cannot penetrate) wall covering and the wall.

OTHER WALLPAPER CHOICES

The following are more options in wallpaper materials. However, because each presents an installation challenge (of one sort or another), it's best to have these professionally hung.

▶ **FOILS**—These are composed of thin sheets of aluminum foil (containing the color and pattern) that are adhered to a paper or cloth backing known as a scrim. There may also be a layer of polyester between the foil and the backing to prevent water in the wall covering paste from contacting the foil. Because they wrinkle easily, they require an absolutely smooth wall surface.

▶ MYLAR—A DuPont trade name, Mylar refers to a particular kind of polyester film that has been combined with aluminum or vinyl sheeting. It is applied over decorative wallpapers with a variety of backings, but unlike foil (with which it's often confused), Mylar will burn.

▶ SOLID PAPER—Wall coverings made of solid paper without any vinyl—whether inexpensive or costly—tear very easily.

▶ FLOCKED PAPER—With a raised-pattern finish in silk, rayon, nylon, or cotton, flocked paper has a texture that resembles damask or cut velvet.

> INSIDER'S TIP: Buy high-quality, machine-printed, pretrimmed paper (wallpaper from which the *selvage*, or unpatterned side edge that protects it during shipping and handling, has been trimmed at the factory).

▶ HAND-SCREENED PAPERS—Each color in a hand-screened paper is applied with a separate handmade and hand-placed silk screen, which means they are among the most expensive wall coverings. Very dramatic, they have a unique three-dimensional appearance.

▶ MURALS—Frequently depicting nature or some historic event, a mural opens up a room, especially if the strips are hung across a large area of wall. You must, however, hang the panels in the order specified by the manufacturer. For a striking look, try hanging a single-panel mural in the middle of a large wall, framed, on either side, by paper that coordinates with the mural's background.

HOW IT MEASURES UP

Although wallpaper usually comes packaged in double rolls (or two-roll bolts), it is priced by the single roll. Clearly, this was a ploy cooked up at a wallpaper sales convention, where it was decided that it makes wallpaper sound less expensive if you advertise the price of only *half* of the minimum purchase! Anyway, to determine how many rolls of wallpaper to buy,

SIZE OF ROOM (FT)	CEILING HEIGHT				
	8FT	9FT	10FT	11FT	12FT
	# OF SINGLE ROLLS REQUIRED Although wallpaper usually comes packaged in two-roll bolts, it is priced by the single roll.				
5x6	8	8	10	11	12
8x10	9	10	11	12	13
10x10	10	11	13	14	15
10x12	11	12	14	15	16
10x14	12	14	15	16	18
12x12	12	14	15	16	18
12x14	13	15	16	18	19
12x16	14	16	17	19	21
12x18	15	17	19	20	22
12x20	16	18	20	22	24
14x14	14	16	17	19	21
14x16	15	17	19	20	22
14x18	16	18	20	22	24
14x20	17	19	21	23	25
14x22	18	20	22	24	27
16x16	16	18	20	22	24
16x18	17	19	21	23	25
16x20	18	20	22	24	27
16x22	16	21	23	26	28
16x24	20	22	25	27	30
18x18	18	20	22	24	27
18x20	19	21	23	25	28
18x22	20	22	25	27	30
18x24	21	23	26	28	31

you need to measure the wall space in the room you will be covering and take into account any pattern repeat.

To do this: Measure the height and width of each wall (including openings), using your steel tape measure. Now, multiply the height by the width of each wall and add the figures together. Subtract the square footage of windows and doors (since you won't be applying wallpaper on them). You should also come out all right if you simply deduct 15 square feet for every average-size door or window. For larger or unusually shaped openings, however, stick with exact square footage. Most single rolls of wallpaper contain approximately 36 square feet, regardless of the length or width of the paper. For instance, a roll 27 inches wide will be about 16 feet long, while a roll 24 inches wide will be about 18 feet long. To allow for cutting and trimming, however, figure about 30 usable square feet of wallpaper per roll. Therefore, divide the total square footage of wall space by 30. If you have a fraction remaining, buy an additional roll.

PREPARING FOR CHANGE

In order to get ready for your new look, you will need the following:

► A table on which to lay out the wallpaper. To protect the tabletop, cover it tightly with clear plastic and brown kraft paper, which comes in a roll. Avoid using newspapers to cover this table because newsprint will bleed through onto the wallcovering.

► Drop cloths to cover your furniture, which should be gathered in center of room (if it can't be moved out of the area altogether, which is always preferable). Buy the inexpensive plastic variety, available at the paint store.

> **INSIDER'S TIP:** Before you begin to hang wallpaper, unroll the paper and inspect it for flaws. Reroll it with the back side out to relieve the curl and make it easier to handle later.

> **INSIDER'S TIP:** The pattern repeat is given in inches on the labels or in the wallpaper book. For patterns that have wide matches, add 1 or 2 single rolls to your purchase.

- A ladder (aluminum is more expensive than wood, but you'll see it's a small price to pay if you try dragging a wooden one around for any length of time). Remember, you can always rent.

- A painter's pad with which to moisten prepasted paper.

- A yardstick for measuring and cutting.

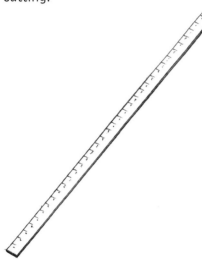

- A level to mark a perfectly straight line.

- A razor knife with a package of new, sharp blades to cut wallpaper.

- A wide putty knife for use with the razor knife for trimming the paper at baseboards and ceilings. The putty knife holds the paper in place; the razor does the cutting.

► A 12-inch smoothing brush with slightly firm bristles to remove air bubbles and wrinkles once you get the paper up.

► A seam roller to set smooth, tight joints between the edges of the wallpaper. Or use a window squeegee.

INSIDER'S TIP: Save wallpaper scraps for repairing tears or stains later on. (See below for instructions.) In the meantime, be sure to store the scraps in an inconspicuous location, where they'll be exposed to the same amount of sunlight as the paper on the walls. This will allow for a similar degree of fading.

TAKE IT OFF

If your walls are already wallpapered, it's usually best to remove the paper before applying the new wall covering. Even when an existing wall covering looks good, professionals usually recommend removing it because moisture from the paste used to apply the new wallpaper can loosen paper that's been holding well, spoiling the new covering.

REMOVING OLD WALLPAPER

How you remove the old wallpaper will depend on the kind of paper that's on your walls. Strippable paper is the easiest to remove, since you can pull both the vinyl coating and the backing off the wall in one easy step. Starting at a seam, you simply pull the paper off gently and slowly at an angle that allows you to keep both hands near the wall.

With peelable paper, you follow the same procedure to pull off the vinyl coating, but the fabric or paper backing remains on the wall.

To remove the backing and to remove other wall coverings that aren't strippable or peelable, you'll have to rewet the adhesive that holds the paper to the wall. Only when the paste is wet can you pull it off the wall.

If your paper has a nonpeelable, nonporous covering (such as vinyl or foil), moisture applied to the surface won't soak through the adhesive. For this reason, the adhesive will have to be removed. To accomplish this as easily as possible, simply wet the wall with a sponge or short-handled mop dipped into a solution of 1 gallon of very hot water mixed with $1/2$ cup of white vinegar.

Wet one wall at a time, or only as much wall surface as you can keep wet and work on before it dries out. Apply the moisture, let it soak in, and then rewet the surface before it dries. You may have to wet the wall several times. The paper should be as wet as a soaked jar label ready to be peeled off. This can take up to 15 minutes. Working down

from the top of the wall, scrape off the wallpaper with a putty knife, being careful not to chip or otherwise damage the wall surface. If the paper doesn't pull away easily, wet it again. Removing multiple layers of wallpaper usually works best if you tackle one layer at a time. Make sure no particles are left behind by going over the area with a steel wool pad before giving it a final rinse with the water/vinegar solution.

Repair any cracks, holes, or other wall damage (as described earlier in this chapter on pages 65–68, when painting walls). Then wash the wall from the bottom up with a solution of trisodium phosphate—TSP, available at any hardware store—and water (follow the package directions for mixing).

> **INSIDER'S TIP:** Make a patch by taping a piece of the wallpaper scrap over the damaged area. Be sure to line up your pattern. After you have drawn out a cut design, use your razor knife (with a new blade) to cut through both layers. Remove damaged piece and paste new piece onto the wall.

PRIMING

In general, wallpaper goes on more easily if you've applied primer-sealer to the wall. Primer-sealer keeps the surface from absorbing moisture from the adhesive, allowing the paper to adhere more readily. It also protects the wall from damage when the covering is removed later on.

Choose a primer-sealer specifically designed as an undercoat for your type of wall covering. Using a roller, apply it at least 24 hours before hanging the wall covering so the wall will be thoroughly dry. (Follow the manufacturer's directions regarding drying time.)

Some professionals believe that alkyd primer-sealers bond to walls better than water-soluble acrylics. Acrylic primer-sealers, however, are easier to use and clean up. You'll want to use alkyds in high-moisture areas, over an *alkyd paint* (see page 69), or if it is recommended by the wallpaper manufacturer.

When you're hanging a semitransparent paper over a colored wall, use a color-coordinated primer-sealer. You can also have the primer mixed to match the paper's background color, so that any hairline seam cracks will be less obvious.

INSIDER'S TIP: Moist areas, such as bathrooms and outer walls, are often susceptible to mildew stains. If you see mildew, you need to remove not just the stains but the underlying mildew itself. Mildew is primarily caused by a fungus living on damp organic material. To kill the fungus and remove the stains, scrub the walls with liquid bleach or a solution of half bleach and half water. Then wash the walls with a solution of trisodium phosphate and water (follow package directions) and rinse well. Let the washed surface dry completely (at least 24 hours). Finally, apply a coat of alkyd (oil-based) primer-sealer into which you have mixed a commercially available fungicide additive (inquire about the specifics at a hardware store). To prevent mildew from reappearing, choose a fairly thick wallpaper and add a fungicide to the adhesive (again, ask about specifics at a hardware store). If possible, install a good fan and/or more effective window openings to provide adequate ventilation.

HANGING IN THERE

Before you start to cut, think about where you'll hang both your first and last strips, as well as how you'll hang the wall covering around obstacles. Solving potential problems before you start is much better than trying to do so while you are holding strips of wet wallpaper.

If a strip ends at an outside corner, cut it back approximately ¼ inch to prevent the paper from fraying and peeling at the corner. A plastic or wood outside corner molding can be installed to cover the ¼-inch space. First, look for the least conspicuous place in the room; usually it's over a door or in a corner near an entrance. Then locate a good starting point. Or you can start at the room's focal point, a fireplace or large window, for example, and work in both directions toward the end points. At the focal point, you can center either a *strip* or a seam.

Taking one possible layout, determine where the seams will fall by holding up a roll of your wall covering where the first strip will hang. Note where the edges rest. Flip the roll over sideways to find the next seam location. Continue to work your way all

around the room in this manner. Try to avoid having seams fall closer than 4 inches to such obstacles as corners, windows, and doors. That kind of placement wastes paper, and narrow pieces may not adhere well to the wall. Also, you'll want a seam near the center of any fixture so you can fit the paper around it without having to cut a long slit.

If seams fall in awkward spots, pick another starting point and work your way around again; each room usually has several possible starting places. When

you decide on start and end points, mark them on the wall.

ESTABLISHING PLUMB

Because most walls are not plumb (perfectly vertical), you'll need to establish a plumb line and use it to align the first strip. You'll also need to establish a plumb line every time you turn a corner.

Begin by adding ¼ inch to the width of your wallpaper. Measure this distance from your starting point and mark the wall near the ceiling. By making your mark *away* from a point where seams will meet, there is less chance that it will show through.

To draw a plumb line, you can use either a plumb bob or a carpenter's level. With a plumb bob, rub light-colored chalk along a plumb bob string with a weight. Place a tack in the wall at the mark you just made and tie the end of the string to the tack so that the point of the plumb bob, or weight, dangles just a fraction of an inch above the baseboard. Once the weight stops swinging back and forth, press the lower end of the string against the wall. Pull out on the middle of the line until it's taut and then let go. The vertical chalk mark left on the wall is the plumb line.

If you opt for the carpenter's level, start by holding it vertically on the wall, placing one edge against the mark you made. Adjust the level until the bubble that designates the plumb is centered. Draw a line in light pencil along the level's edge. Move the level down and

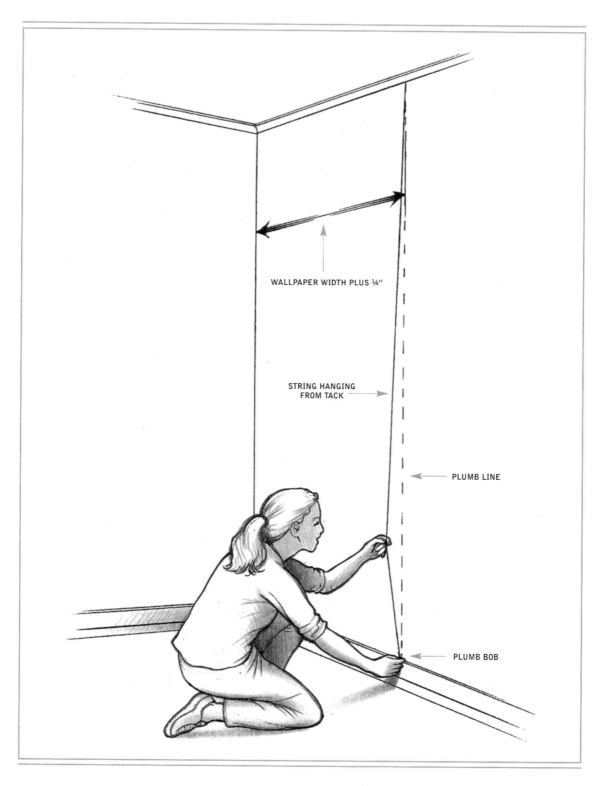

WALLPAPER WIDTH PLUS ¼"

STRING HANGING FROM TACK

PLUMB LINE

PLUMB BOB

repeat, connecting lines until you have a floor-to-ceiling plumb line.

Be sure that you hold the level steady and that the bubble remains absolutely level; even a slight variance from plumb will cause problems.

MAKING THE CUT

For visually pleasing results, any design in the wall covering should look nice at the ceiling line. To avoid chopping the design in an awkward spot, plan to have a full design element fall just below the ceiling line. If you can keep a plain background area at the top edge, any variation in ceiling height won't affect the design. For wallpaper with a *drop match*, place two strips on a table, match them, and then use a straightedge to find the best breaking point across both strips.

CEILING LINE

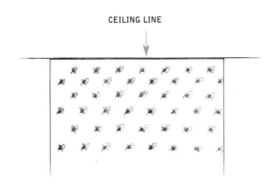

To cut a strip, measure the height of the wall. On the wallpaper roll, locate the design element you want at the top edge, measure 2 inches above that, and cut across the paper with a razor knife and straightedge. Or make a straight crease at that point, keeping the edges aligned as you fold, and cut along the crease with utility shears. Measure the length of paper you need, add 4 inches, make the bottom cut. Roll the strip bottom to top, pattern side out.

At first, cut—and hang—one strip at a time. As you develop confidence, and if your paper has a *random match* or a *straight match* with a short repeat, you can cut several strips in a row. (Be sure to number them lightly on the back.) Cut only enough strips to reach the next obstacle, such as a window or corner.

When you're cutting subsequent strips for a drop match, the best way to ensure that the pattern matches is to hold the roll up to the wall. Leaving a minimum 2-inch top allowance, match the pattern to the adjoining strip and make a crease where the top of the wall and ceiling meet. It should be a tight, neat fit. After placing the roll on the table, make the top cut at the crease. Measure the wall length plus 4 inches and then make the bottom cut.

> ☞ **INSIDER'S TERMS:** A random match is a pattern or texture having no design elements that need to be matched between adjoining strips. A straight match is a pattern in which the design flows directly across the strips, so the design elements at the top of adjoining matched strips are the same on both sides.

SOAKING THE PREPASTED PAPER

Place a water tray on a towel on the floor next to your worktable. Align the tray so its long side is parallel to the long side of the table. Fill the tray two-thirds full of lukewarm water. Now, immerse the loosely rolled strip in the water for 10 to 15 seconds (or as rec-

> ☞ **INSIDER'S TERM:** Booking means relaxing a pasted strip of wall covering by folding the pasted sides together so the ends overlap and the edges align. (See below.)

ommended by the manufacturer). Then, grasping the top corners of the soaked strip, pull it up slowly, about 1 foot per second, letting any excess water fall back into the tray. Finally, place the strip, pattern side down, on the table and book as described below (unless the manufacturer advises against *booking*).

NOTE: If you're not booking your paper, you can place the water tray on the floor directly beneath the wall area the strip will cover.

BOOKING

To promote even adhesion, wallpaper needs time before it's hung to absorb the paste. Moistened paper also expands slightly; if it's hung too quickly, the paper expands on the wall, causing bubbling. To let the strip relax, you book the paper. Most wallpapers, except foils and a few others, require booking.

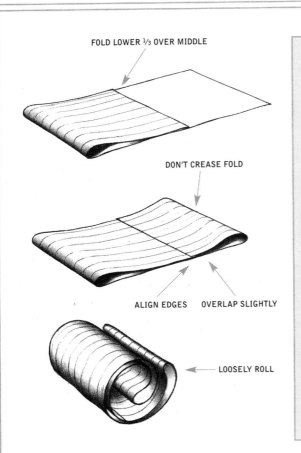

FOLD LOWER ⅓ OVER MIDDLE

DON'T CREASE FOLD

ALIGN EDGES   OVERLAP SLIGHTLY

LOOSELY ROLL

INSIDER'S TIP: To avoid having air bubbles and/or lumps, carefully smooth the wall covering as you go. Minor bubbles usually disappear when the strip is dry. However, if there are a lot, you probably rolled down the surface too many times. Use a razor knife and slit an X in the center of the bubble. If your paper is patterned, cut to follow the lines as best you can to ensure invisibility of the repair. Gently lift each corner and brush the adhesive on the underside of the paper and the wall. Press into place, sponge off any excess paste, and roll seam edges.

Begin by folding the bottom third of the strip over the middle, pasted sides together, being careful not to crease the wallpaper at the fold. The edges should align neatly. Then fold over the remaining portion of the strip until it overlaps the bottom cut end slightly, again aligning the edges neatly.

If you have pretrimmed paper, you're ready to roll the strip loosely, place it in a large plastic bag, and close the bag.

(This creates an evenly humid environment in which the paper can relax without drying out.)

If you need to trim your paper, check that the edges are precisely aligned. On one side, line up a straightedge with the trim marks. Using a sharp-bladed utility knife, cut through both layers.

After waiting the booking time recommended by the manufacturer (usually 5 to 15 minutes), you're ready to hang your first strip. Remember not to cut the second strip until the first one is hung.

HANGING THE FIRST STRIP

With your stepladder positioned next to the plumb line on the wall, unroll the first booked strip but don't unfold it. Then, holding the strip by the upper corners, slowly unfold the top portion, letting the rest of the strip fall down.

Allowing the strip to overlap the ceil-ing line by about 2 inches, place the top portion of the edge close to but not on the plumb line. Then press the strip to the wall at the ceiling line just hard enough so that the paper sticks to the wall without sliding down.

Next, adjust the paper until the side edge is perfectly parallel with the plumb line, picking up the strip as needed but being careful not to stretch the paper. If necessary, move the top corners so the paper hangs without wrinkles.

2" OVERLAP

PLUMB LINE

Using a smoother and spreading out from the seam, gently smooth the top portions of the strip so the paper, adhesive, and wall make firm contact. Remember to smooth the paper into the ceiling edge as well. Unfold the rest of the strip, aligning and smoothing it as you did the top portion. When the entire strip is straight and smooth, run a seam roller or sponge along the edge.

To trim the ceiling and baseboard edges, use a razor knife, keeping a broad/putty knife between the razor blade and the wall covering to ensure a straight cut and to protect the paper. To ensure smooth cuts, don't move both the broad/putty knife and the razor at the same time. And change blades often.

Wipe any excess adhesive from the wall covering, ceiling, and baseboard with a clean, damp sponge. Rinse the sponge often. Before continuing with the next strip, clean and dry your hands.

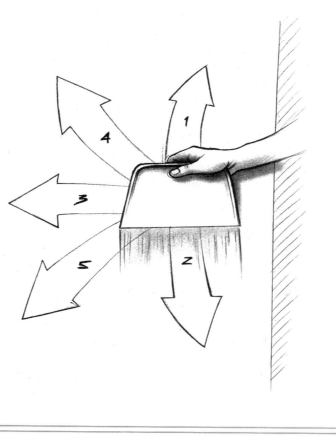

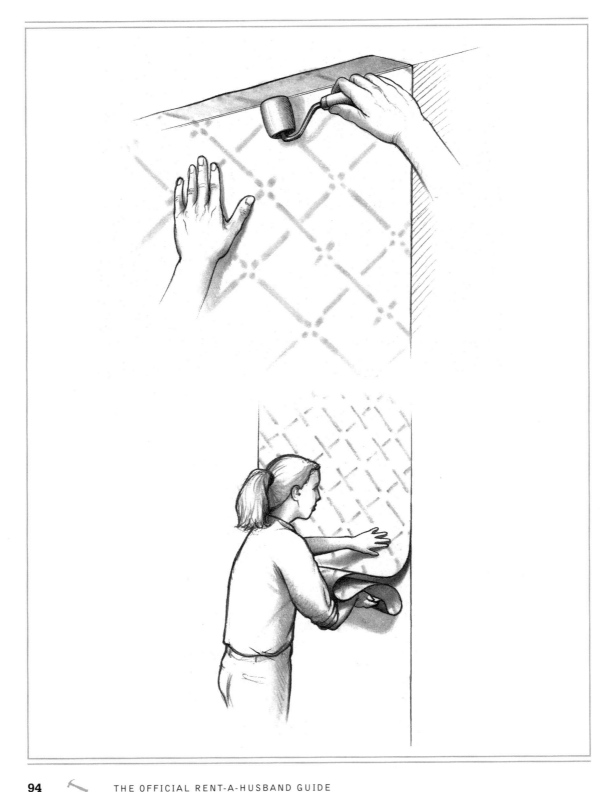

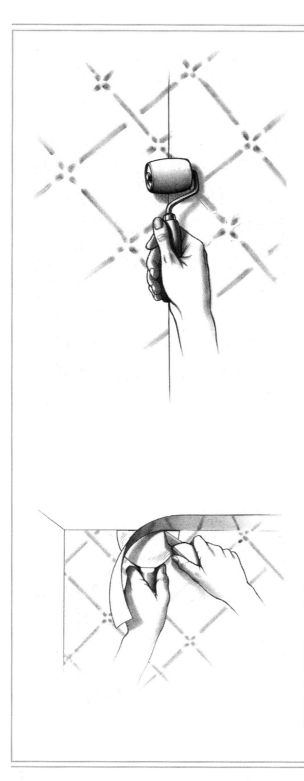

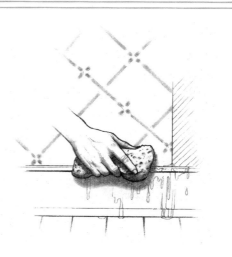

:'Q: **INSIDER'S TIP:** Unplumb surfaces: As you work around the room, you may find that the pattern doesn't always match at seam lines or that design elements at the top look crooked compared with the ceiling edge. Your difficulty probably stems from the fact that your walls and ceilings are not plumb. In general, hanging the wallpaper straight (along the plumb line) helps the overall appearance more than having the pattern match exactly. With a boldly patterned paper, however, you may need to favor the pattern break at the ceiling over having the paper plumb. Try to make corrections in inconspicuous spots.

HANGING THE SECOND STRIP

When you hang the second strip, you'll create a seam where this strip meets the first one. In most situations, a *butt seam* is the best way to join two strips of wallpaper, since it's the least noticeable.

Prepare the second strip (in the same manner as the first) and hang it, following these directions for creating a butt seam: Unfold the top portion of the second strip on the wall, as you did for the first one. With one hand, work from the top down to align the second strip with the first, spreading your fingers broadly to create even pressure. Move your hand firmly but gently, trying to move not just the edge but the entire strip.

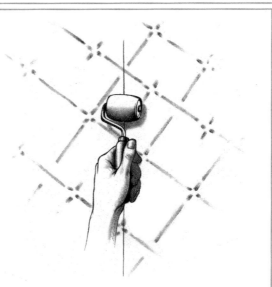

Use the other hand to hold as much of the strip as possible off the wall so you can align the edge without stretching the wallpaper. When the edge of the top portion of the strip butts tightly to the adjoining strip, unfold the rest of the strip and finish aligning the seam. Then smooth the strip and trim it along the ceiling line and baseboard; wipe it clean. Finally, after checking that the seam is lying flat, smooth it using light pressure.

> ☞ **INSIDER'S TERM:** A butt seam is a method of seaming two wallpaper strips by pushing their edges together firmly.

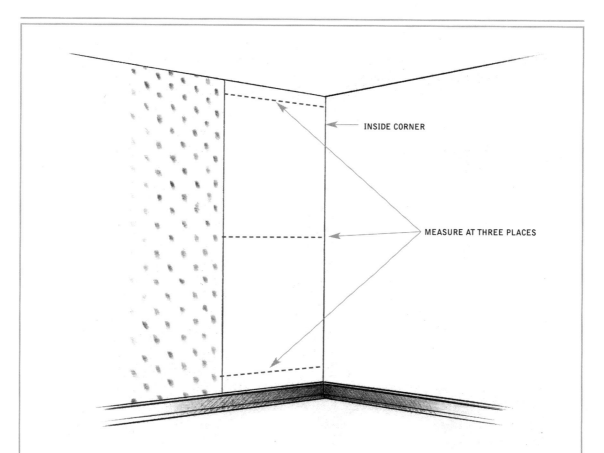

INSIDE CORNER

MEASURE AT THREE PLACES

COVERING CORNERS

Wallpapering around inside and outside corners requires special attention, especially because adjoining walls may not be plumb.

For inside corners: Pushing a strip of wallpaper into an inside corner and then continuing that strip on the next wall can result in puckered, crooked paper. Instead, it's best to split the strip and hang some on each wall.

First, measure from the preceding strip to the corner at three different (equidistant) heights. Then cut the strip vertically ¼ inch wider than the widest measurement; don't discard the leftover paper. After pasting and booking the strip, butt it to the preceding one and smooth it firmly into and around the corner. To help the strip lie flat in the corner, snip the overlaps at the top and bottom.

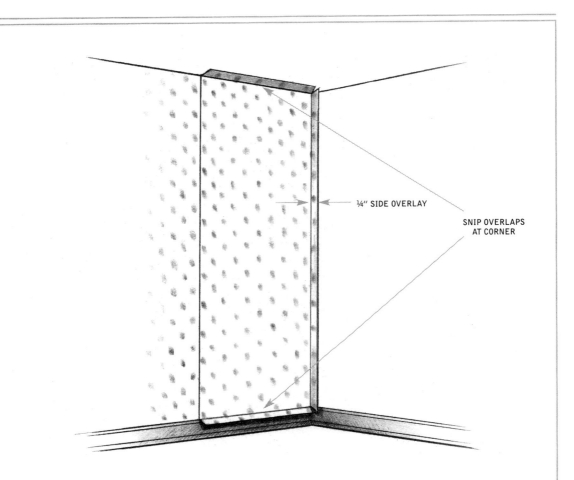

¼" SIDE OVERLAY

SNIP OVERLAPS
AT CORNER

Measure the width of the leftover piece of wallpaper. From the corner, measure that same distance plus ¼ inch on the adjacent wall and make a plumb line. Paste and book the strip.

Position the strip's uncut edge next to but not on the plumb line; let the edge in the corner overlap the previous piece ¼ inch.

This overlap, called a *lap seam*, allows you to make the paper on the sec-

ond wall plumb. Any pattern misalignment at the seam is usually less noticeable.

> **INSIDER'S TERM:** A lap seam is a method of seaming two strips of wallpaper by overlapping one edge over another.

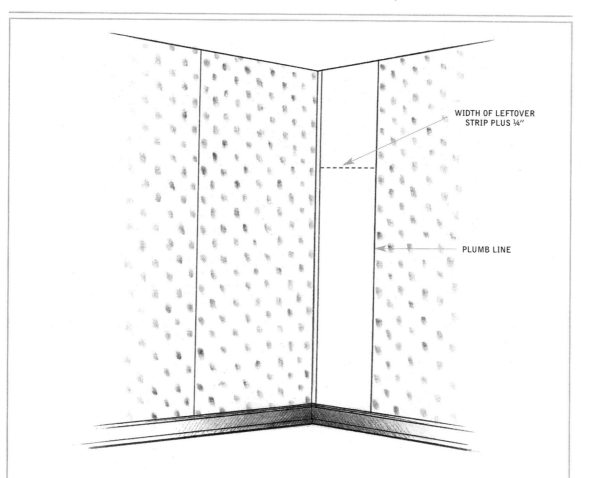

WIDTH OF LEFTOVER
STRIP PLUS ¼"

PLUMB LINE

For outside corners: To hang around an outside corner, butt and smooth the new strip to a previous one, snip the top and bottom overlap at the corner, and smooth the strip.

Drop a plumb line on the new wall at a distance equal to the width of the next strip plus ¼ inch. Then measure the distance between the plumb line and the edge of the corner strip at several incremental heights: If the measurements

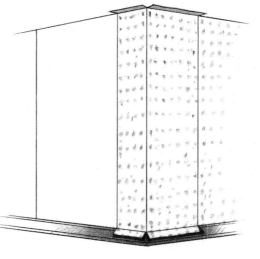

are the same, the new wall is plumb and you can hang the next strip as for a straight wall.

For a wall that's only slightly out of plumb, you can do the following: If the distance from the plumb line to the previous strip is greater at the bottom of the wall than at the top, slit the next strip partway from the top down, working within a background area of the design; slit from the bottom if the upper distance is greater.

Next, align the near side of this strip with the preceding one and the far side

> **☞ INSIDER'S TERM:** Double-cutting a seam is a method of seaming two wallpaper strips by overlapping their edges together firmly and cutting down through the middle. Peel off the excess.

with the plumb line; adjust the length of the cut, and overlap the edges of the slit until the strip is smooth and plumb. Then *double-cut* the overlap.

An alternative to the technique just de-

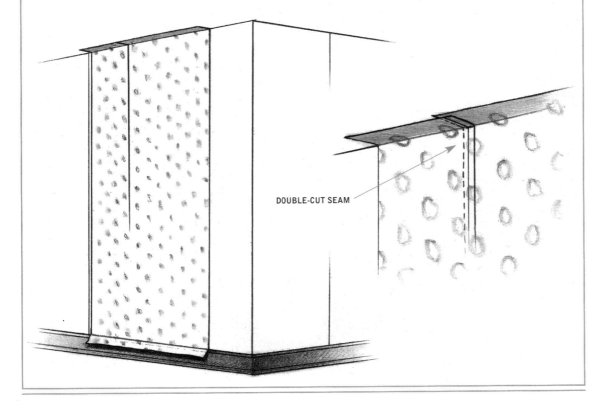

DOUBLE-CUT SEAM

scribed is to hang the new strip parallel with the plumb line and use a lap seam where the strips meet. If a strip ends at an outside corner, cut it back approximately ¼ inch to prevent the paper from fraying and peeling at the corner. To cover the exposed ¼ inch, install a plastic or wood outside corner molding that can be glued or nailed on.

WALLPAPERING AROUND OPENINGS

Don't try to custom fit such areas as doors, windows, and other large openings by meticulous measurement and advance cutting. Instead, hang the strip as you normally would, but with the following difference: Cut the excess material to within 2 inches of where you'll trim. Using sturdy scissors, cut diagonal slits to the corners of the opening.

With a smoother, press the wall cov-

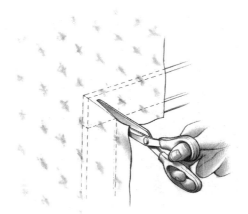

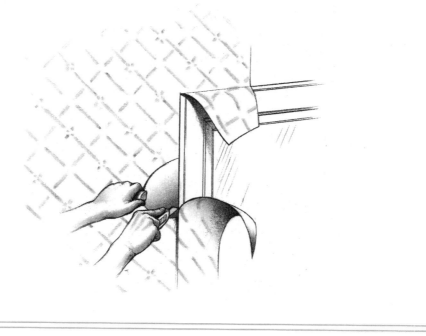

ering into place along all the edges of the opening. Use a razor knife to trim the excess material around the opening's frame, protecting the covering with a broad/putty knife. If the molding is intricate, make scissor snips.

ELECTRICAL OPENINGS AND FACEPLATES

Be sure to turn off the electricity to the room if you haven't already done so. (This is a daylight project!) Now remove the faceplate.

Hang the wallpaper as you would normally, letting it cover the opening. Then, using a razor knife, make an X-shaped cut over the opening, extending the cuts into the corners. Carefully trim the excess paper around the edges.

> **INSIDER'S TIP:** If wallpaper wrinkles or will not butt properly to the adjoining strip, it's probably not aligned correctly at the top. Don't try to stretch or force it. Instead, gently pull off the strip and reposition it on the wall.

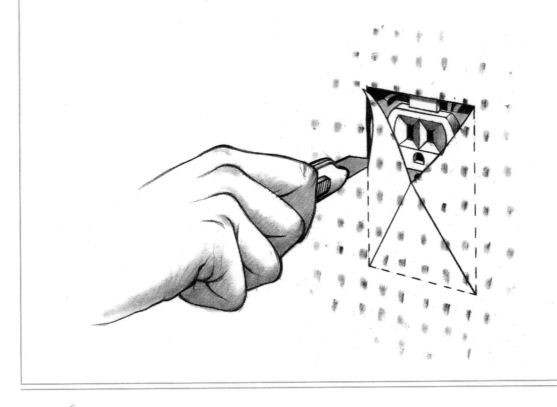

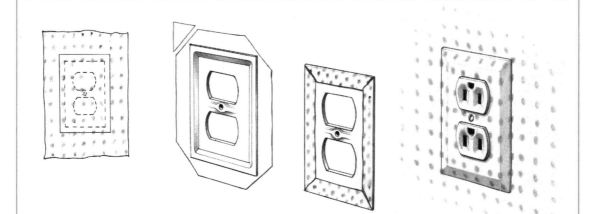

INSIDER'S TIP: Separated seams: If seams pull apart as the adhesive dries, you may have used too much or too little adhesive when pasting, the strip may have dried out after booking, or it may have stretched as you hung it. Applying a little seam adhesive just under the edges often helps; or use a small brush to apply more adhesive to the backing at the seam edge. Press firmly and wipe away any excess glue. If the adhesive has already dried, your only solution may be to color the exposed area with a special mixture of artist watercolors and pigmented primer-sealer (inquire at your local hardware or paint supply store).

For a nice finishing touch, you can cover the faceplate to match the paper that surrounds it. Sand and prime the faceplate and apply vinyl-to-vinyl adhesive to the right side of the faceplate and to the wrong side of a scrap of wallpaper. Hold the faceplate over the opening, aligning the screw holes. Place the pasted scrap over the faceplate, adjusting the scrap until it matches the pattern on the wallpaper.

With the scrap lightly tacked to the faceplate, lift both off the wall and place them face down on a table. Trim the scrap to within ½ inch of the edge of the faceplate, cutting the corners. Fold the paper over and press firmly. Finally, cut the faceplate opening with a razor knife and screw the faceplate over the opening.

There. Rooms with a brand-new view!

Something's Afoot:
Flooring

Once the fate of Rent-A-Husband's "reputation" hinged on the innocent misuse of a single pronoun (or, to be more exact, *half* a pronoun). It was very soon after the opening of his business that Rent-A-Husband received a call from a customer named Laura. She explained her husband had recently gone to work for a Japanese-based firm and in the process they'd been transferred to a new city where they'd just bought a home. She went on to say her husband was currently in Tokyo undergoing orientation, and she wanted to get the house into the best possible "living order" before he returned, starting with the retiling of the kitchen floor. (We should mention here—and you'll understand why in a minute—that her husband's secretary, a native of Japan, had just arrived in the United States for her first assignment and was struggling to learn English as quickly as possible.) Now, back to the kitchen. Since no work had been done on the floor in many moons, some preliminary measures were necessary prior to actually putting down the tiles. Ironically, the day they were installed turned out to be the same day Laura's real husband was scheduled to return.

And return he did. Anxious to get home from the airport, he called his secretary en route for his messages, and that's when things started to break down. For although she was making excellent progress in English, her one weak area was with the proper usage of—you guessed it—pronouns. As such, the last message he received from his wife was relayed to him as follows: "Don't come in through the back door because Rent-A-Husband is laying some*one* on the kitchen floor all afternoon." Who could have imagined the trouble just one less "*thing*" would cause!

WALK ALL OVER ME

If the expression "footprints in the sands of time" conjures up images of your kitchen floor, you've come to the right place. Here is where you are going to learn to rock the very foundation on which you stand. But before taking the first step in the direction of the new floor, it's important to have a bit of general background on the replacement options available. The most popular types of flooring are *vinyl tile, ceramic tile,* and *wood strip.* And although wood laminate is a relatively new and improved version of the former (as far as ease of installation), we are limiting our advice in this chapter to strictly the non-wood varieties. Wood flooring (of any sort) is simply too advanced for the beginner to attempt to install. So if you just can't live without the look and feel of wood underfoot—at this point—call in a professional.

LAYING VINYL

Vinyl flooring (also known as "resilient flooring") is available in two basic formats:

squares, which are 1-foot square pieces (most often with a self-adhesive backing), and sheet flooring, which comes in 6-foot- and 12-foot-wide rolls (and is typically attached with a *notch troweled*—on adhesive). The installation of sheet flooring is an excellent project for beginners, as long as the area being covered is relatively small. But because it is hard to handle, trying to manage sheet flooring for a large room can make first-timers feel as if they're wrestling a bear. It's best to get some practice under your belt before movin' on up to the grand ballroom.

> ☞ **INSIDER'S TERM:** A notched trowel is a rectangular metal or plastic blade with a handle on the top and notches of varying shapes and dimensions along the edges. It's used to spread adhesive (mastic) for tiles and panels of all kinds.

OUT WITH THE OLD

The first thing you need to consider before putting down a new floor is the old one. While some people actually do install one floor right on top of another, this type of "pentimento" serves only to raise your room and lower the quality of your flooring job. You simply never get as professional-looking a result by leaving the old floor down. And if you're going to do it at all, you may as well do it right—right? That said, be forewarned: Ripping up old linoleum is a job that should be reserved for deserters from the army and other such miscreants. In other words, don't expect the time of your life. However, with a little patience, it is absolutely something you can handle; and it will certainly be time well spent.

In addition to your basic tools, this job will require:

► A pry bar.

► A razor knife.

► A sanding block and paper.

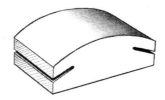

► A lacquer thinner.

► Fix-All or a similar patching compound.

Now, proceed as follows:

Using your putty knife, a hammer, and a prybar, gently remove the baseboard and shoe molding (if there is any) covering the edges of the old flooring material. Since these pieces are already cut to fit, you should number, save, and reuse them. If there is a metal threshold strip at the doorway, remove the screws or nails holding it in place and pull it up.

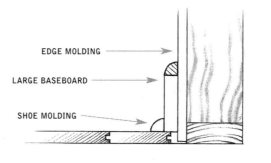

EDGE MOLDING

LARGE BASEBOARD

SHOE MOLDING

Starting in one corner, see if you can pry up an edge of the old flooring material. If you're lucky, it will peel right off, but usually it's not that simple.

Scrape the old flooring material up, one section at a time, using a putty knife and working it back and forth under the edge. Try dabbing a little lacquer thinner or other adhesive remover near the edge to make the task a little easier. (Since solvents are extremely flammable and the fumes can be hazardous to your health if you breathe them for any length of time, always make sure you have good ventilation and keep all solvents away from flames. Also, always remember to wear gloves and any other protective clothing recommended by the manufacturer of the material you are using.)

Once the old floor is removed, use your putty knife and a solvent (or adhesive remover, available at hardware stores) to scrape off as much of the old adhesive from the subfloor as possible. Fill in any holes or irregularities in the subfloor with Fix-All or a similar patching compound (much as you would when "prepping" walls for paint or paper). When the patches are dry, sand them flat. If the surface is really a mess, con-sider installing a ⅜-inch or ½-inch un-derlayment material (such as plywood, which is made from layers of wood veneers glued together) over your existing subfloor material. Remember, you will not get the best result without a completely clean, flat surface on which to "build."

Now, if your floor is all prepared, it's time to move on to giving it a new look.

INSTALLING TILE SQUARES

Since most tile squares are 1 square foot in size, you first need to figure out how many you'll need to cover the area you're working on. To do this, multiply the length of the floor times its width. Now add 10 percent to allow for cutting waste. To get started, you'll need:

▶ A tape measure.

▶ A chalk line.

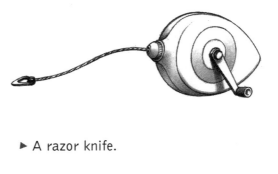

▶ A razor knife.

► A long carpenter's square.

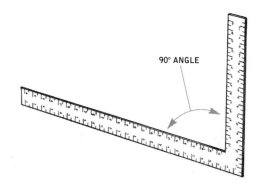

90° ANGLE

Your first task is to find the center of the room. This is easily accomplished. First, measure one wall of the room near the baseboard and mark its mid-point. Now, measure the opposite wall and again mark its midpoint. Either have a helper hold one end of your chalk line on one of your marks or weigh it down firmly with a brick or another heavy object so the string stays on the mark while you pull the line taut across the second mark and snap a line.

Repeat this process with the other two walls and again snap a line between your marks. You should now have a chalk-marked "+" in the middle of the room. Use your square to see if the lines of the "+" are truly perpendicular.

Without removing the paper backing

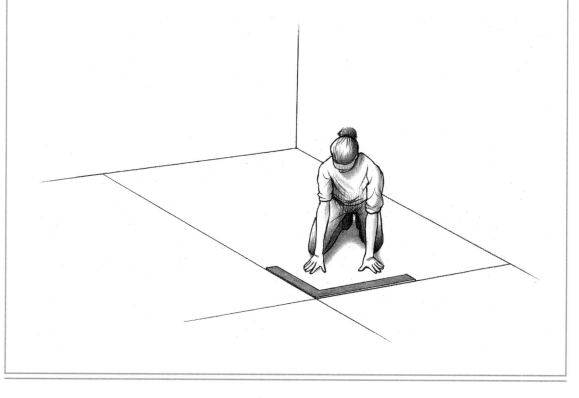

(this is just a "test run" to see how the pattern falls), lay a row of tiles along what seems to be your straightest coordinate, from the center of the floor all the way to both walls. Since nothing in life is absolutely perfect, you'll most likely have room for only part of a tile at each edge. Adjust the row if necessary to equalize the gap. Half a tile at each edge is ideal.

After you've adjusted your first test row, lay a second row along the other arm of your "+," again starting from the center. Once more, adjust the rows to equalize the gaps at both edges. Carefully mark the new position of your center tile.

With your layout adjusted, snap a re-vised chalk line. (Simply measure the number of inches you have moved the center tile off the original line, then snap a parallel line that same number of inches over.) Remove (or at least smudge) the original chalk line so you don't get confused.

To double-check your perpendicular line in the center, use a long metal carpenter's square, then snap a corresponding chalk line. Check your layout with a tape measure; measuring 3 feet along one axis and 4 feet along the other. The hypotenuse (angle) between those two points should measure 5 feet if you've got a perfect right triangle.

Clear your work area to make sure your starting point is perfectly clean and grit-free (a whisk broom and dust-pan should accomplish this task nicely). Now it's time to pull the paper backing off your first piece of tile. Examine the back for a directional arrow. It really doesn't matter what direction you choose, but you'll want to set all the tiles going in the same direction.

> 💡 **INSIDER'S TIP:** For best adhesion, the tile and all materials should be kept at a room temperature of at least 70 degrees for 24 hours before and after it is laid.

Very carefully place the first tile along the lines you've marked. Remember, that first tile is always the most critical, since it will determine the lay of all the others. Additionally, the glue on self-adhesive tile tends to be pretty aggressive, so you won't have a lot of "play" once you set it down. Therefore, *take your time and try to get it right!*

Proceed by working along your axis and lay another four or five tiles, butting them tight against one another. Clean as you go with your whisk broom to make sure the surface is grit-free before you set each tile. To help keep the edges in a straight line, use a straight-edge or carpenter's square as a guide. Ideally, the tile edges will precisely follow your chalked line. Once you set your first tile, however, you're committed and must follow the line dictated by the tile. A slight variation really won't make much difference in an average-sized room. However, if you find yourself deviating greatly from your chalk line after just four or five tiles, you may want to consider pulling them up and starting again.

Once you have your first row of four or five tiles down, go back to the center and lay a tile or two along the other axis. The important thing is to butt each tile edge tightly against one another.

Don't get too carried away laying tiles straight out along the second axis; as soon as possible, begin to fill in the "stair-step" tiles. Continue working from the middle outward until the entire area that takes full tiles has been covered.

You'll need to cut partial tiles to fill in around the perimeter of the room. You can, of course, simply measure the gap with a tape measure, and then cut a section of tile to fit.

At the doorways, the finished tile

should reach to the middle of the opening. Be sure to cut the tile an inch or two longer to give the metal threshold (which will eventually go on top) plenty to hold on to for a firm grip.

If you run into odd angles or curves, use thin cardboard, kraft paper, or even a paper bag to create a template that will help you cut the tile accurately.

Finish up by reinstalling the shoe molding or baseboard around the perimeter. Cover the tile edges at doorways with the metal threshold strip.

REPLACING A DAMAGED TILE SQUARE

If only a couple of tile squares are damaged, it's a fairly simple matter to pull them up and replace them. With any luck, your tile pattern (or something very similar) will still be available. (If your pattern went out while Elvis was still king, it's probably time to give some serious thought to a new floor!) Now, back to the matter of repair . . .

Start the process by heating the damaged square with a blow dryer, or lay a thin, soft cloth over the top of the tile and rub gently with an iron set on medium heat. Next, use a putty knife

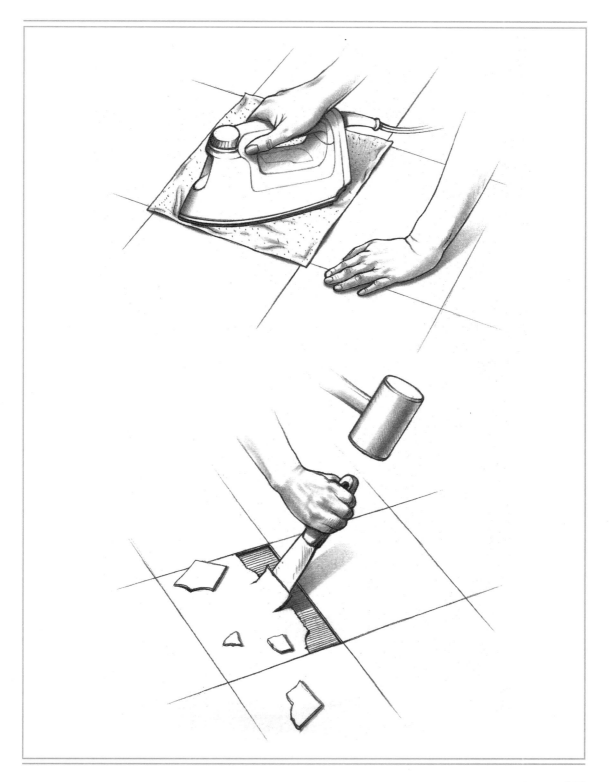

and a mallet to pry up the defective tile, being careful not to damage the adjacent tiles. If necessary, use a razor knife to cut the damaged tile into two or more pieces, and remove one piece at a time. Scrape as much of the old adhesive out of the vacant spot as possible; it's important that the surface where you'll set the new tile be clean and perfectly smooth. If necessary, dab a little adhesive remover or solvent on a clean rag, and gently wipe up any excess adhesive (but be careful not to get the solvent on or under the adjoining tiles!).

Look to see if there's an orientation that makes a difference in the floor's pattern before you set the new tile in place. Also, check the fit before you remove the paper backing (for self-adhesive tiles) or spread the adhesive (for glue-in-place tiles). On occasion, it may be necessary to trim the new tile slightly.

Now, if the fit seems okay, remove the paper backing (for self-adhesive tiles). For troweled-adhesive tiles, carefully spread a thin layer of a compatible tile adhesive with a serrated trowel *on the empty floor space*, being careful not to smudge adhesive on an adjoining tile. Set the new tile in place and push down firmly.

> **INSIDER'S TIP:** All resilient floors are subject to indentations caused by heavy loads resting on small or uneven surfaces. Protect your floor by removing any small metal domes from furniture legs; try to substitute large, load-spreading furniture rests. The broad bases on the rests spread the weight over a larger area and prevent mars and dents. Choose rests that are flat and smooth, with rounded edges to prevent cutting the tile.
>
> **INSIDER'S TIP:** Older tile may contain asbestos. When in doubt, have an expert evaluate the composition of your old tile before beginning. *Do not* attempt to remove any tile yourself that might contain asbestos.

INSTALLING SHEET VINYL

As previously mentioned, maneuvering sheet vinyl and getting it to stay in position tends to be a tricky business. If you start to feel a panic attack coming on fairly soon into the game, the room in which you've chosen to lay your floor is probably just too large. To preserve your sanity in the wonderful world of sheet vinyl installation, keep the room on the small side!

With that in mind, here are the supplies you'll need to tame the beast:

► Weights (cement blocks wrapped in old towels or buckets of water).

► Scissors.

► Vinyl adhesive.

► A small-toothed notched trowel.

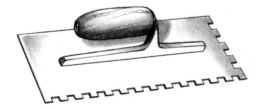

► A rolling pin.

► Kraft paper and masking tape.

► A razor knife (with new blade).

► A straightedge.

Sheet vinyl comes in 6- and 12-foot rolls. If possible, buy enough to allow for a seamless installation. (Draw your room out on graph paper and take it with you to the flooring store if you need help deciding how much vinyl to buy.)

Prepare the room by removing all the furnishings, including the covers on the floor registers and the shoe molding along the baseboards. When you remove shoe molding, number the pieces so you can replace them in the same order. If no shoe molding exists, remove the baseboard.

Vinyl is a lot easier to work with when it's warm, so plan ahead. Set the roll in the sun for a few hours before you begin, or lay the vinyl flat in your living room and cover it with an electric blanket to warm it up. While the vinyl is warming, use your whisk broom to make sure the floor where you'll be working is clean.

> **INSIDER'S TIP:** If you're working on a bathroom, have a handy friend or plumber help you remove the toilet before you start.

Now, here comes the tough part. You'll need to trim the vinyl almost to its final size in order to get it neatly "curling up the walls." But since walls aren't perfectly square, you can't simply transfer the exact dimensions and cut. While every situation is different, generally it's easiest if you start with the longest wall. Lay the vinyl in place, with about 3 inches extra rolling up the wall on the long edge. To keep the vinyl from shifting while you work, weigh it down with cement blocks wrapped in old towels or buckets filled with water.

With the scissors, cut your material *roughly* to the dimensions of the rest of the room, allowing somewhere between 3 and 6 extra inches all around. Work slowly and carefully, making sure you take off only what you need to remove to get the vinyl to lay flat. Try not to let the vinyl nick or tear (although that's a lot easier said than done!).

If your layout requires lots of jogs and angles, one alternative is to make a paper template that is the exact size and shape of the area to be covered. Tape together lengths of heavy kraft paper with masking tape until you have a piece big enough to cover the area. Use scissors to trim it to size, then tape the template firmly in place on your sheet vinyl and cut around the outline with a razor knife. If you're worried about getting the size and shape exact, you can leave an extra ½ inch to 1 inch all around, although this may make it a little harder to get the vinyl into place and will require extra cutting later.

When you've gotten the vinyl cut more or less to shape, use a straightedge to guide your razor knife as you cut along the walls. Press the straightedge hard into the corner to make sure you are cutting close to the wall. Trim concave (inside) corners using a succession of gentle, scooping cuts (it usually takes less of a cut than you think, so work up to it slowly!). For convex (outside) corners, make a vertical cut in the material at the corner. Here again, take it slow so you don't cut too far.

For curves (such as around the toilet base) or odd angles, use lightweight cardboard or heavy paper to make a template.

Once you've got the vinyl cut to shape, you can heave a sigh of relief and pat yourself on the back; the hard part is over! The next step is to apply the adhesive, which is accomplished by first gently rolling back half the vinyl.

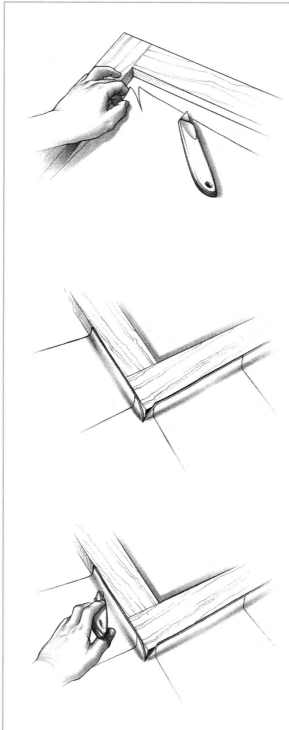

(Again, weigh down the remaining half to make sure it doesn't shift in the process.) Now, sweep the exposed floor again with your whisk broom, just to make sure you haven't tracked in any bits of sand and there are no vinyl trimmings in the way.

Working from the center outward, apply a thin coat of adhesive to the floor with a small-toothed trowel. It may look too thin to hold, but this stuff has an alligator's tenacity. The biggest mistake you can make here is to get it on too thick, which will give the finished surface a mushy, dimpled look.

Now, using the rolling pin, roll the vinyl into place on top of the adhesive. Once the first half is firmly in place, move your weights over to the side you just put down, and do the other half. (Just remember to work the adhesive from the center of the room toward the edges.)

Clean the new flooring with a solvent that has been recommended by the manufacturer. It is important to clean up any adhesive that may have spilled or oozed up onto the surface. Then roll the flooring so that it sets firmly and flatly in the adhesive. Lean heavily on a rolling pin and work your way across the floor. Start at the center of the room and roll firmly to remove any air bubbles.

After the floor has been cleaned and rolled, replace the baseboard and shoe molding.

REPAIRING SHEET VINYL

Just because you have one seemingly unsightly tear or burn in a sheet vinyl floor, you don't necessarily have to rip it out and replace the whole thing (especially if time hasn't dimmed the memory of your first go-round!) Frequently, the bad spot can be patched so the repair is hardly noticeable. To proceed, you'll need a piece of matching vinyl slightly larger than the area to be replaced. If whoever installed the floor didn't happen to leave a few extra scraps lying around (look under your sink or in the basement), you may be able to pilfer a piece from under the refrigerator or another inconspicuous location. Cut a patch that's 1 to 2 inches larger than you need. Lay the patch over the bad spot, making sure you match the pattern. Tape the patch firmly in place with wide masking tape or electrician's tape.

Load up your razor knife with a fresh blade and, pressing firmly through *both* layers, cut the patch to size, using a metal straightedge as a guide. If possible, follow a line in the pattern to help conceal the cut. Gently pull off the tape and set the patch aside.

Carefully remove the damaged section of flooring and clean off any excess adhesive from the underfloor. Lay the patch in place and check the fit. Trim it with scissors or a razor knife if necessary.

Now, using a notched trowel, spread a thin layer of adhesive in the empty area to be patched. Or, for very small patches, apply the adhesive directly to the back of the patch itself. Fit the patch into place, and carefully wipe away any excess adhesive. To hold the patch in place until the adhesive is thoroughly dry, weigh it down with a heavy object. Fill in any gaps with colored caulk.

LAYING CERAMIC TILE

Although more costly than vinyl, ceramic tile does add a richness and glamour to any room. Also, since ceramic tiles are available in a wide array of colors, shapes, sizes, and finishes (glazed, unglazed, or matte), they provide a truly personalized floor. On the downside, ceramic tiles are more difficult to lay than vinyl, requiring such additional steps as mixing and applying a mortar and grouting, then letting the whole thing set for 2 days. Plus, you need to be certain that your floor will support the added weight of the tiles (especially important for apartment dwellers). However, many people still believe the exquisite result that can be achieved with ceramic tiles is well worth the extra time, effort, and expense.

When purchasing the tiles, be sure to buy the type made expressly for floors,

☛ **INSIDER'S TERM:** The majority of tiles are known as field tiles, which make up the bulk of any ceramic tiling project. Trim tiles are those that add a color accent to the field tiles. Since both tiles are the same size, the exact placement of the trim tiles is simply a matter of personal taste and requires no additional instruction or skill. Bullnose tiles have one or more finished and tapered edges and are generally used as end pieces on walls and countertops.

💡 **INSIDER'S TIP:** Before you leave the store with your precious cargo, ask the clerk to open any sealed boxes so you can check for cracks or breakage.

as they are also available for walls and countertops. (Tiles designed for walls and countertops are much thinner than floor tiles, and will crack very easily if walked on.) As previously mentioned, ceramic tiles tend to be rather expensive, so bring the exact dimensions of your project area with you and get professional assistance in choosing the right number of *field* and *trim* tiles to accommodate your needs. Also be sure to factor in an additional 5 percent of the total surface area to allow for cutting damage.

There is one catch to ceramic tile work that could require you to call in an expert. You'll need a stout (approximately ¾-inch) plywood subfloor topped by a cement backer board. Around tubs and showers, you'll usually want to use a cement board instead of a water-resistant type of drywall known as green board. Before you set the floor tile, you may also need additional plywood to stiffen the surface, depending on the type of subfloor already in place. And for wet applications (shower floors, for example), a waterproofing membrane may be necessary. Have a carpenter or an experienced tile person evaluate your existing surfaces and add plywood and other backing material as necessary.

Finally, before we begin, a couple of words about tools and materials. For a small job (or if you're just beginning and have plenty of time), you can buy an inexpensive mechanical tile cutter. This works by scoring the surface of the tile with a blade and providing a guide to help you snap the tile in two along the score mark. If you're doing a large job, however, rent a good electric (wet) tile saw at your local tile store.

Be sure to ask the salesperson to show you exactly how to use the saw, and be certain you understand its safety features.

In addition to the cutter or saw, here's what you'll need to get started:

▶ A tape measure.

▶ A notched trowel.

▶ Thin-set or mastic.

▶ Acrylic admix.

▶ Spacers.

> **INSIDER'S TERM:** A subfloor is the floor surface below a finished floor. It is usually made of sheet material like plywood, except in older houses, where it is likely to consist of diagonal boards.

- A float.

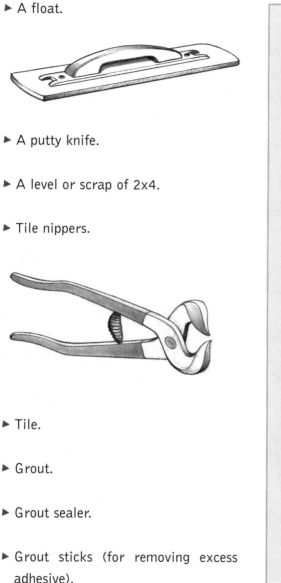

- A putty knife.

- A level or scrap of 2x4.

- Tile nippers.

- Tile.

- Grout.

- Grout sealer.

- Grout sticks (for removing excess adhesive).

- A sponge.

- Clean, soft rags.

☞ **INSIDER'S TERM:** Thin-set adhesives (used to set tiles) come with organic, cement, and epoxy bases. Organic bases, called mastics, are water-resistant, but they can irritate the lungs and skin if extra protection (rubber gloves and masks covering the mouth and nose) is not worn during their use. Cement bases are excellent for applying tiles to concrete or masonry subfloors. Epoxy is the strongest base and provides high bonding power.

☞ **INSIDER'S TERM:** Acrylic admix is an additive that strengthens tile adhesives and grout.

☞ **INSIDER'S TERM:** Spacers are little white plastic crosses (available at hardware stores) that range in size from $\frac{1}{16}$- to $\frac{3}{8}$-inch thick, and measure less than 1 inch across. They're used to maintain even spacing between tiles prior to applying grout.

☞ **INSIDER'S TERM:** A float is a tool used to smooth the surface after grout has been applied.

The most critical part of setting tile is laying it out well to start.

After you have snapped the chalk lines along the intersection at the center of the room to be tiled (refer to tips for laying vinyl tile squares—see pages 108–10), it is, once again, best to lay out a test row or two to help gauge your margins and make sure you have the look you're after. If you're planning to use trim tiles as well, include their placement in the dry run.

Use a notched trowel to spread a layer of thin-set mortar, mixed to the consistency of toothpaste (follow the

package directions), over an area of no more than 2 or 3 square feet. That way, you'll have time to place and adjust the tiles before the adhesive begins to set. Lay each tile with a firm set-and-twist motion to settle it uniformly into the mortar. Check the level of each tile compared to its neighbor with a carpenter's level.

Remember to use tile spacers between tiles to help you maintain an even spacing distance.

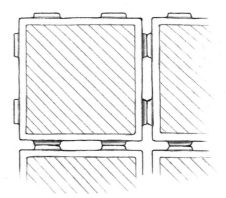

When setting partial tiles, it is a good idea to wait to apply the adhesive until you've already cut the partial tiles to fit, as individually crafting them can be time-consuming.

Once all the tiles have been set, gently clean any excess adhesive from the surfaces and grout lines with a minia-ture screwdriver. Wait 6 to 8 hours and

> **INSIDER'S TIP:** To patch the areas around the sink and toilet, use a specialty tool known as tile nip-pers. (Since tile cutters will cut only straight lines, tile nippers are used for irregular cuts, which are made by nipping away small pieces of tile.) For more intricate cuts, make a cardboard template and cut the tile around it. You can also use small grinding stones in an electric drill to make curved cuts.

then pull out the spacers using needlenose pliers or a nail, being careful not to inadvertently dislodge a tile. (If one or two spacers are especially recalcitrant, just let them stay.) Clean up your tools immediately after using them.

Let the tiles set for the length of time recommended by the manufacturer of the adhesive you have used. Tiles can break very easily if they are walked upon at this stage.

GROUTING

A fluid cement product that's used to fill spaces between ceramic tiles or other crevices, grout is applied with a rubber-faced float (available at any tile or hardware store). Spread the grout over the face of the tiles and force it down into the joints between them. Be sure all the joints are filled.

When the surface is well covered with grout, working across the tiles on a diagonal (2 square feet at a time), scrape off the excess with the float. As you remove the excess, check to make sure the joints are filled and there are no air pockets.

Remove the remaining grout from the surface of the tiles with a sponge dampened with clean water. Wipe the

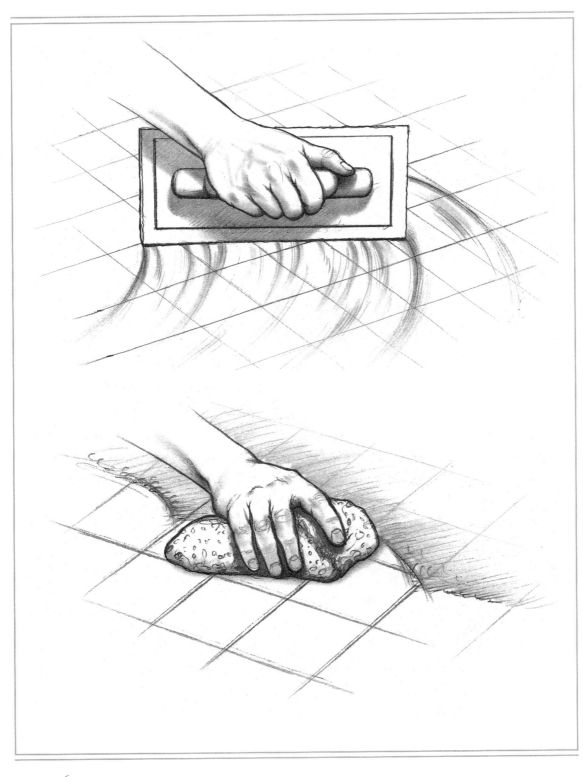

tiles and rinse the sponge frequently, changing the water when it gets dirty. Get the tiles as clean as possible. Then wait about 30 minutes for a thin haze to appear, and wipe it off with a soft cloth.

Some grouts take several days to "cure" (or harden); check the length of time suggested by the manufacturer. Meanwhile, put plywood over the floor to keep from stepping on the new grout. When cured, the grout should be sealed.

Inquire at the tile store as to the best sealer for your purposes. The sealer seals unglazed tiles so they won't absorb stains, but it also is beneficial for use with glazed tiles because it seals the grout against staining. Use a foam-rubber roller (available at tile or hardware stores) to apply the sealer, according to package instructions. Allow 24 hours to dry.

REGROUTING TILE

If the grout between your tiles begins to loosen, take early preventative action. Otherwise, you will find yourself replacing the tiles instead of just the grout.

First of all, remove all loose grout using a beer-can opener. If the grout is too hard for this opener or if you have a lot of regrouting to do, you can purchase a special grout saw (quite an inexpensive item) at a tile store.

Mix 1 cup of phosphoric acid (available at any hardware store) into 1 quart of water. Wearing rubber gloves and using a sponge, wash all of the affected area with the diluted acid. Then rinse with fresh water.

Mix the grout according to the manufacturer's instructions. Apply the grout to the tile joints by wiping diagonally in several directions with a rubber-edged tile float.

Wipe off the excess grout with a damp, but not saturated, sponge. Be careful not to remove too much from the joints. After the grout dries (about 24 hours), wipe the tiles again to remove any residue.

REPLACING A CRACKED OR BROKEN TILE

Since it is difficult—but certainly not impossible—to remove a cracked tile without damaging the surrounding good tiles, you must be extra careful when removing the cracked one. Start by scraping away the grout surrounding the tile, and try to pry up the tile with a putty

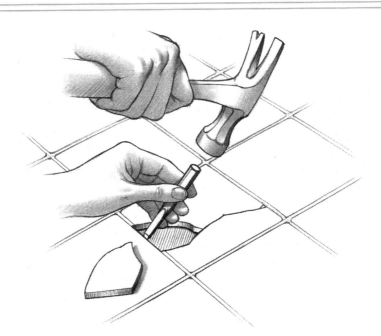

knife. If you can't pry it loose, use a small cold chisel (an inexpensive item available at tile and hardware stores) and a hammer to break the tile into small pieces and pry them up. It's best to wear protective glasses while doing this. Work from the center of the tile out toward the edges to avoid damaging the surrounding tiles.

To remove the adhesive from the floor (beneath the tile you've removed), use a flat, wide chisel. With a notched trowel, "butter" the back of the new tile with adhesive, and spread a thin, even amount in the empty space on the floor, as well. Press the new tile into place and wipe off any excess adhesive

with a damp sponge. Allow it to dry and then grout and seal (as described on pages 123–24).

CARPET CARE

Laying carpet is an involved process that's best left to the pros or a more advanced do-it-yourselfer. For stains on existing carpet, however, we offer the following quick and easy solutions.

OUT, OUT DAMNED SPOT(S)

Time does march on—and in the process, leaves its tracks (mud, footprints, pet stains, and the drips, drops, and spills of daily life) all over your carpets. Like a constant "work in progress," your rugs and carpets maintain an all-too-accurate account of the comings and goings of those whose lives cross them every day. In this section, however, we're going to show you how to readily and easily remove many of those trouble spots, distant memories you can well live without!

CARPET STAIN REMOVAL

The first thing to find out when you're thinking of buying a carpet is what it's made of. Synthetic fibers such as nylon, acrylic, polyester, or polypropylene stain less easily than those made of natural fibers. This is because they aren't as absorbent. Bear this in mind when making your purchase.

Don't apply *any* cleaning solution to a carpet without first testing it on an inconspicuous spot or a piece of scrap. Put a few drops of the solution on the carpet, then hold a paper towel against the treated area for 5 seconds. If the dye runs, it's time to give up on the do-it-yourself approach and call in a professional cleaner.

Even if your carpet is colorfast, stain removal can be a process of trial-and-error. If a certain solution doesn't work

in the time allotted, apply it again for a little while longer. If you still have no luck, try a different solution.

Be careful not to make the problem worse when you're trying to remove a stain from a carpet. When applying a liquid to treat the stain, always use the smallest amount that will do the job. (Remember, it's easier to add than take away.) If you apply too much liquid, it will soak the carpet backing and possibly ruin the finish on the floor underneath.

Always blot stains; never rub. This will keep the stain from spreading.

ODOR REMOVAL

To absorb carpet odors, sprinkle the offensive area with baking soda. Wait 15 minutes, then vacuum. For especially pungent smells, let the baking soda remain overnight before vacuuming. *Use this technique only on dry carpets*, and be sure to test a small, hidden area for color-fastness before applying the baking soda to the entire carpet.

WATER-SOLUBLE STAINS

Most water-soluble stains can be removed from carpets if you attack them while they're still fresh (wet). Apply a solution of ¼ cup mild dishwashing liquid, 1 quart warm water, and 1 tablespoon white vinegar. Using an electric mixer, whip the solution into a stiff foam. Apply the foam with a soft brush. Scrape away the soiled foam with a dull knife, then wipe off the residue with a damp sponge. Rinse the stain with a little cool water on a sponge; then blot it with paper towels.

OILY STAINS

For oily stain removal, your best bet is a cleaning fluid such as Energine (available at hardware stores). Check the label on the carpet to see if the cleaner is safe for your fiber. If no label can be found, you can test a little fluid on an inconspicuous area. If the label or test indicates it's safe, dampen a sponge with the fluid and apply it to the stain. Blot it with paper towels. Repeat as long as there's an improvement. Finally, apply a mild solution of dishwashing liquid and water, then blot again.

An alternative technique for getting oil stains out of carpeting is to liberally sprinkle stained area with cream of tartar. Let it stand for 24 hours, and brush off or remove with a vacuum cleaner.

GREASE STAINS

For set-in grease stain removal, dip a bar of Lava soap (available at hardware stores) in warm water and rub it on the spot. Rinse very well, as any soap left in the carpet will lighten the area in which it remains when the carpet dries.

Another way to remove a set-in grease stain is to apply a few drops of turpentine, soak that up with cornmeal or kitty litter, and then vacuum. Follow up by dampening a cloth with a cleaning fluid (such as Energine) and blotting the remaining spot. You don't need to rinse this.

OTHER STAINS

To remove fruit juice stains, shaving cream will do the trick. Be careful to apply just a little, however, or you'll have trouble getting the cream out of the rug. Spray just enough on your hand to cover the stain, and allow it to sit for a minute or two. Now blot the cream with a sponge dampened with club soda. Repeat the process as necessary until all the stain is gone.

Ballpoint ink can be removed from carpeting by covering the affected area with salt. As the ink is absorbed, vacuum up the salt and repeat the process.

You can also get ballpoint ink out of carpeting by blotting the ink with a milk-soaked rag, then brushing the milk with an old toothbrush. Just be sure to rinse the milk out of the rug thoroughly, or you'll just be replacing one stain with another (not to mention the added odor of spoiled milk!).

You can remove a bloodstain from carpeting by covering it with equal parts meat tenderizer and cold water. Allow the mixture to sit for half an hour, then sponge it off with cool water. Alternately, try sprinkling the stain with salt, then cold water. Gently blot the area with a sponge, then wipe up the mixture.

Coffee will come out of carpeting if you attack the stain early on—while it's still fresh. Blot up the excess coffee, then rub the stain with a mixture of 1 tablespoon white vinegar, a squirt of mild dishwashing liquid, and 1 cup of water.

If your carpet or rug has become your pet's own personal toilet, make a solution of 1/3 cup of white vinegar and 1 teaspoon of baking soda. A little dishwashing liquid added to the mix enhances its effectiveness. (Don't worry about the initial fizzing, it will subside shortly.) Dip a rag in this mixture and gently apply it to the stained area. Blot up the mixture with thick rags. If the stain is near the wall, and the culprit was a male cat, it's a good idea also to wash about 18 inches up the wall. No need to rinse.

Another trick for getting urine odor out of carpeting is to sponge the spot with club soda, then vinegar. You don't need to rinse, and this will reduce the incidence of repeat offenders by "unmarking" the territory—at least as far as the feline and/or canine is concerned!

Rust stains on carpeting require a mild solution of oxalic acid (available from hardware stores and drugstores) and water. Use the oxalic acid with caution, and never leave it in a spot that's accessible to children or animals; it's an active poison. Put a few crystals in a glass and cover them with hot water. Let them dissolve in the water overnight. Then, wearing rubber gloves and eye protection, brush the solution on the stain. Let it sit for half an hour, then blot the area dry with a rag.

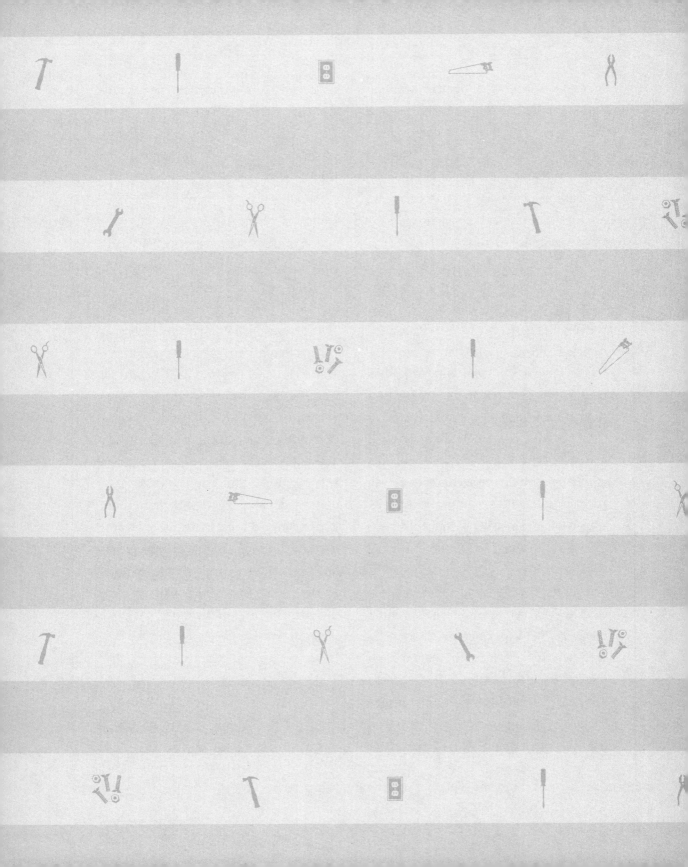

CHAPTER 6

Bringing on the Reinforcements:

Hiring a Contractor

Often the greatest show of strength lies in simply knowing when to ask for help. Never to be confused with accepting defeat, understanding your limits and realizing when it's time to reach out for assistance is, instead, a vitally important step on the road to any real success (including home improvement).

With a full 25 percent of Rent-A-Husband's business comprised of "righting the wrongs" of other contractors, it's increasingly clear that there's no valor in a job that's just completed as opposed to one that's well done. There are just some things best left to the pros.

However, the process of hiring a contractor can make some people feel like a lamb being led to slaughter. Just how are you supposed to know when the

right one comes along? And equally important, once you do make the hire, how do you know he's living up to the promises he made when he was trying to woo you? The truth is, most people don't—not instinctively, anyway. That's where the information in this chapter comes in. After reading it, you'll be able to size up a contractor with the best of them—and better still, you'll learn how to keep tabs on the work in progress.

STARTING THE SEARCH

The home improvement business is full of contractors, ranging from those who are responsible, talented, and honest—the kind who have sawdust in their veins—to downright crooks who are only interested in renovating your bank account and hitting the road before you know what hit you. You just have to know how to locate the former because, rest assured, they're out there. One of the biggest traps homeowners fall into as they start seeking a contractor is pretending to know more than they do about the project. And while it's human nature not to want to appear ignorant, trying to "fake it" tends to make one an easy mark for crooks. So, when such an individual tells you the chimney needs to be replaced because the thingamajig is cracked, you might pretend to know what he's talking about and tell him to go ahead and do what needs to be done, but it would make more sense to do a little homework and get the facts.

Spending the time to read this book and, hence, get better acquainted with your home will pay big dividends when it comes to dealing with contractors. You'll be far less likely to fall for dishonest claims, exaggerated estimates, and unnecessary repairs.

Before you decide to do any renovation (especially a major one), it is wise to give it some serious thought. For example, how long do you plan to stay in the place you're renovating? If you're intending to move sometime soon, it may not be smart to invest a lot of money unless the work will substantially increase the equity in your home.

Also, will the end result truly be worth the expense? After all, there's a chance a combination sauna/bowling alley won't hold the same appeal in five years! Just remember before you start looking for a contractor, have a well-considered plan in place.

Equally important, do your research. Look for things you like about your friends' homes, things you've admired in magazines, and things that have caught your attention on television home shows. Once you have an idea of what you want, learn as much as you can about what the job will require. This will boost your confidence when you begin interviewing contractors.

GETTING DOWN TO BUSINESS

When it's time to do the actual hiring, don't let your fingers do the walking (or research) for you. It's not that honest contractors don't advertise in the Yellow Pages (or on television, for that matter). It's just that the best way to learn about a contractor's reputation is to ask questions of people who know. Since an honest contractor should be more than happy to provide a client list, interview homeowners for whom he's completed jobs in the past. If he hesitates to provide you with such information, keep looking for contractors.

The people who work at local lumberyards and hardware stores deal with contractors all the time and can usually provide great insight. In fact, what they're willing to say about your prospective choice will speak volumes. In addition, you're entitled to check a contractor's credit rating as part of the selection process. You can't go through a credit bureau, however, without his prior approval.

> **INSIDER'S TIP:** For work involving structural changes, you should have detailed drawings done by a certified draftsman or an architect.

Homeowners who've completed projects similar to the one you have in mind are another great source of information. The guy may have done a great job on someone's deck, but if you're doing something that requires good solid interior finish work, he may be the wrong candidate. After all, there are specialists in every field. You wouldn't go to a proctologist for a toothache, now, would you?

Once you do locate a homeowner with a completed job similar to the one you have in mind, ask a few questions. And don't be embarrassed; I'm sure you'd gladly do the same for someone else.

Was the contractor on time?

Did he show respect for your home and belongings as he worked?

Did he do a good job of cleaning up after himself at the end of each day?

Did he stick to the agreed-upon budget? (Of course, as Murphy's Law has taught us, there are certain times—which are out of our control—that unexpected problems do crop up, but they should be obvious and clearly reasonable.)

Was the contractor available to answer any questions that arose?

Did he keep the homeowner apprised of the progress of the job?

If there were any problems since the work was completed, was the contractor willing to resolve them?

Most important, would the homeowner use this contractor again?

Arrange to meet three contractors (a good number) who are possibilities. Don't hide the fact that you're shopping around; it works to your advantage. Discuss what you want to have done and inquire about each one's similar experience. Offering to show you jobs he has in progress and also ones he's completed is a good sign that he's on the level.

After the first interview (if they were equally impressive), explain exactly what you want and ask each of the three to submit quotes (a detailed written bid). This quote should include materials, pricing breakdowns, and a building schedule with a defined completion date.

Try to be as informed as possible about the requirements of your project before speaking with the contractor. Ask questions and expect answers you can understand. However, bear in mind, if a particular candidate can't be clear discussing your project with you at the kitchen table, he won't be able to do so once the job is in progress either.

Don't expect contractor(s) to get back to you the next day (unless what you're doing is pretty simple), but it shouldn't be next month either. After looking over the bids, see how they compare. They should all be in the same range, both price-wise and in the way the candidates approach the job. Be wary of extremes: bids that are either too high or too low.

When making your final choice, do you automatically accept the lowest bid? Isn't that the point of the three-bid system? Not exactly. The bidding process is also a chance for you to size up the bidders. If you have an uneasy feeling about the lowest bidder, take a closer look at the others in the running. Remember, it's your home and your money, so don't rush into anything you're not entirely comfortable with.

GENTLEMEN, START YOUR ENGINES

Once you've made your final choice, sit down with your contractor and go over everything in detail. It's a whole lot easier to make alterations on paper before the work begins than it is once the job is in progress.

It's extremely important that your materials and supplies lists are complete and final plans are clearly understood by both parties. You can be sure the contractor doesn't want surprises on the job any more than you do. Misunderstandings tend to center around what materials and supplies the contractor is expected to provide as part of the bid, as opposed to those that the client is expected to provide. Pay extra attention to these points before signing off on anything.

The final contract between you and your contractor should include names and addresses of both parties; scope of the project; completion date; payment schedule; signature and date; and general conditions of the work. Although it's mostly self-explanatory, let's take a closer look at a couple of the sections.

PRICE—Agree on a price that includes everything necessary to do the job and make sure the contractor understands that it's etched in stone. As previously mentioned, you should bear in mind that sometimes there are unavoidable circumstances (i.e., natural disasters such as floods, ice storms, tornadoes, etc.; loss of power; labor strikes; illness or death of owner) that can cause changes. Just be prepared to be reasonable about the unexpected.

PAYMENT SCHEDULE—Don't ever pay all the money on signing. Depending on the scale of the job, the payment schedule may be broken into any number of payments, based on completion of phases. Phases are points in the construction when specific work should be completed—such as rough construction, installation of plumbing and electrical, etc. The most common payment schedules for home renovations are based on three payments (pages 136–38). But proceed with caution.

Most often the contractor's biggest outlay of money comes at the beginning of the job when he has to buy materials. That's the reason some contractors will give to try to convince you they need a large payment up front. But unless you can verify that your money is going directly to a supplier to pay for materials, here's the problem: Usually the contractor will buy from the supplier on credit and use your money for something else. Now there's nothing wrong with this, unless he skips town or stays in town but doesn't finish the job. You see, if he's dumped a load of lumber purchased on credit on your lawn and he's missing in action, the supplier will come after *you* and very likely put a lien on your property (in other words, the supplier will go after you and your home in an attempt to recoup his losses).

And if a contractor bails out on a job, the subcontractors as well as the suppliers will usually have between 60 and 90 days to file a lien on your property for payment. This can be very serious because in most cases they *will* collect, even if it means foreclosure. In some states, parties are required to tell you if they're filing a lien; in other states, they can do so without your knowledge. For your own protection, it's very important to investigate the lien laws in your state and to understand how they affect you. If you have any questions, it's wise to check with an attorney who's knowledgeable in this area.

In some instances, subcontractors will file a lien on the property that will stay in effect until the work is finished. The only way to find out if a lien has, in fact, been filed (prior to a lawsuit) is to check with your local registry of deeds. This is just a formality, however, and is done to guarantee that the homeowner won't sell the property while the job is in progress. In this case, you have to make sure that you all sign release of lien forms when the work is completed.

WORKING OUT A THREE-PAYMENT SCHEDULE

Now, let's look at a three-payment schedule as an example of how to set one up.

THE FIRST PAYMENT, made on signing the contract, should never be more than one half of the total budget (depending upon such variables as the amount of material required versus the labor).

THE SECOND PAYMENT should be made at about the halfway point in the work schedule. This should also be at a point before the walls are sealed so the electrical and plumbing work can be checked to be certain everything is up to standard and code. (The builder is legally responsible for calling in all building inspectors to check this work. Once an "accepted" permit—of which you should receive a copy—is issued,

the walls can be sealed.) Remember, the rule of thumb is that the contractor pays for his mistakes and you pay for yours.

THE THIRD PAYMENT should be scheduled on completion of the job. In the best of all possible worlds you should hold a portion of the final payment until things have settled down and you've had a chance to see that everything's just as you want it. Don't forget, you have to live there long after the contractor is swinging his hammer at another locale!

As the work nears completion, you and the contractor need to agree on what is left to be done. This agreement is called a *punch list*. It contains everything necessary to complete the entire job. The most important task you'll have as the job finishes is to keep track of what's left to do . . . so stay on top of things. And since it's common for contractors to hire subcontractors for jobs like electrical and plumbing, it's important to find out who's responsible if a subcontractor's work is unacceptable. No matter how responsible the contractor is, he's undoubtedly a busy man, and once he's gone, it's going to be hard to get him back. So just make sure to take care of every conceivable item before he's gone.

Finally, don't forget that contractors depend on repeat business and referrals from customers for future jobs; his work should reflect that quality and attitude. Since it pays him more than once to do a good job for you, don't settle for anything less than you expect (within the bounds of reason, of course!).

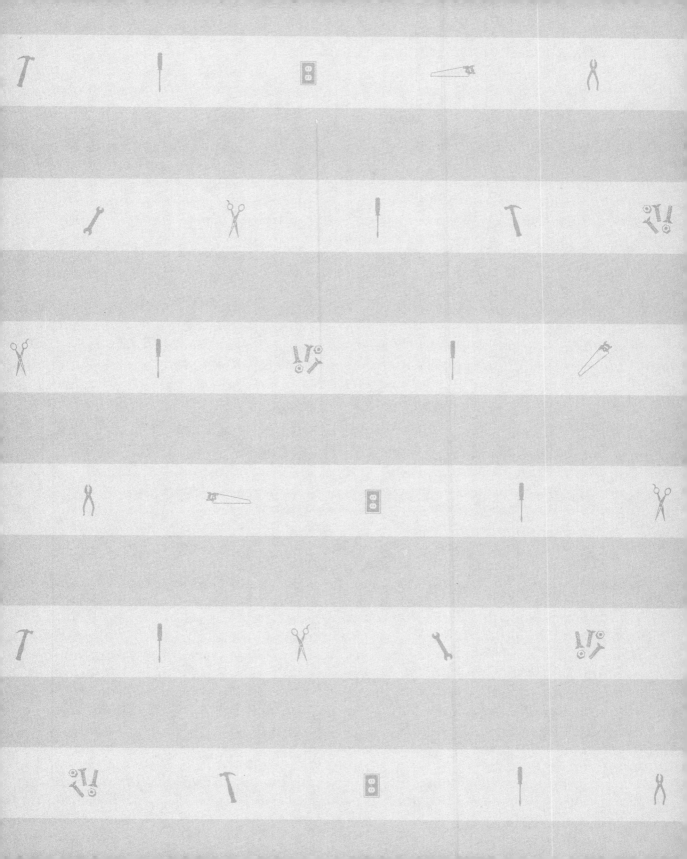

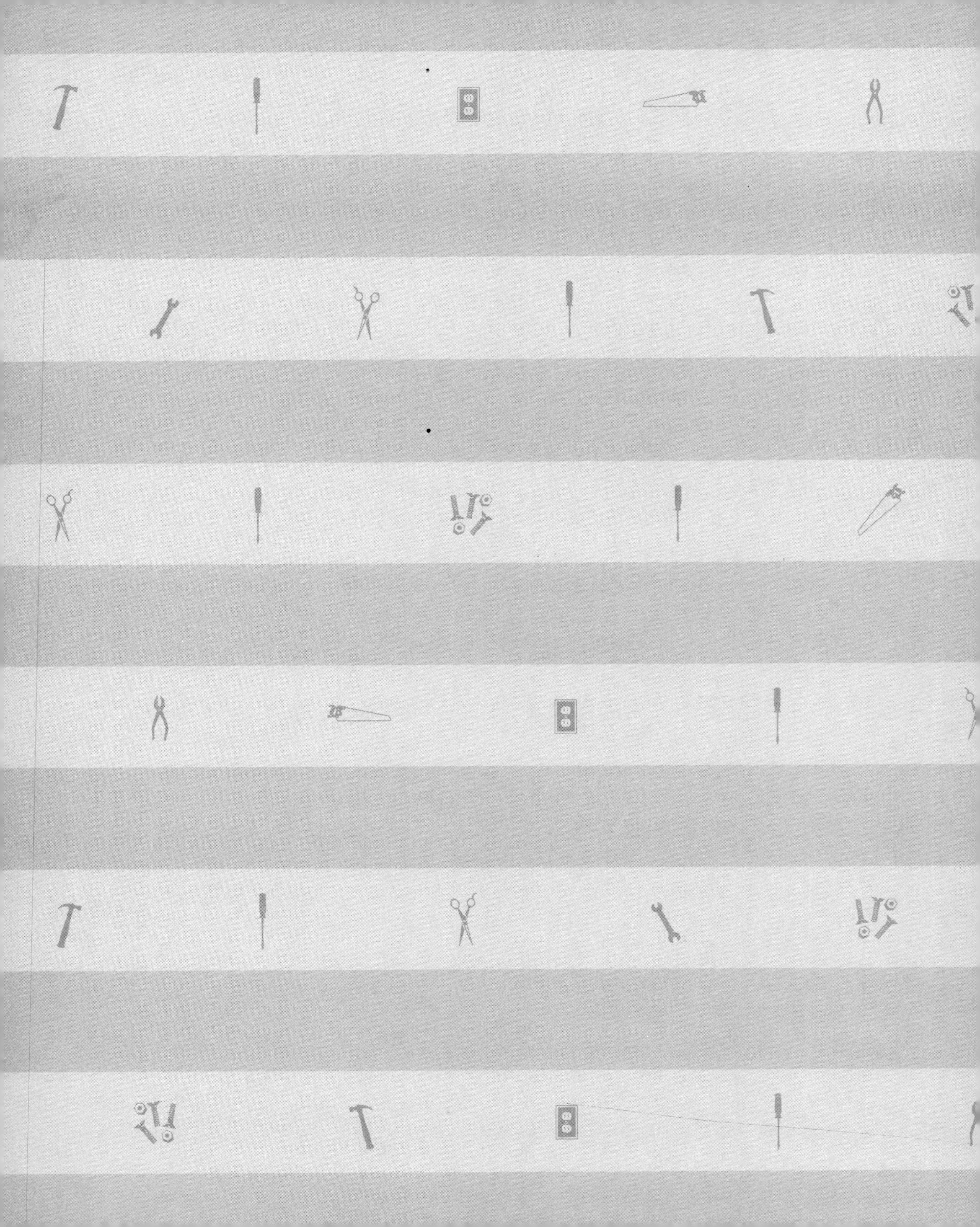

PART

2

Room
for Improvement

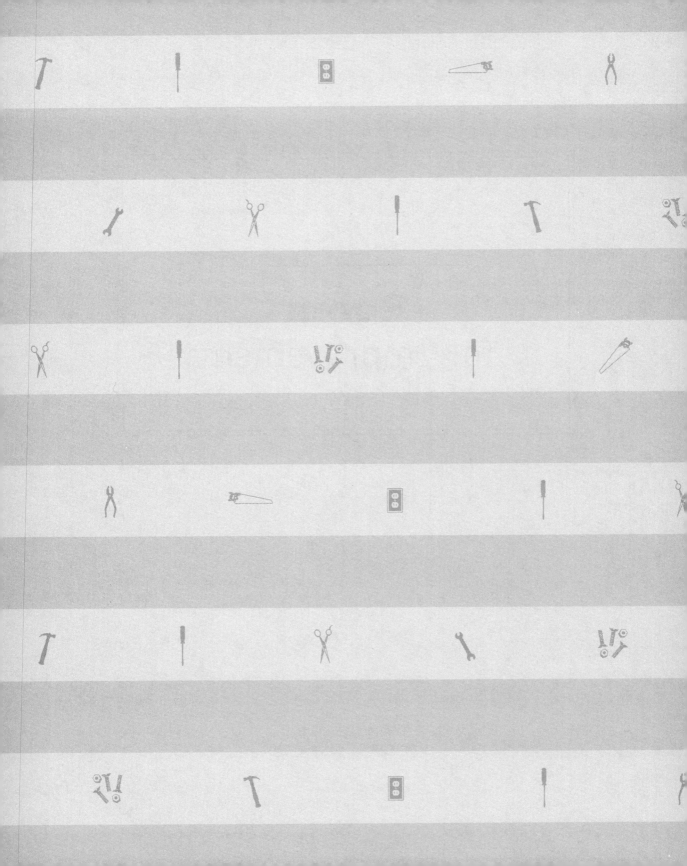

Downsizing:

A Storehouse of Ideas

SPACE: MAXIMIZING WHAT YOU'VE GOT

Obviously, the phrase "a place for everything, and everything in its place" was coined quite some time ago. Long before the advent of CDs, VCRs, video megastores, and the Home Shopping Network. Certainly, decades before the consumer-driven eighties. Somewhere in the back of your mind, you just know there's got to be an easier way. You're fed up with not being able to locate *what* you want *when* you need it. But where to start? Well, you're about to find out.

The first step on the road to becoming the master/mistress of your storage domain is to assess the space you have. As you do this, think about what you require from it; and how it can best be made to fit your needs. Remember, you must learn to control the space; don't let the space control you! And be sure to evaluate *all* areas—not just the obvious horizontal ones but those vertically aligned, as well.

Houses and apartments are full of "empty spaces," which, like "empty calories," are there but not doing anyone any good. If you take a moment to visualize your home, you'll realize there all kinds of areas—nooks and crannies created by pipework and other architectural features, spaces under the stairs, closets, landings, extra high ceilings, basements, and attics—that are severely underutilized.

Sketching a rough layout of your dwelling—room by room—will give you greater insight into the options and limitations of its layout and hence, a better understanding of what you actually have to work with. Think in terms of spaces rather than rooms. You can manipulate your space according to your personal needs and create something much more original and dynamic in the process.

Before we tackle the unique requirements of each room (on a chapter by chapter basis), let's take an overall look at some of the most useful and easiest to acquire storage solutions available.

STORAGE UNITS

There are three basic types of storage units or systems to choose from: built-in, modular, and freestanding. Here's the inside scoop on each:

BUILT-IN UNITS

A built-in unit provides good insulation against cold and sound, and since it can be made to the full height of the room, it maximizes wall, floor, and ceiling space, as well. Built-in closets can be designed to do everything from fitting

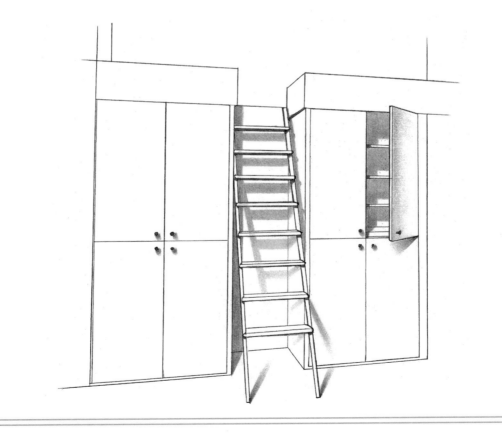

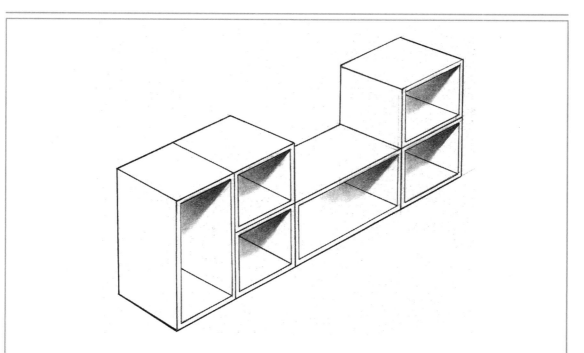

into a fireplace alcove to turning a corner; and those with sliding or folding doors and/or interiors that can pull or swivel out on a hinge are also great space maximizers. However, one disadvantage to a built-in unit is that—like money when you die—"you can't take it with you" if you happen to move.

> 💡 **INSIDER'S TIP:** Always measure precisely before buying anything related to a built-in unit. Even a fraction of an inch too large or small can make a crucial difference in the end result.

MODULAR UNITS

Known for their versatility, modular units are composed of cubes, shelves, drawers, and cabinets that can be adapted or enlarged to suit your individual needs. Try arranging them alongside one another to cover a whole wall, or stacking them on top of each other to form a pyramid for "staggered storage." In addition, shelves and desktops can be placed over separated modules; and they're excellent storage vehicles for such items as CDs, videos, games, or any other items you want put away for safekeeping.

FREESTANDING UNITS

If you have a nomadic soul and tend to move around often, or if you just like to change your surroundings from time to time by rearranging the furniture, freestanding units are a choice you should consider. Although they do not have the "internal versatility" of modular units, prefabricated freestanding units are—as a whole—quite easy to take apart and reassemble, and they can be incorporated into an existing piece of furniture or a kitchen storage unit. In addition, the drawer kits come with side and corner pieces, and in some cases molded inserts can be added to create extra compartments.

SHELVING IT

Well-placed shelving helps maximize space because it can be built into alcoves and corners or in the dead space created by the slope of an attic roof. Shelves can enhance the architectural features of a room while housing a multitude of books and assorted objects. Ideally, all shelving systems should be adaptable so they can be moved to another room, extended, enlarged, or adjusted to hold different contents.

There are three main types of shelving: wall-mounted (adjustable and non-

INSIDER'S TIP: When using freestanding units as room dividers, always make sure to weigh them down at the bottom to prevent them from toppling over. Also, don't make them too tall.

adjustable), freestanding, and built-in. The strongest and most expensive variety is made from hardwood, with the grain running in the direction of the shelf length. Softwood, particleboard, and plywood are not as solid as hardwood, but are the most commonly used materials for indoor shelving. More specifically:

▶ **PARTICLEBOARD**—Readily available, reasonably priced, and supplied in standard widths, particleboard can be cut to the required length. Composed of wood chips that are glued together, the hard-glazed-faced particleboard wipes clean very easily.

▶ **PLYWOOD**—Varies quite a bit in strength and cost, but can prove sturdier than solid hardwood (although it may not be as attractive). Plywood is created when three or four layers of veneered wood are stuck together with a powerful adhesive. It's available in ¼-, ½-, ⅝-, and ¾-inch thicknesses, with the plywood gaining strength with increasing thickness.

▶ **SOFTWOOD**—Inexpensive, but softwood (such as pine and balsam) is prone to warping.

▶ **GLASS SHELVES**—Used for ornamental, lightweight display; when built into a window they allow light to filter through, providing a perfect spot to show off small plants and glass objects.

▶ **METAL OFFICE SHELVING**—The least expensive choice, metal office shelving can be spray-painted and also provides the best support for heavy loads.

SHELVING SUPPORTS

A shelf collapses when it is unable to hold its load or because the supports are not securely mounted to the wall. Supports must, therefore, be strong, spaced at reasonable intervals (16 to 24 inches apart, so they are aligned with the stud in the wall), and attached to a wall with screws long and thick enough to anchor them firmly. A variety of shelf supports is available for the do-it-yourselfer; with some kinds more suitable for a flat wall and others designed to fit into an alcove. Remember, *the heavier the load or the thinner the shelving material, the closer together the brackets should be*. To be exact:

For strong, built-in shelving, use brackets or wooden or metal supports that run along underneath the shelf to support its back edges and that are secured to the wall.

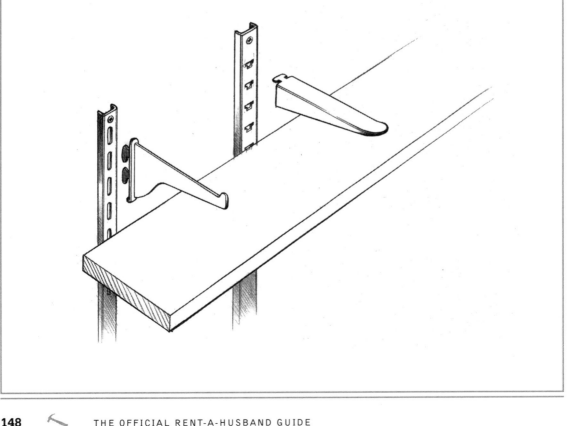

For adjustable shelving, use metal or wooden uprights with slots at intervals for shelf brackets so you can vary the distance between shelves.

For lightweight adjustable shelving, use pegs, dowels, plastic studs, clips, or wires that are inserted into holes in wooden uprights.

There now . . . you're ready for the fun part. You're about to learn how to shelve it, hook it, hang it, file it, contain it, and (finally) find a permanent home for all the clutter that's been hogging the space in yours. So get ready to take charge!

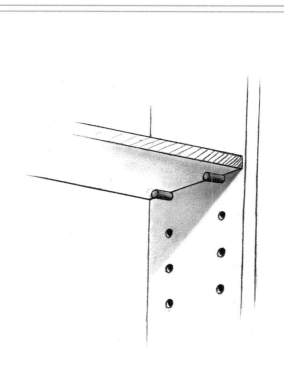

MOUNTING YOUR OWN SHELVES

The shelves that are the least expensive and often the easiest to install are the wall-mounted variety. A popular adjustable style is the track and bracket version. It has metal tracks screwed directly to wall studs or into a solid wood backing that is attached to the studs. Brackets clip to the tracks and support the shelves. Since these brackets are easily moved, shelving may be adjusted to different heights. If the shelves are to support heavy items such as books, the shelf supports must be attached to studs in the wall. As previously mentioned, the studs are most often 16 to 24 inches apart and are covered with drywall. To ensure that you don't hammer or screw into any concealed wiring, tap along the wall lightly with a hammer and listen for a change in sound between the hollow board and the solid stud. When the time comes, you will make your drill holes at the spot where you hear a dull sound.

Bear in mind, if the wall is solid, you must make sure it isn't damp or crumbling (in which case, you'll find cracks and soft material) before you start to mount your shelving. To check, bore a hole with a small masonry drill (which you can rent) in an inconspicuous spot at the base of the wall. Screws will not grip on their own in solid brick or plaster walls, so, in most cases you will have to use a wall anchor that matches the screw size.

Partition or hollow walls are too thin to allow a screw to grip sufficiently. Therefore, wall anchors are needed to hold the screws in place. These are inserted like a closed umbrella into a predrilled hole in the wall. Once inside the wall cavity, the anchors spread out to hold the fixture in position. Specifically, "solid wall anchors" (lead anchors for masonry; plastic for plaster or drywall) expand to grip the inside of brick or plaster walls when the screw goes all the way in. "Hollow-wall anchors" (also known as "Molly bolts") have metal shoulders that expand as you turn the bolt. And "spring toggle" anchors have twin arms that spring apart inside the wall cavity.

Knowing this, you can begin your shelving project by drawing a plan of your proposed design to scale on paper. (Just do your best; no one expects Frank Lloyd Wright–quality here!) Carefully mark the positions of the up-

SOLID WALL ANCHOR

SPRING TOGGLE ANCHOR

HOLLOW WALL ANCHOR

rights on the wall with a pencil and make note of all light switches and electrical outlets you encounter along the way. Now, attach the top of the first upright loosely to the wall (with strong tape). Use a 6-inch level to align the upright, and mark the point for the bottom screw. Have a helper hold the second upright in position while you lay a shelf between the two and place a level on it. Mark the screw positions.

Attach the brackets or uprights with screws that are long enough to go through the wall and into the stud to a depth of at least ⅝ inch. Always attach the fixture securely to a stud, so the shelves can carry a reasonable amount of weight without pulling loose from the wall.

Another shelving option, freestanding units (often used as bookcases), generally come in two heights. Units with three or four shelves are 27 to 36 inches high, the same height as a desk or work surface. Bookcases 60 to 72 inches high have six or more shelves. The standard depth for shelving is around 12 inches. The distinct advantage to having freestanding shelving is that the units can be repositioned whenever you want, providing greater flexibility for the design of any room.

Many furniture manufacturers offer ready-to-assemble freestanding units that are both inexpensive and easy to assemble. They may have such options as drawers and cabinet doors so that the unit can be customized. Finishes vary, but be aware that shelves covered with laminate veneers are usually made of particleboard. Shelves made of solid wood will be stronger and more resistant to sagging over time.

For safety's sake, it's a good idea to attach tall bookcases to the wall behind them. Some manufacturers provide a safety strap—a ribbon made of tough woven nylon—used to attach the top of the bookcase to a wall stud with wood screws.

The most expensive shelving option is built-in. Because it requires careful measuring and cutting to create a precise fit, installation of this type of shelving is best left to a professional. Also, since built-in shelving is destined to become a permanent feature of your home, you need to give considerable thought to its appearance and location before the actual construction begins.

QUICK STORAGE FIXES

While room-specific storage/organizational suggestions will be provided in the corresponding chapters that follow, here's a roundup of some of the "generic" quickest and best:

▶ If you haven't got a spare closet, attic, or basement (attention apartment dwellers!), try storing long, narrow items such as skis, snowboards, and surfboards under beds. Alternately, line them up across two ceiling beams.

▶ Use containers designed for other purposes—such as the compartments of a fishing tackle box for storing jewelry, cosmetics, or craft supplies.

▶ Using insulating cork (thicker than other types of cork), make a bulletin board to hang in the kitchen or home office.

▶ Striped deck-chair canvas easily becomes a wall-hung organizer when you add lots of different-sized pockets. Sew large paper clips and/or hooks into the bottom for notes or gloves, and hang the organizer on the back of a door.

▶ If you have a hallway with a high ceiling, build a pulley system and hang bicycles near the top; or hang bikes on a wall with spikes.

▶ Create storage pockets by edging shelves with strong carpet binding, tacked firmly at intervals, leaving gaps wide enough for hanging scissors, letter openers, and the like.

▶ Hang wicker baskets on the kitchen wall—one for each member of the household—and put letters, telephone messages, and personal odds and ends in them.

▶ Fasten a hinged, fold-down board to the wall so that it can be "put into action" in a flash when you need extra counter space.

▶ Use two filing cabinets to make a base for a desk and to provide extra storage.

- See-through storage drawers are easy to install under any surface.

- While there are organizers on the market for everything from hair bows to loose change, there's nothing stopping you from making your own, once you get the general idea. Since you need only basic cutting, sticking, and sewing skills, turn it into a family project by having the kids join in!

A FINAL NOTE: Reassessing your storage needs is an ongoing project. Every six months, take another look around and ask yourself whether the current systems are still doing the job. If you need to make some adjustments to cover new or different areas, and to keep things running smoothly, don't delay. Remember, we are not static creatures and our homes must change along with us to accommodate the "flow"!

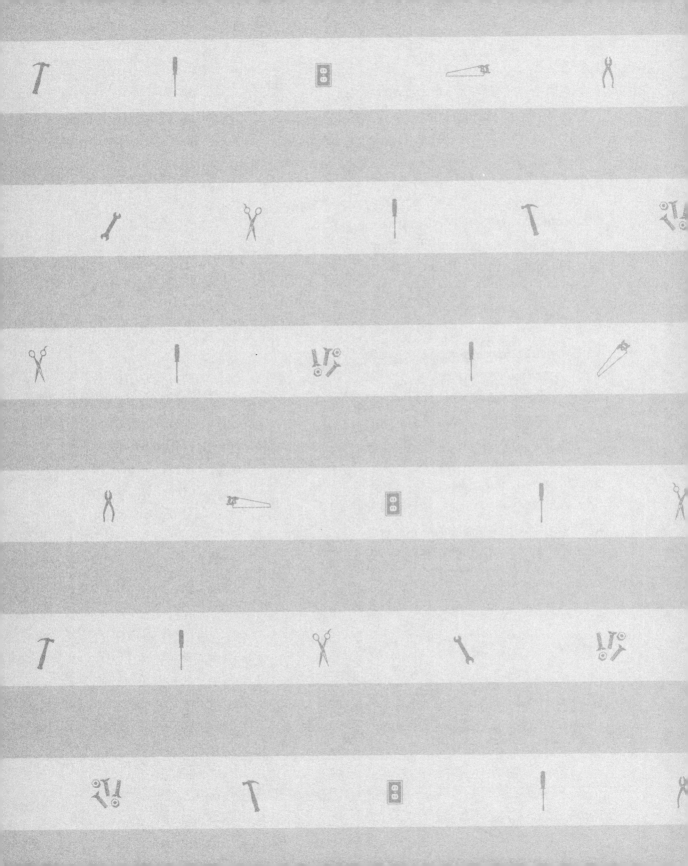

8

Kitchens

Much more than just a room where food is prepared, the kitchen truly is the heart of the home. As such, you must think carefully about how you currently use your kitchen and the ways you'd like to improve it. Crucial to your ultimate satisfaction will be how efficiently the room's three activity zones—the sink area, the food preparation area, and the food storage area—operate, both individually and in combination. A well-configured kitchen should facilitate all activities that take place in it, since the way you interact with the machines and elements in your kitchen (as well as in other areas of your home) determines the room's overall efficiency or *ergonomics*.

Of course, a lack of organization is often due to a lack of space (particu-

> **INSIDER'S TERM:** *Ergonomics* is a buzzword that refers to the relationship of people to machines, in order to maximize work efficiency. Therefore, an ergonomic kitchen is one that actually enhances one's ability to function optimally in it.

larly in the case of apartment dwellers). But if structural changes of any kind are out of the question, what's a person to do? The answer lies in two words: space exploration. Think carefully about whether your kitchen's spaces (cupboard, wall, ceiling, and floor) are all being implemented to the max. Is there perhaps a piece of furniture elsewhere in the house that could be put to better use in the kitchen? A dresser (hutch), for example, offers a lot of space for china. Also, think about which storage areas are already packed to capacity and which might afford you a little more room.

DIVIDE AND CONQUER

The most important step on the road to maximizing the potential of your kitchen is to group its paraphernalia into three categories: items you use every day; things you hardly ever use; and those that simply never see the light of day. Once you've done the separating, the organizing can begin. Start by making a charitable donation of any usable items from the last group and throw away the rest. The second pile, which might consist of utensils and gadgets you rarely use or china brought out only on special occasions, should be packed and stored away in a relatively inaccessible place (such as in the basement or on sturdy closet shelves). Now, you're left with only the most important pile: your first. So, it's time to subdivide.

Begin by separating the contents of this pile according to function: all cooking implements together; all eating ones; cleaning ones, etc. Using existing storage, along with a few carefully placed additions, you will be able to find a home for each item that's as appropriate to its role as the cutlery tray is to the knife. Now, let's concentrate on the room's three main areas.

> **INSIDER'S TIP:** Label specific cupboard shelves for designated items. That way, you don't have to perform as a one-man band when putting away groceries. Solicit the help of other household members, who no longer have the excuse that they don't know where anything goes!

THE BIG THREE

When rethinking the sink area, you must first keep in mind all of the activities you use yours for: washing dishes; preparing food; arranging flowers, etc. Focus on which of them take priority and which items you need close at hand to accomplish these tasks most effectively. Go one step further and ask yourself which you would like to conceal.

Although it's very tempting to store everyday tableware inside your dishwasher (the "never-ending cycle"!), for organization's sake, do try to unload it after each use. Slimline models are ideal for one or two people, as they're much more energy efficient than the full-size models when only a few dishes are being washed regularly.

If your kitchen is designed with a double sink, decide which side is to be used for washing dirty dishes and which is reserved for food preparation. Plan the surrounding storage space to correspond with these activities. Obviously, the dishwashing sink needs a place for cleaning products and dishcloths, as well as a drainage area for wet dishes, and a garbage bin for plate scrapings (remember, not everything goes in a garbage disposal!). Plate racks offer additional storage, while providing an attractive and practical way of draining dishes. The sink in which food is prepared requires an empty work surface nearby for foods, as well as a space for everything associated with preparing it—knives, chopping boards, pots and pans, etc. In addition, don't overlook the areas below, above, and around your sink(s). The space under your sink is the obvious place to store unsightly things like cleaning products and a trash can; above the sink is more suited to display cabinets. The surrounding worktop is best for storing cooking utensils. Try using large stoneware jars for this purpose.

> **INSIDER'S TIP:** Your storage arrangements should reflect your shopping habits. The more frequently you shop, the less storage space you will need.

> **INSIDER'S TIP:** Resist using your oven for extra storage space. Although you may remember that you put something in there, don't count on anyone else to look before turning it on!

Since food is the central theme of any kitchen, the importance of efficient food storage cannot be emphasized too much. Besides, organization just makes cooking a much more pleasurable experience. Divide groceries into categories, bearing in mind that different foods require different storage conditions.

Items such as cookies, crackers, sugars, and flours, for example, last longest at room temperature, while fruits and vegetables keep best in a cool, dark spot.

When it comes to cold food storage, always buy the largest refrigerators and freezers your kitchen will accommodate. (Remember, they run more economically when kept well stocked.) And if members of your household consume food with the speed of light (anyone with growing boys, in particular, knows what we mean), chest freezers might be a good option. However, since they take up a lot of floor space, chest freezers are best kept in a utility room or garage. Also, when freezing, don't forget to label the items, including both content and date.

If cupboard space is particularly tight, a utility cart on wheels is a good investment for storing canned and packaged food. Available in a wide array of sizes and designs, the newer models represent true utilitarian style. Not only can you stack them as deep as you want, but they also come in handy when you're unpacking groceries, as they can be pulled as close to the bags as you need. Store dry foods such as pasta, rice, flour, and dried fruit in airtight containers, preferably in cabinets since their flavor is affected by light, heat, and moisture.

Food preparation is still the "soul" of the kitchen, even if you spend more time microwaving frozen dinners than you do preparing cordon bleu. If a cast-iron range serves as the centerpiece in your kitchen, making a display of heavy-bottomed cast-iron or copper pans adds a very dramatic touch. As we all know, the only thing that's more annoying than listening to someone banging around, looking for a specific pot or pan, is when you're doing so yourself. But there's really no need. There are plenty of attractive pan racks for this purpose, including ceiling racks with butcher's hooks and freestanding pot stands. If you don't display them, pots, pans, and pan lids are best kept together in a tall wire unit where you can see exactly what you have. Remember not to store such things up high, where they can come tumbling down every time you open the cupboard door—a bruised foot is better than a cracked skull!

Now, think about what you actually use when cooking. Do you need wooden spoons handy? Oven gloves? Recipe books? Spices? Is there a surface nearby where you can put down heavy, hot pans? There is no need to have every appliance you own on display. If, for example, your popcorn popper or pasta machine is used fairly rarely, it makes sense to put it up high and out of sight. Strive to keep all the accessories together. Few things are more frustrating than getting the food processor out, only to end up spending 15 minutes hunting for the right blade. It tends to take all of the fun out of puréeing!

INSIDER'S TIP: If you are short on space for storing spices, try adding a narrow shelf to the back of one cabinet. And store spices alphabetically or group by category so you spend less time looking for the one you want when you need it.

INSIDER'S TIP: Unplug countertop appliances immediately after use. Keep them away from water and never touch them with wet hands.

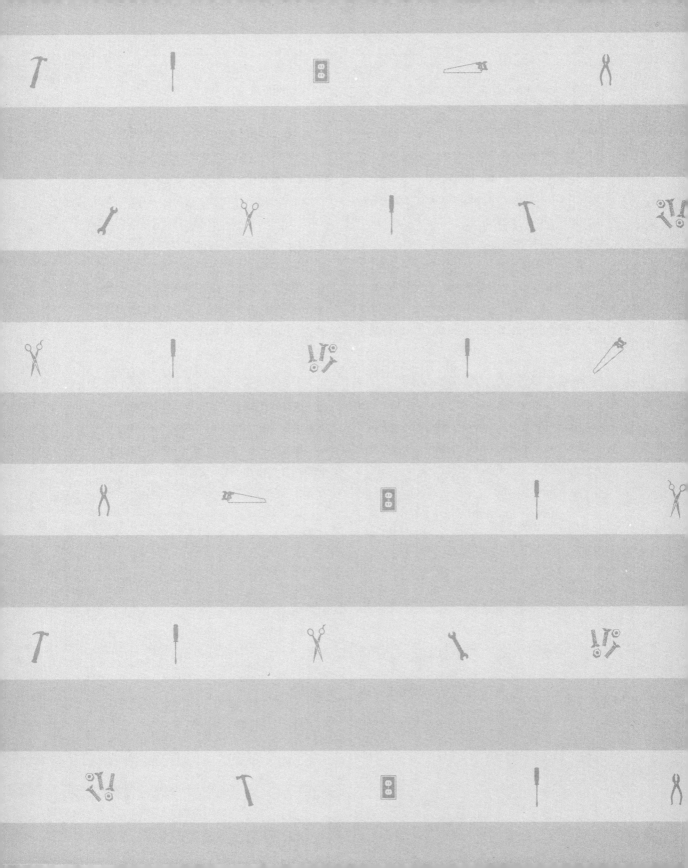

9

Bathrooms

In today's hustling, bustling households, bathrooms are frequently the last bastions of privacy. (And for those with small children, even this refuge isn't always sacred!) Nonetheless, the bathroom is, ideally, a place for unwinding, pampering yourself, enjoying a refreshing shower or a long, luxurious bath. However, since the bathroom also tends to be the smallest room in the house, efficient storage can be a problem. Every bit of space must be used as effectively as possible to ensure your bathroom isn't a storage washout!

INSIDER'S TIP: Since a bathroom conceals (and often reveals) the most intimate truths about personal habits, you should keep this in mind if it's shared with other members of the household or if it's accessible to visitors.

SIZING UP THE SITUATION

The first step toward maximizing the storage potential of your bathroom is to make an honest assessment of how efficiently your current system is working. For example, where are you now storing such necessities as toiletries, towels, paper products, and bathroom cleaning supplies? Are appropriate refills (soap, toilet paper, hair care products, etc.) readily available when you need replacements? Are hampers and wastebaskets conveniently located for drop-offs and pickups?

Remember, the bathroom is, like other rooms in the house, just a series of zones: bathing, shaving, and applying makeup, for example. And while these activities may take place within the same area, they each require their own storage solutions.

Work out what you use the bathroom for, who else uses it, and how much time each of you spends there. Then make a list of all the things that need to be stored.

If you're working with an existing bathroom, you might already have come up with some storage solutions, but if you're designing a bathroom from scratch, it's worth thinking about these factors when you draw up your initial plan. Always make sure to include provisions for adequate ventilation.

If you are starting from the beginning, it's worth showering your bathroom with a little attention. Take the opportunity to consider where you want to position such things as towel racks, toilet paper holders, and fitted shelves before you lift a single new tile. Always try to make use of awkward spaces. Corners, for example, are perfect places for triangular shelves. And don't overlook windowsills that are conveniently located for storing extra items. Installing floor-to-ceiling shelves is your best option if you want a lot of extra storage space. And don't forget so-called "dead" areas like the backs of doors or the space over the toilet. Once you look at it architecturally, as a whole, even the tiniest bathroom is bursting with possibilities.

When you choose shelves, drawers, hooks, or towel racks, look closely at the material they are made from. Since bathrooms are, by nature, hot, steamy places, you want fixtures that

INSIDER'S TIP: Install one or more simple hooks inside your bathroom vanity to hang curling irons and blow dryers.

INSIDER'S TIP: Small or narrow spaces feel more open and inviting when you create an optical illusion by adding mirrors. Choose a size and design that fit your space. Or try mirroring an entire wall for a surefire space enhancer.

can withstand a range of temperatures, as well as condensation. Laminates are the most practical choice, but more attractive options include treated wood, toughened glass, plastic, or wicker.

> **INSIDER'S TIP:** Cosmetics and lotions attractively packaged in glass bottles and jars, as well as decanters full of colorful bath salts and oils, make striking (and relatively inexpensive) additions to bathroom displays.

> **INSIDER'S TIP:** A tiny space will never look big and airy, so indulge in a bright, bold palette for maximum effect—even if the rest of your home is more subdued. Think of a small bath, especially a powder room, as a little surprise for visitors.

Nooks between the ends or sides of tubs are an ingenious storage area for towels, while small chests and narrow but deep cabinets can be placed under sinks. Don't forget, accessories sold to customize kitchens, such as pullout metal baskets, towel rails, and wastebaskets, can just as easily be applied to the bathroom.

CLUTTER CONTAINMENT

Once again, start by paring down your possessions. After all, do you really think you'll ever use that old tube of lipstick you wore in college or take the half-finished bottle of medication that has long-since expired? The time has come to rid yourself of all those fading old bars of hotel soap, half-empty bottles of shampoo (which made your hair look flat, anyway), and your ex-husband's decrepit toothbrush. As always, the key to successful storage is to keep like with like.

You can buy ready-made holders for makeup and makeup brushes, nail-care equipment, and cotton balls. But don't limit yourself to the conventional alone—use your imagination! Wicker baskets are an excellent place to start and can be used to hold everything from magazines and towels to toilet paper rolls. Nylon bags with strings are the perfect home for children's bath toys.

Also, consider customizing containers intended for other purposes—cigar cases, pencil holders, and wine racks (which make unique and accessible storage for rolled towels) all offer possibilities, so let your imagination run wild!

The only rule you need apply is that the scale of the item(s) to be stored matches the scale of the container it is to be stored in.

If you are extremely cramped for space in the bathtub/shower, buy a shower caddy that can be hung from the showerhead to hold shampoos, conditioners, and shower gels. Suction-pad bathroom accessories are ideal in a home where you either don't want to or can't fix permanent shelves or hooks.

SUPPLEMENTAL STORAGE

The time has come to subject your towels, sheets, and pillowcases to a ruthless inspection. Eliminate those that are gray and tattered, as well as the ones that give you nightmares when you sleep on them.

Make enough space only for the ones you really use and like and decide how many of these should be hidden away and how many should be displayed. Obviously, clean towels should be readily available; however, don't stack them in a single vertical tower that will fall over when one is removed. It's best to arrange them into two or three manageable stacks (by size) on narrowly spaced shelves.

If condensation in the bathroom prevents you from storing linens where you want, try fitting cabinet doors tighter so that when they are closed the shelves stay dry. Good ventilation should guard against the buildup of condensation.

INSIDER'S TIP: If you have enough drawers in your bathroom(s), assign one to each member of the household.

INSIDER'S TIP: Light is crucial to a small space. Bring it in with a window, skylight, overhead fixture, or wall sconces, and bandy it about with mirrors, a shiny metal faucet or sink, and crystal accessories.

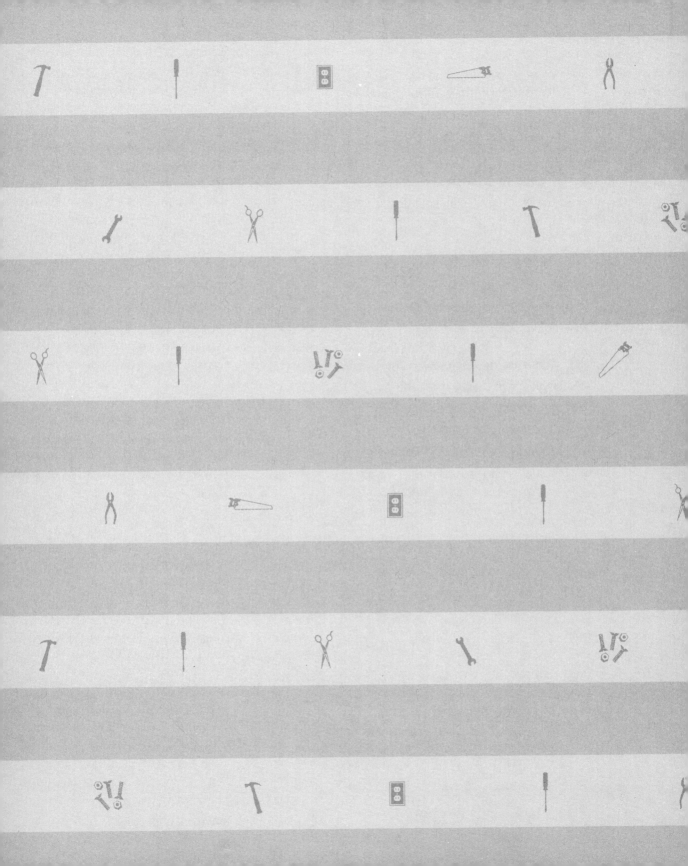

10

Living Rooms

As the nerve center of the home, the living room is the place where family members congregate to talk, read, or simply relax. But the living room is more than just the main communal space. It is also where guests are entertained. And, due to the increasing trend toward combination spaces that incorporate both dining and living areas, this part of the home is entirely open to new interpretations. Creating a successful living space isn't just about providing a comfortable, clutter-free place to relax—it's about making sure the design works at every level and for everyone who uses it, as well.

SIZING UP THE SITUATION

Since living rooms have so many different functions, you must begin by assessing what these are: watching television, listening to music, studying, entertaining friends, talking on the phone, etc. And be sure to include all members of the household, bearing in mind that you need to make space for such things as toys, CD collections, homework, hobbies, and so forth. Give some thought to whether any of these activities can be transferred to other areas of your home. Perhaps it's possible to create a study, play, or entertainment area elsewhere.

STORAGE SOLUTIONS
YOU CAN LIVE WITH

The style you set for the living room will probably dictate the type of storage systems you employ. If you don't have a separate family room, you'll need to do a little compromising. For example, if you want to keep a television, VCR, DVD player, and/or a sound system in the living room, you can purchase an entertainment cabinet that closes up to hide the equipment when not in use.

Perhaps the easiest way to maximize storage space in a living room is with bookcases. They come in such a variety of shapes, sizes, and styles that you can literally put them anywhere. The spot in living rooms that is the most underused is between and/or beneath windows. Try positioning identical bookcases between several windows to increase storage and display room. Another option is to install built-in bookcases that surround the room. Customized bookcases have the advantage of going all the way up to the ceiling and they become part of the room's décor. They can even be designed to look like walls.

You can find numerous antique pieces that look at home in contemporary living rooms. Trunks, chests, or even lobster traps (with a piece of glass cut to fit on top) work well as coffee tables, and old medicine cabinets are perfect places for housing everything from passports to picture albums. If antique furniture isn't your particular style, there are many contemporary designs to select from. The least expensive option is to choose those you assemble yourself. If you buy modular systems, you can add to them as your collectibles increase. Although you won't have the beauty of solid wood, the laminated boards from which most modular pieces are constructed come in a wide range of finishes, and many are suitable for painting. If you're furnishing your home from scratch, try not to make snap decisions based on aesthetics alone. Rather, consider how well a piece of furniture will serve the function you require and whether it will fit into the overall scale of the room. Since manufacturers' catalogs give dimensions, there's no need to rely on luck.

The most expensive type of furnishings are built-in pieces with customized interiors. However, if you're working within a small space, it's probably a very worthwhile investment. Such a piece can do the work of many and fulfill a wide range of functions. If you happen to buy a home that already has built-in furniture, think twice before you eliminate it. You might be able to salvage the interior storage and change the exterior so that it's more in keeping with your taste.

To create an innovative new look, try replacing the doors, or painting and stenciling them.

If your living room has alcoves, you could choose to build shelves or cabinets into these spaces—either floor to ceiling or low-level styles. And remember, storage is not just about large pieces of furniture, but about small containers, as well. Everything you use should have a home of its own, chosen on the scale of the items it is going to house. Boxes, jars, tins, and baskets are all excellent storage devices, and all have the advantage of being portable. Keep in mind that if you store like with like, you will never have difficulty finding anything again!

> **INSIDER'S TIP:** If you have a fireplace, take advantage of the space during the months it's not in use by placing an attractive basket inside the hearth and using it to conceal books, toys, needlepoint, or whatever you don't want lying around. Just be sure to remember to remove it before starting the first fire of the season!

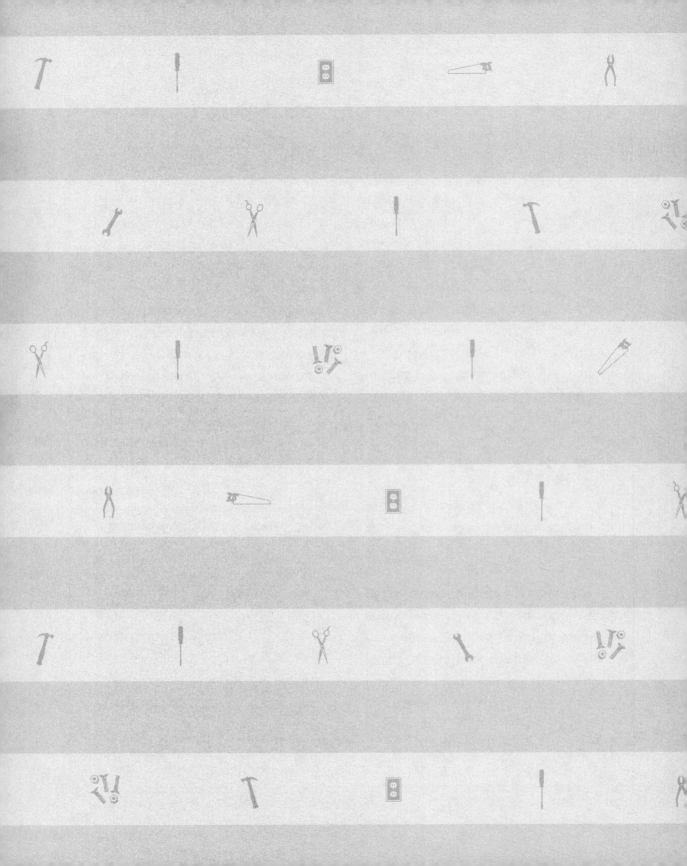

11

Bedrooms

A private sanctuary away from the maddening crowd, your bedroom is an oasis where you retreat at the end of the day to relax, rest, and rejuvenate your spirit. A personal refuge where your most precious possessions are kept, and your most intimate moments are shared. But can these activities truly be enjoyed to the fullest in a room littered with last week's newspapers, piles of dirty clothes, and half-empty soda cans? I think not!

The time has come to pull yourself together starting here . . . starting now. Your clothes need to be organized, your bedside table needs clearing, and your drawers could undoubtedly benefit from a good overhaul. Only then will you find the peace that has eluded you. Easier said than done? Actually, it's easier

than you think! For, once again, it all comes down to the *d* word: discipline.

Since bedrooms tend to be the places we use to stash things away from the view of visitors and other members of the family, the first step is to turn a discerning eye on the shoes under your bed and the forgotten odds and ends hidden away in every corner.

> **INSIDER'S TIP:** Old suitcases make great storage spaces for everything from photo albums to out of season clothes.

While some people find comfort in food or drink, other satiate their desires by surrounding themselves with all sorts of unnecessary items (in other words, clutter). But the fact of the matter is, it's impossible to find true comfort sleeping in the middle of piles of junk.

SIZING UP THE SITUATION

At first glance, bedrooms might not seem that complex. But take a closer look at yours. Besides sleeping (and other activities carried out in bed), what else do you use it for? You may desire a haven in which to read, meditate, and write letters. Or perhaps you need to work in there at a computer or work out there at a minigym. Who else shares this room with you, and what does he or she use it for? Is this where you store your clothes and shoes? What else do you keep in there: books, luggage, old gym socks?

Only by making an honest assessment of your needs can you ascertain which areas are screaming the loudest for attention. Once again, study the available space and make a note of any "dead" portions that could be used more effectively.

> **INSIDER'S TIP:** You can uncover yards of extra space for seasonal or seldom-used belongings by utilizing under-bed storage boxes. Such items as blankets and pillows, winter wear in summer, and holiday decorations all fit nicely; just be sure to tape a list of the contents on top of each box to find what you're looking for in a flash.

ORGANIZATIONAL TIPS TO SLEEP ON

The simplest way of utilizing under-utilized space to the fullest is to install a wall storage system. It can hold everything from personal files and records to electronic equipment or just about anything you're willing to keep in sight. And units with drawers can hold things you don't care to look at, including clothes, which frees up space on shelves in the closet and drawers in your dresser. Conventional dressers can store more items than just socks and underwear. Sweaters, slacks, and seasonal clothing can also find a home in your dresser. In the process, you'll free up space that these items might take up in your closet. In addition, armoires provide room for hanging clothes and their interior shelves will hold any number of storage boxes and bins.

> :bulb: **INSIDER'S TIP:** Sloping ceilings do not necessarily mean limited storage space. An attic bedroom can take advantage of space in the eaves for shelving and drawers. However, the shelves must be built in, as each shelf will vary in depth.
>
> :bulb: **INSIDER'S TIP:** By curtaining off an alcove or section of a room, you can create an inexpensive way to provide basic storage.

CLOSET ORGANIZATION

If clothes are stored properly, they look better and last longer. That's a fact. For this reason, you should have adequate hanging space in closets so that the garments are well ventilated and shoulders and sleeves don't get caught in the door or rub against surfaces. The best combination in a closet is one of both long and short hanging space, shelves, and drawers.

However, organizing your wardrobe is not just about having enough folding and hanging space. It's also about facing up to what it is that you really wear and what is merely hanging around. It's about getting rid of all the excess clutter in your closets, as well. If you've ever moaned that you don't have a thing to wear (and who hasn't?), in spite of the seemingly endless array of shirts, skirts, pants, jackets, and dresses before you—the time has come for some selective culling.

> :bulb: **INSIDER'S TIP:** Always store white garments away from direct sunlight, as it tends to make them yellow.
>
> :bulb: **INSIDER'S TIP:** If you don't own a conventional dressing table, try mocking one up with available pieces of furniture. A generous-sized mirror propped on a dining table makes a wonderful alternative. Add a wicker trunk underneath for storage and an extra surface; put an array of baskets, bowls, and cake stands on top to create a charming and attractive home for personal treasures.

Set aside some time to take a long, hard look at your clothes, because this is your local charity shop's lucky day! They're about to receive a donation, and you're about to gain some much-needed space. The parting is quite painless, trust us! Simply gather together a pile of clothes that you no longer wear. The first items to go in the pile are anything you haven't worn in two years, whether it's because of the fit, fashion, or simply the fact that you never liked it as much when you got it home as you did at the store. Do the same with shoes, belts, hats, and gloves. And feel good about this process; somebody, somewhere, needs these clothes more than you do and they'll be very grateful for them. Just be sure to pack the wearable castoffs into heavy-duty plastic bags and deliver them to the aforementioned charity shop *that very day*—before you have a chance to change your mind.

Now, review what's left. Make a new pile, this time consisting of anything that can be put into long-term storage—whether in the attic or at the dry cleaners. Entries here should include out-of-season clothes and coats, as well as items of sentimental value (like your wedding dress). Wrap, box, and label everything.

Surprise! The remains of the day are the items you actually wear!

> **INSIDER'S TIP:** Drawers are more expensive than shelves. Allow for different depths of shelving for a less costly alternative.

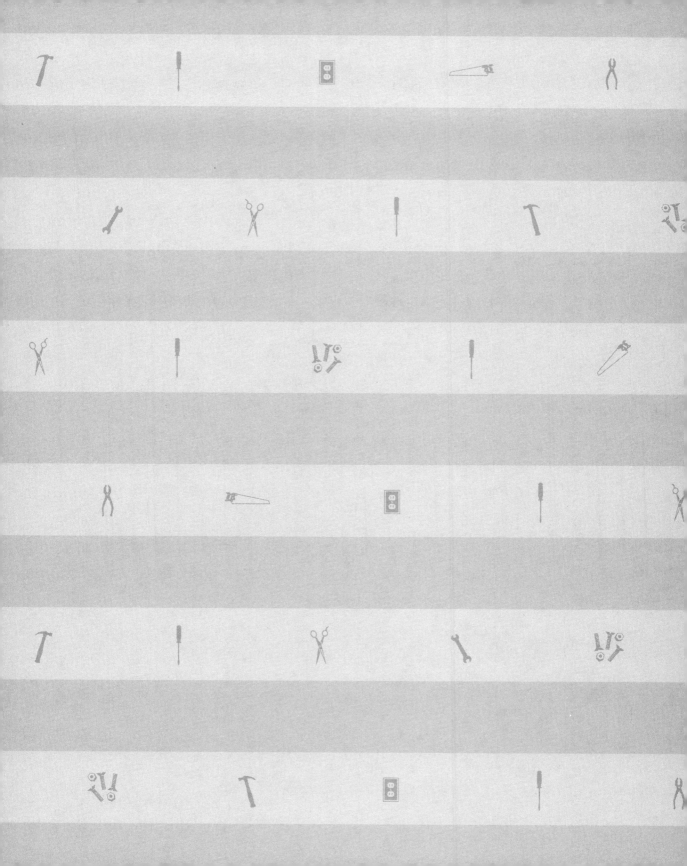

Children's Rooms

A child's room is more than just the place where they sleep. It's also the place where they play, entertain friends, listen to music, watch television, and engage in any number of other activities. A child's room really is a mini-world that demands a great deal from just four walls!

While adults generally prefer to keep items that aren't used on a constant basis out of sight, children are quite the opposite. The goal in children's rooms is to organize the clutter in a manner that allows the room to look neat, while enabling the child to find what he or she is looking for without delay. Of course, as children get older, their storage needs change, both in terms of what will need storing and how accessible it must be. So make it easy for both them and you—deal with the present, but look to the future. It's a fallacy that children like to live in a mess—too often they're simply not provided with enough suitable storage options to function otherwise.

Children's rooms are actually prime examples of one-room living at its most difficult: one person's clothes, activities, and possessions all crammed into a space that's two sizes too small. (And if the room is shared with a sibling, the problems are only compounded.) In this situation, annoyances such as drawers that stick, shelves that are too high, and toy boxes that are in a constant state of disarray all conspire to keep a child fighting perpetual chaos. Even teenagers don't intentionally live like livestock. More often than not, it's a simple case of overcrowding compounded by poor organization.

ROOM TO GROW

The most important thing to consider when assessing the space for your child's room is the way in which his or her needs are going to change as time progresses. Flexibility is key here. The same furnishings you start out with can serve your growing child very well through the years, if you don't lock yourself into juvenile themes. Regardless of how cute baby furniture looks in the store, children really do grow at warp speed, so it pays to think ahead. This is where modular systems of furniture really come into their own, providing desks, spare beds, private cubbyholes, and underbed storage, all of which can be reconfigured as the child gets older.

A baby, him- or herself, takes up very little space. The clothes are tiny and he or she hasn't yet had a chance to acquire a taste for collectibles. But the accompanying paraphernalia: That's what requires the room! Cribs, playpens, strollers, walkers, high chairs, baby swings, giant teddy bears, etc., all take up a substantial amount of space. Storage for this age really needs to be adult-orientated, to make changing, feeding, bathing, and dressing the baby as easy as possible. So, for example, wherever your baby's changing table is, make sure that there's a shelf nearby for all the necessary diapers, lotions, and baby wipes.

If you decide to buy a complete baby-changing unit, look for a style with drawers and a fold-up changing table that can convert into a dresser later on.

As a baby becomes a young child (in the blink of an eye!), low-level storage for toys, games, and books becomes of primary importance, particularly if you want to encourage your child to participate in the cleanup detail. Take a cue from nursery schools, whose personnel have spent decades perfecting the art of storage for young children. Employ lots of boxes, baskets, and bins. Try using Plexiglas boxes with covers (which en-

> **INSIDER'S TIP:** Deep drawers tend to get messier faster than shallow ones; if possible, avoid too deep drawers.

able you to see what you're storing), as well as cardboard, wire-mesh, and wicker containers. They're widely available in home-improvement centers, hardware stores, and through mail-order catalogs. Remember, look for storage units that are easy for a young child to handle, will stand up to abuse, and have no rough edges or heavy lids.

Developing a storage system will become a priority at this stage. There should be containers for every size and type of toy. Plastic stackable baskets are a very good investment. Buy them in several primary colors and develop a simple coding system that your child can easily learn. For example, use red for Legos, blue for blocks, and yellow for crayons. The young child's room is not only a place for playing, but a place for learning, as well. Strive to make it a stimulating, well-defined, and warm environment, with simple but strong color schemes and patterns.

THE CHILD'S BEDROOM

As children grow bigger, let's say until the age of twelve, they need a great deal of storage for the many possessions they tend to acquire. Toys, books, dolls, action figures, games—the list goes on—all figure prominently in your child's life at this time, followed right behind (much sooner than you'd ever expect!) by computers, video games, and sound systems.

> **INSIDER'S TIP:** If children share a room, you can create privacy for them by hanging ceiling-to-floor roller blinds, cut to size, down the middle.

> **INSIDER'S TIP:** For a neat and colorful display, keep stuffed animals and toys in a hammock (a small blanket hung from a line), suspended from one corner of the room.

A space for creative play is needed, but equally important is a space for friends to spend the night. Fortunately, the child is growing in proportion to his or her possessions. You, therefore, can make use of both high- and low-level storage facilities. And always buy any new furnishings for your child's room with an eye for how many things it can contain.

To promote neatness, locate the storage for a particular activity near where the activity takes place. For example, keep art supplies near where your child draws or paints, and games close to where they are played.

TEEN CENTRAL

Naturally, as children become teenagers, their needs change once again. They want a more adult look. At this level of one-room living, there need to be areas for entertaining, working, relaxing, and sleeping. Display is still important, but now it will consist of concert tickets and the like.

Unless you're the rare exception, don't expect to be able to order your teenagers to be orderly. All you can re-

ally do is provide enough space for them to store their possessions, should they want to. Then just hope for the best.

At this age, clothes are a primary obsession, so provide as much wardrobe space as possible. This needn't be a major acquisition, nor sacrifice on the part of another closet shareholder. A pole on wheels (like those found in a department store), along with a couple of clothing organizers with compartments, should suffice.

Such innovative sleeping quarters as a high-level platform bed, with space underneath for a desk or a small sofa bed, are most often preferable to bunk beds at this point. Futons are also very popular with teenagers because they provide an inexpensive seat as well as a spare bed for overnight guests.

Storage racks, in which to keep collections of videos, DVDs, computer games, and CDs in an orderly fashion, are another necessity.

Most important (maybe not to them!) is a study space, away from the madding crowd (younger siblings, in particular). At minimum, this should consist of a desk with drawers (or a table with a small filing cabinet) and shelves, positioned in a quiet, well-lit area.

A cork bulletin board for posting reminders should help your teenager stay on track and, hopefully, put him or her in a serious frame of mind. (At least you'll be giving it the old college try!)

When it comes to personal products and toiletries, such as items for the skin, hair, and teeth, the same rule applies: Always store like with like. Different-colored baskets can separate razors from moisturizers, hair gel from shaving cream. If, after your best efforts and advice, you still don't seem to be getting through to your teen, simply close the door and walk away!

INSIDER'S TIP: A loft bed makes optimum use of the floor space, since so many activities take place within the footprint of the bed. Because the sleeping area is on top, the area underneath is free for study, play, or storage. One more, slightly costlier sleeping option for the teenager is a Murphy bed. When not in use, the bed folds into a unit in the wall and clears the deck for activity below.

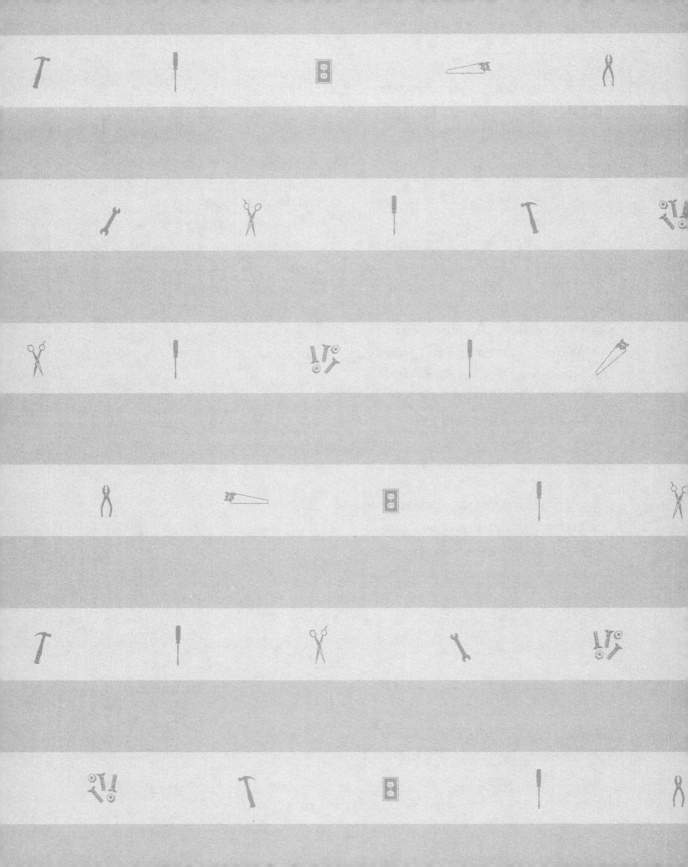

13

Unexpected Spaces:

Finding Them in Places
You've Never Thought to Look

If first impressions really are the most lasting, the importance of having a clutter-free, welcoming entrance hall can not be overstated. Therefore, it's crucial to apply strong organizational skills to this area so that you can manipulate the space to your own advantage.

Entrance halls should boast good lighting for both day and night, warm and welcoming color schemes, and attractive storage for everyone's coats, umbrellas, etc. But a well-organized hall shouldn't stop there. Frequently, it offers little pockets of space that are like discovering gold—once you know how to utilize them.

EXPLORING SPACE

Imagine yourself a stranger, entering your home for the first time. As you walk through the front door, take a look around. Ask yourself if the first impression is a favorable one. Unfortunately, because halls are usually not considered rooms in their own right, there is a tendency to treat them as little more than dumping grounds. But worry not, there's much that can be done to improve this situation. In fact, halls happen to be one of the easiest areas in the house to reorganize.

Start by eliminating all the junk that tends to accumulate in the area. You know, the keys, mail, coats, hats, and umbrellas that are the first things most people unload the moment they walk through the door. A small table, shelf, or bench near the front entrance should serve as a convenient drop for small items, such as keys and mail (try to read and handle on a daily basis to avoid a buildup). A key rack conveniently positioned on the entrance hall wall ensures that you will always know where to reach for your keys, at a moment's notice. And if there's no closet in the area, consider adding a coat rack near the door.

Of course, bookcases and display shelves are natural storage solutions because you can build or purchase them to fit a specific space. And both benches with underseat storage and desks with shelves above them fit very nicely into many hallway configurations.

Put any out-of season clothing and shoes (that might just be "hanging around") into long-term storage elsewhere. And while it's still fresh in your mind, give some thought as to how you can avoid collecting clutter in the area in the future.

Is there room for one big piece of furniture, such as an old-fashioned chest or a hutch, for example? If you do decide to buy a new furnishing for the hall, just be sure to invest in a piece with maximum storage potential.

You also need to consider lighting. How much and what specific type of artificial light is needed? One of the best ways to focus on a special feature (artwork, for example) is with a spotlight. It provides a very elegant and dramatic look.

PERSONAL HIDEAWAYS

If you're lucky, you may find that the space under the stairs is actually large enough for a writing desk or even a small home office. If not, a compact storage shelf or cabinet will usually fit.

> **INSIDER'S TIP:** If you have an especially wide hall, make it functional by converting part of it into a small office. Set up a space-efficient desk (with filing space underneath) flush against the wall. Add a chair and a phone and you're ready to rock 'n' roll!
>
> **INSIDER'S TIP:** An underutilized alcove can easily be transformed into a small breakfast nook or reading room.

Take a fresh look at alcoves and other blind spots. Can these be converted into places for storing "extras" like magazines or other odds and ends that haven't found a permanent home elsewhere in the house?

In your quest to unearth new spaces and use them efficiently, don't lose sight of what the hall and stairs are really all about: traffic. People use them to get from one area of the house to another, so make sure you don't get so carried away with manipulating the space that the space starts to manipulate you!

INSIDER'S TIP: According to the ancient Chinese practice of *feng shui*, the state of your surroundings has a subtle effect upon your mental state. It is believed that this can ultimately affect your health and fortune. If, therefore, the entrance to your home is cluttered, you are greeted each day with things that stand in the way of your goals. Practitioners of *feng shui* believe that clearing your front entrance of obstacles may allow you to do the same with the obstacles in your life. Just a little food for thought.

INSIDER'S TIP: Convert a walk-in closet into a minioffice. If you tend to be claustrophobic, keep it open by removing the doors.

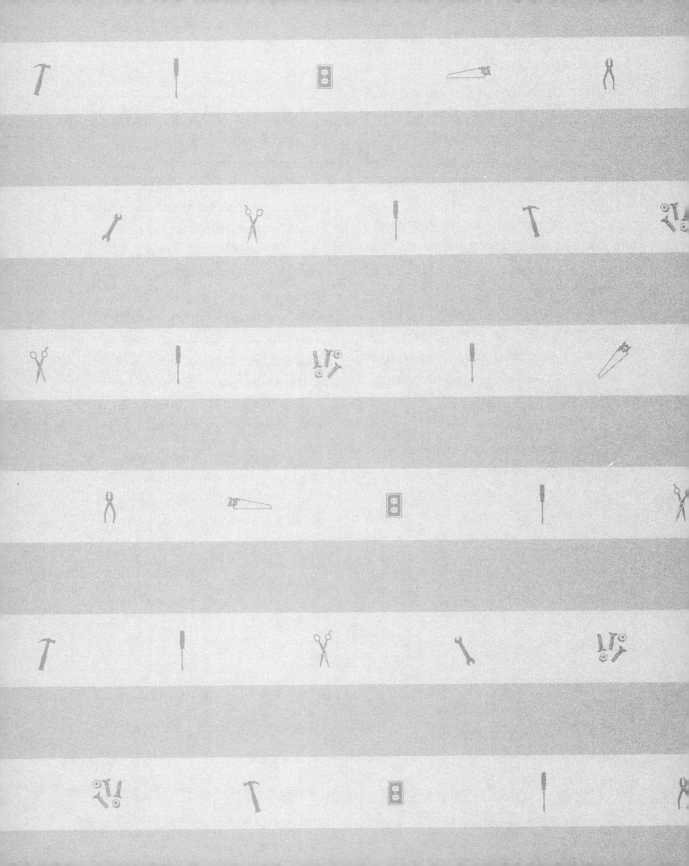

Minding Your Own Business:

The Home Office

Every year the number of people working from home increases dramatically. While some are self-employed or have negotiated an arrangement with their employer, many others are pursuing interests they hope will lead to professional independence in the near future. Even in households where people are employed full-time outside the home, there are often a computer, printer, fax, and phone in a corner of the kitchen or a bedroom. Whatever the reason for working at home, the need for adequate and accessible storage cannot be overstated. Without it, important documents, correspondence, and supplies will undoubtedly be misplaced, buried, or relegated to the proverbial "the dog ate it" excuse pile.

It is, therefore, crucial that you approach the organization and maintenance of your home office with the same degree of professionalism you would bring to a workspace in a more traditional setting outside the home. With that in mind, the first order of business is to assess your actual storage needs. To assist you in this (seemingly daunting) task, we've developed the following step-by-step approach—guaranteed to get your home office in user-friendly shape before the 5 P.M. whistle blows!

SIZING UP THE SITUATION

No matter how you arrange your office, the most practical and convenient way to organize your materials and equipment is to establish three "working" zones. Start by making a list of everything you plan to house in your office—from pencils and paper clips to research materials and file folders. Once you have the list completed, go through it—item by item—and decide into which of the three zones each entry should be placed.

The first, or primary, zone is made up of materials used on a daily basis such as pens, pencils, notepads, reference books, and files relevant to your current work project(s). These items should all be stored within arm's reach (no more than 28 to 30 inches away). And be sure to include your vertical reach area, as well as the areas at your sides and behind you.

Your immediate work area should include an open desk or table surface and a well-designed office chair. If you consult many reference books during the course of a day, a bookshelf should be positioned in proximity, as well. Desks and workstations often have built-in storage for primary-zone items, such as a shallow pencil drawer for small office supplies and large drawers customized for files. Compact desktop shelf units and rolling file cabinets both provide flexible storage space for frequently used items.

INSIDER'S TIP: A word about proper seating: Since the human spine is slightly S-shaped, the back of a well-designed office chair is curved to fit this part of the human anatomy. Take your time when choosing this very important piece of office equipment and be sure to "test drive" all candidates before selecting a chair to take home.

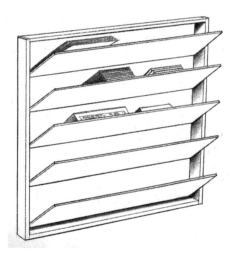

A plastic wall organizer hung over your desk accepts a variety of clip-on accessories that are movable and keep clutter off work surfaces. And for more extensive, primary zone storage, wall-mounted shelving that rests on movable brackets attached to steel tracks is an excellent and versatile choice. A wide lower shelf on such a unit can even be used as your work surface/desk.

Items that are not necessarily used every day, but still must be readily available, fall into the second zone. Since every kind of work has its own storage inventory, this group might in-clude such things as piles of periodicals for a writer or fabric and wallpaper samples for an interior decorator. Storage facilities for the second zone—which include a variety of file cabinets and shelving—should be placed a few steps from your desk, preferably around the perimeters of your office.

Since file cabinets and shelving are both available in a wide array of sizes and styles, the following is a more in-depth look at each category.

FILE IT

Made in two basic formats, file cabinets are either vertical or lateral. Vertical file cabinets are 24 to 28 inches deep and about 15 inches wide.

Cabinets for legal-sized documents are approximately 19 inches wide, with file folders facing the user as the drawer is opened. Vertical file cabinets fit well at the end of a desk or a table and some are even equipped with wheels to conveniently roll underneath work surfaces.

Lateral file cabinets are 30 to 48 inches wide and 15 to 20 inches deep. Designed to be placed against walls, their file folders are either front- or side-facing. Both vertical and lateral cabinets are available in two- to five-drawer heights. The format you purchase should be the shape that works best with the configuration of your office.

> **INSIDER'S TIP:** Try to route electrical cords and cables so you can locate office equipment away from your immediate work area.

File cabinets are obtainable in everything from sleek steel units with baked-on enamel finishes to traditional wood varieties. But no matter what style you choose, be sure the units have top-quality drawer slides—the mechanism that holds the drawer as it is opened and closed. The best drawer slides have ball-bearing rollers, are fully extendable, and work smoothly and effort-

lessly even when supporting a fully loaded drawer.

Be extra careful when loading file cabinets and opening drawers. Although most file cabinets remain stable when a single drawer is extended, they tend to tip over if two loaded drawers are opened at the same time. For safety, some file cabinets have catch mechanisms that prevent two or more drawers from being opened simultaneously. Others have counterbalance weights installed in their frames to prevent mishaps.

SHELVE IT

The big difference between shelves and cabinets is that everything on your shelves is also on display. While shelves look great with books, plants, or knick-knacks, loose papers and office supplies are best stored out of sight.

Office equipment such as fax machines and printers also belong in the second zone.

The third zone is made up of such nonessential, infrequently used items as old tax returns and extra paper for your printer. If space is a problem, consider storing such materials in another room or at least out of the immediate vicinity. This will serve to maximize space in your office area. Milk crates, cardboard file boxes, and stackable bins all make great containers for out-of-room storage. (Just be sure to clearly label the contents of each.)

Now, there is a fourth zone, but it's made up entirely of dead weight. You know, those odds and ends you realize (in your more lucid moments) you'll never really need again, but somehow haven't been able to part with. Experts agree that a certain level of ruthlessness is necessary when dealing with this category.

First, don't stop to read anything, write anything, or spend a lot of time even thinking about anything connected with this zone. And for heaven's sake, don't put items aside for later consideration. Undoubtedly, that's what you did the last time this stuff was brought to your attention—five years ago! Just close your eyes and toss it. Not only will you feel empowered by the experience, but considerably lighter, as well.

MADE TO ORDER

Home office designers agree that one reason we keep piles of paper around is that they remind us of things we're afraid we'll forget if they're out of our sight. A final key to the clutter-free office is to tame those paper tigers by replacing the jumble with a more organized personal system. A good planning calendar can combine appointments with addresses, contact lists, and to-do notes. Alternately, a growing amount of "personal organizing" computer software can do the same.

To keep current concerns visible, use bulletin boards, blackboards, or white boards. But remain vigilant, any of these tools can harbor clutter if you're not careful.

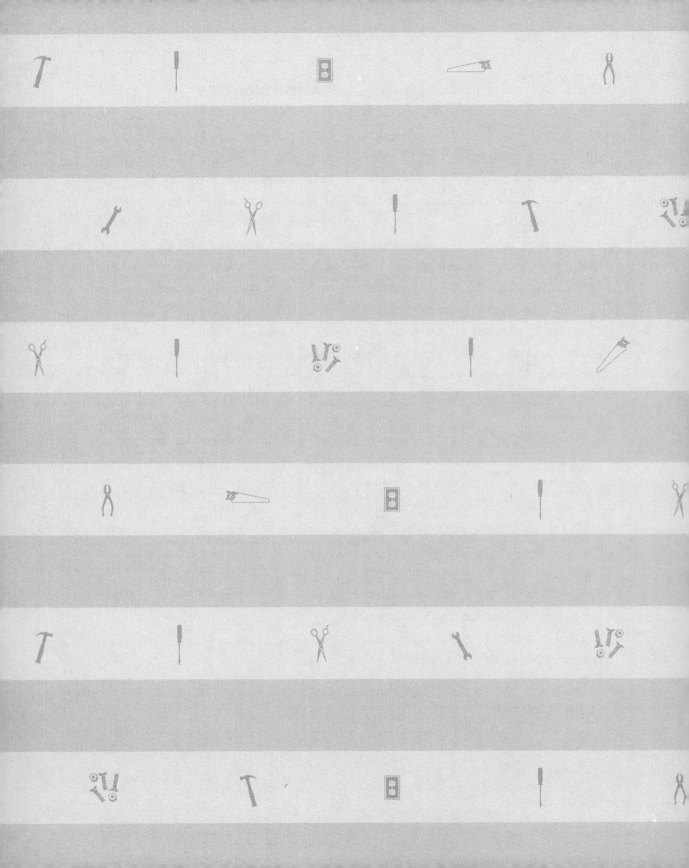

PART

3

Home Safety
From the Inside Out

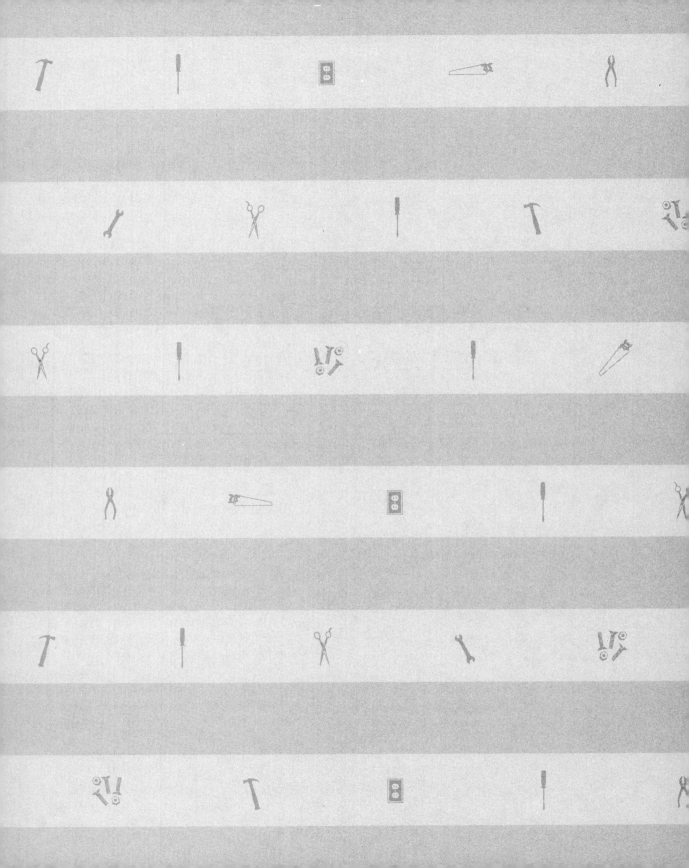

15

Indoor Security

Not long ago, Rent-A-Husband received a panic-stricken call from a woman in desperate need of having her living room carpet removed. The urgency was precipitated by the fact that her four-year-old son had ingested dangerous carpet-cleaning chemicals when some of his toys and snacks fell on the floor before going into his mouth . . . a floor covered with carpeting still slightly damp from a recent cleaning.

We're told the little boy had such a severe reaction to the chemicals that his entire body swelled up. And by the time he reached the hospital (where his problem was thankfully resolved), he'd spiked a temperature of more than 105 degrees. Unfortunately, others similarly struck haven't been so lucky. According to the U.S. Department of Health, over 1,100 cases of people suffering the exact same reaction to these products have been reported in this country alone since 1995, but time wasn't on the side of those who failed to receive a prompt diagnosis and they didn't survive the incident.

The key to preventing such disasters lies in understanding where the danger exists.

SAFE AIR

How long can you hold your breath . . . a minute or two? Don't try to find out. The fact is, the fresh air that fills our lungs and provides our blood with a steady supply of oxygen is something we tend to take for granted. But how long can we continue to do so? The dramatic increase in incidents of asthma and other respiratory ailments (among people of all ages) in recent years should be some indication that the air within our homes might not be as safe to breathe as we'd like to believe. Could yours be tainted with fumes or particles from any of the following harmful substances?

Major classes of indoor air pollutants include:

▶ Biological contaminants such as bacteria, mold, and pollen, as well as house dust.

▶ Chemical by-products such as formaldehyde, benzene, and other harmful chemicals present in construction materials, cleaning supplies, paints and solvents, and a wide variety of other items.

▶ Radon, a radioactive gas that is found in the ground and in groundwater (see pages 199–200).

Combined with industrial pollution, which may be in the vicinity, and extremely high or low humidity levels, the above pollutants can be present in varying concentrations in any particular household.

BIOLOGICAL CONTAMINANTS

Bacteria, mold, and fungi thrive in areas that are frequently damp or wet. And while warm and humid weather usually provides the friendliest breeding ground, the most important step at any temperature is moisture control.

Be alert to signs of trouble brewing, such as stuffy odors, condensation on walls and windows, water stains, and areas where books, papers, magazines, clothes, furniture, and other items become damp or moldy. Some people are allergic to mold. If you think you might be one of them, speak with your physician. He or she can diagnose symptoms related to a condition known as "biological pollutant" sickness. To assist your doctor in making such a determination, be prepared to answer the following questions before your visit:

▶ Do you have frequent headaches, fevers, itchy watery eyes, a stuffy nose, a dry throat, or a persistent cough?

▶ Do you feel tired or dizzy all the time or have breathing difficulties?

▶ Did any of the above symptoms appear after moving to a new home?

▶ Do the symptoms disappear or become less intense when you leave your home and return when you come back?

▶ Have you recently remodeled your home or performed any energy conservation projects, such as installing storm windows or weather stripping? Did the symptoms occur after the residence became more weather-resistant?

▶ Have you experienced any recent water damage in your home or does it generally feel more humid? Are you able to see moisture on the windows or on other surfaces such as walls and ceilings?

▶ Have you acquired any new pets?

▶ Do the symptoms get worse after exposure to hay or fields, raking dry leaves, a lawn being mowed, a damp basement, or after consuming foods and drinks prepared by fermentation such as beer, wine, sharp cheese, sauerkraut, pickles, or mushrooms?

▶ Do you have a known allergy to penicillin, which is made from mold?

To minimize moisture buildups in basements or laundry rooms, vent clothes dryers to the outdoors. If there aren't enough vents on the roof of your home, install additional units to keep attics and crawl spaces dry and reasonably cool or warm. Do you think your ventilation is adequate? You can tell by seeing if your attic surfaces are damp or more than a little warm to the touch during hot summer temperatures. If they are, ventilation must be improved. For another opinion, ask one or more reputable contractors to take a look at the situation and supply you with suggestions (and quotes) for remedying it.

Mold frequently develops where water pipes enter the space in a cupboard below a sink. Another potential problem can occur in the surplus water trays of self-defrosting refrigerators. Try sprinkling a small amount of borax—a natural mold fighter—over the area and wipe clean a few hours later. This will usually remove and/or prevent mold from forming. Repeat as needed.

In the bathroom, run the exhaust fan when you take showers or baths. Clean shower stalls and other damp surfaces with mild disinfectants and be sure to include the shower curtain and liner. Mold often begins to grow in the grouting between bathroom tiles and in the caulking seams between the tub and shower unit and the wall. Check to see if the caulking and grouting in your bathroom are still intact. If not, repair any damaged sections.

Empty the water trays in air conditioners and refrigerators frequently. And pay special attention to your household humidifier . . . its benefits may well not outweigh its risks. Although humidifiers do add moisture to air that's too dry for comfort—a common problem in the low-humidity conditions of winter—they also frequently become breeding grounds for biological contaminants. This is because they contain standing water for long periods of time. An effective way to combat bacteria growth is to clean "cool mist" and ultrasonic humidifiers daily and to use only distilled water in them.

Another persistent cause of moisture is damp or wet carpeting. It provides an effective medium for the growth of mold, especially in basement or lower-level bathrooms, bedrooms, or family rooms. To dry your carpet, use a dehumidifier and one or more large fans to constantly move air over the wet fabric.

In basements that tend to leak or collect moisture, take care of these problems by patching cracks in the walls and floor, renewing the drainage tile system around the building's foundation, keeping sump pumps in good operating condition, painting damp walls with a water-sealing basement paint, and periodically cleaning and disinfecting the floor drains with a commercial drain cleaner. But it's not enough to plug the leaks—the foundation must be sealed off from the outside air as well, since air that enters a home from the

> **INSIDER'S TIP:** Keep a lot of houseplants around. More than just items of decor, plants do an effective job of cleaning the air we breathe by filtering out pollutants. It's nature's way of keeping the air clean.

soil can contain considerable amounts of moisture. Consult a professional, as this sort of maintenance is not for the novice do-it-yourselfer.

RADON

A radioactive gas that's produced by the gradual breakdown or decomposition of radium, radon is an element that occurs naturally within ground and groundwater in varying (usually very small) concentrations. Because the air pressure inside a home is usually lower than the pressure in the soil around the building's foundation, this difference acts like a vacuum that can draw radon in through cracks in the foundation and other openings.

The fact that radon exposure is hazardous to humans was suspected years ago in Germany and Czechoslovakia, when a large percentage of miners in those countries developed lung cancer while working in areas with high concentrations of radon.

Some of the many ways radon can enter a building include:

► Through cracks and voids in basement side walls, foundations, and floors, or through openings around drains, sump pumps, joints, and pipes.

► Through areas that builders have left unfinished.

► Through dirt-floor basements.

► Through water drawn from a private well that may contain radon, which subsequently gets released into the house.

► Through low air pressure—which can increase radon levels—caused by large appliances (such as a furnace or clothes dryer) that draw air into the house, by a warm indoor temperature during cold weather, and by chimneys and other exhaust fans.

You should contact your local or state environmental agency or health department, and ask what they recommend before making any decisions about testing for radon. Some agencies provide free testing services, or, at the very least, they may be able to tell you, based on your location, if you are in a known radon area. If a government agency will not perform the test, you can purchase a radon kit at a local hardware or building supply store and complete the test yourself. Just make sure that the kit has passed the Environmental Protection Agency's testing program, or is state certified. Look for the phrase MEETS EPA REQUIREMENTS on the package. Alternatively, you can have a commercial testing service come to your home and perform a radon test.

The results of the radon test should be read and interpreted by health department officials, who will help you decide if additional tests should be performed, and—if necessary—what steps should be taken to try to reduce the radon levels in your home.

CHEMICAL PRODUCTS

A number of common household products can produce harmful fumes or particles. A rather common pollutant, which can be found in varying ·(usually small) concentrations within many homes, is formaldehyde. It can be emitted by such everyday items as waxed paper, room deodorizers, facial tissues, permanent press clothing, plywood, and urea-foam insulation used in construction.

Benzene and trichloroethylene, found in such products as paint thinners,

> **INSIDER'S TIP:** Whenever a choice is available, use exterior-grade pressed wood products such as plywood and fiberboard because they contain phenol resins, not formaldehyde-producing urea resins. If your home has urea-foam insulation, make sure the insulation is not damp and that there are no cracks in your walls.

> **INSIDER'S TIP:** To get rid of formaldehyde the natural way, keep philodendrons, spider plants, golden pathos, bamboo palms, corn plants, and chrysanthemums. To keep benzene at bay, try English ivy, dracaenas, gerbera daisies, and peace lilies. And for trichloroethylene, again, go with dracaenas and chrysanthemums.

strippers, solvents, synthetic fibers, rubber, plastics, detergents, wood preservatives, aerosol sprays, cleansers and disinfectants, moth repellents, air fresheners, stored fuel, printing inks, and adhesives, are other potentially harmful substances.

Herbicides, pesticides, and even fertilizers can also prove damaging. Although they may not actually be used within the home, products applied in the yard can still be blown inside by the wind, tracked into the house underfoot, or leached into the house in contaminated water that seeps through porous or cracked foundations. Take note of the warning labels on the cans or packages to determine the potential hazards of any individual product.

CARBON MONOXIDE

Carbon monoxide is a colorless, odorless gas that interferes with the blood's ability to deliver oxygen throughout the body. Sources of this hazardous combustion product include automobile exhaust from attached garages and gas appliances. Lethal concentrations of carbon monoxide are most frequently related to poor furnace maintenance, damaged chimneys, vents, and flues, improper installation of appliances, backdrafting of furnace gases because of excess exhaust, inadequate air supply, or faulty auto exhaust systems, and cause several hundred deaths each year.

Signs of carbon monoxide poisoning include impaired vision and coordination, fatigue, headache, dizziness, confusion, and nausea.

Chronic exposure to low levels of carbon monoxide may contribute to cardiac disease. In fact, one study showed that heart patients exposed to high levels of this gas suffered three times as many irregular heartbeats as those exposed to normal air.

To reduce exposure to carbon monoxide in your home, take the following precautions:

► Vent gas space heaters and furnaces to the outdoors.

► If you have a gas stove, install and use an exhaust fan vented to the outdoors.

► When gas-fueled or wood-burning fireplaces are in use, be sure flues are open before starting the fire.

► Comply with any manufacturer's suggestions for changing filters on central heating and cooling systems and air cleaners.

► If you use a wood stove, make certain the doors fit tightly.

▶ Have a trained professional inspect, clean, and tune-up your central heating system (including furnace, flues, and chimneys) on an annual basis.

If you are concerned, you can have professionals check potential carbon monoxide sources to make sure they are safe.

> 💡 **INSIDER'S TIP:** The flames from a properly adjusted gas burner should be blue with only slightly yellow tips. If the tips are very yellow, the stove is releasing too much carbon monoxide.

FIRE

Perhaps no other word in the English language can ignite feelings of sheer terror more intensely than *f-i-r-e.* According to estimates by the National Fire Protection Association, over two thousand homes in the United States are struck by fire each day, annually claiming four to five thousand lives and injuring tens of thousands more. In addition, the Consumer Product Safety Commission estimates that every year

fire-related property damage is in the billions of dollars.

To effectively protect your home and family from fire requires three things: eliminating fire hazards, installing smoke alarms, and practicing how to respond in case a fire does break out.

Check the following locations to pinpoint potential fire hazards in your own home:

▶ FAULTY ELECTRICAL OUTLETS—The most obvious hazards to look for are overloaded outlets. Naturally, if an overload is significant, it will result in a tripped circuit breaker or blown fuse. View such an event as a warning signal and take steps to remedy the problem (see Chapter 3). Also inspect outlets for cracks, scorched or blackened areas, and loose connections (the inability to hold plugs tightly.) If you notice any of these problems, or if the faceplate feels warm to the touch, have the outlet replaced by a professional.

▶ APPLIANCE PLUGS AND CORDS—Feel them while they are operating; slight warmth is to be expected, but if a plug is hot to the touch, turn the appliance off and unplug it. Have the appliance professionally inspected before using it again. If appliance cords and plugs are frayed, cracked, or burned, they must be replaced (see Chapter 3). Also, remove all appliance and extension cords from beneath rugs or furniture, where they can be abraded and start a fire.

▶ **HEATING EQUIPMENT**—Make sure all electric baseboard heaters, space heaters, fireplaces, and woodstoves are adequately shielded from contact with nearby surfaces and are kept away from furnishings. Electric space heaters should be frequently inspected for frayed cords, broken or loose wiring, and overheating wall plugs.

▶ When a fireplace is in use, make sure a fire screen—which should fit closely around the entire fireplace opening—is in place to prevent sparks from flying out. In addition, don't store newspapers, kindling, or firewood near a hearth and *never* leave a fire unattended.

▶ Woodstoves have to be installed according to local building code regulations, so hire a certified installer for this job. If you live in a home with a woodstove that was installed prior to your occupancy, have it inspected by a building inspector or fire marshal.

▶ If you build fires regularly, have your chimney or stovepipe inspected and cleaned at least once a year. This is particularly important if you live in a northern region and keep a fire going throughout the winter months, due to fume leakage and sooty buildup.

▶ Kerosene-burning space heaters are extremely dangerous and should be avoided whenever possible. In fact, local fire codes in many areas flatly prohibit them. If you feel compelled to use them, follow the operating and maintenance instructions supplied by the manufacturer very carefully. Take care to ensure their tip-over safety switches work, keep heaters at least three feet from combustible surfaces (drapes, tablecloths, and upholstered and solid wood furniture), and never leave a heater in operation unattended.

▶ **KITCHENS**—Check cooking surfaces for grease buildup and if found, clean them by scrubbing with ammonia, followed by detergent and water. Be sure curtains, potholders, and napkins are kept far away from burners and heat, and don't store newspapers or paper bags near the stove. Major appliances such as the refrigerator and dishwasher should also be checked regularly to ensure they are in working order and should be maintained periodically by a qualified service technician. Also keep small appliances clean, dry, and functioning properly. Always unplug them when they're not in use.

SMOKE DETECTORS

Your first line of defense against fire, smoke detectors reduce by half your chances of dying in a home fire, according to the National Fire Protection Association. There are two basic types of smoke detectors: photoelectric and ionization detectors. Photoelectric detectors work by generating a beam of infrared light; smoke interrupting the beam causes the alarm to sound. Since these detectors are sensitive to smoldering fires in upholstery, bedding, and be-hind walls, they are well suited for installation near sleeping and living areas. Unfortunately, since photoelectric detectors also respond to steam, dust, and other airborne particles, they are not a good choice for such areas as bathrooms, laundry rooms, and home workshops. For these areas, ionization detectors offer the best protection. They perform by emitting a minute amount of radiation that electrically charges, or ionizes, the air inside the device. Smoke that enters the detector reduces the electric current that, in turn, activates the alarm.

TO INSTALL A SMOKE DETECTOR

Remove the cover of the smoke detector and hold the base against the wall or ceiling. After locating the mounting screws inside the smoke detector, mark the screw locations on the wall or ceiling with a pencil.

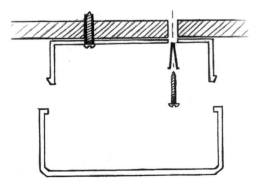

Drill pilot holes a little smaller in diameter than the plastic screw anchors, then tap the screws through the mounting holes in the unit, and screw them into the screw anchors. Tighten the screws, install the battery, replace the cover, and test the unit.

TO TEST A SMOKE DETECTOR

Press the battery test button in the cover of the unit to be sure the battery is connected properly.

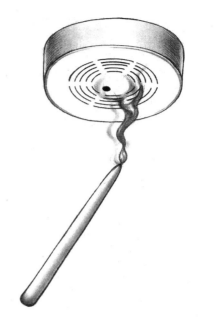

Hold a long (6-inch) lit candle below the smoke detector so that the heated air will rise into the detector.

If no alarm sounds within 15 seconds, blow out the flame and hold the candle so that the smoke rises into the detector.

If there's still no reaction, repeat the procedure. If the detector fails to perform after two attempts, replace the battery.

> **INSIDER'S TIP:** Since it's recommended that smoke detector batteries be changed once a year, it's easy to remember to do it on the day the clocks are turned back each fall from daylight saving to standard time.

FIRE EXTINGUISHERS

The National Fire Protection Association recommends that every home be equipped with at least one fire extinguisher, located in the kitchen. It is preferable, however, to have one on each level of the house. Fire extinguishers are graded by their size, class, and rating. Size refers to the weight of the fire-fighting chemical it contains, while class indicates the types of fires an extinguisher can put out. For example, class A extinguishers are intended only for use on ordinary combustible materials such as wood, paper, and cloth. Class B extinguishers are used for flammable liquids such as grease, oil, and gasoline. Class C extinguishers contain halon gas (which has an adverse effect on the earth's ozone layer); for that reason C extinguishers are no longer manufactured for home use. They are, however, still available in

combination forms such as B:C and A:B:C. Halon extinguishers are extremely effective around such expensive electronic gear as computers, largely because halon expands into hard-to-reach areas and around obstructions, quenching fire in places other extinguishers cannot reach.

A number of fire extinguishers contain chemicals for putting out combination fires. In fact, extinguishers classed B:C and even A:B:C are more widely available for home use than extinguishers designed solely for individual types of fires. For any location in the home, an all-purpose A:B:C extinguisher is generally the best choice.

Rating measures a fire extinguisher's effectiveness on a given type of fire. The higher the rating, the more effective the extinguisher is against the class of fires to which the rating is assigned. To protect one entire floor of a house, we suggest you purchase a model rated 3A:40B:C. This is a relatively large model (about 10 pounds) and costs approximately $50. For use in the kitchen, alone, a 5B:C unit should suffice. This one weighs only about 3 pounds and costs around $15.

Be sure the fire extinguisher you buy

has a pressure gauge that enables you to check the condition of the charge at a glance. Inspect the gauge once a month, and whenever a loss of pressure is indicated, have the extinguisher recharged either where you bought it or through your local fire department.

Every member of the family (except young children) should practice using a fire extinguisher to learn the technique in case a fire does break out. To operate a fire extinguisher properly, stand or kneel six to ten feet from the fire with your back to the nearest exit. Holding the device upright, pull the locking pin from the handle and aim the nozzle at the base of the flames. Now, squeeze the handle, sweeping the nozzle from side to side to blanket the fire with retardant until the flames go out.

> **INSIDER'S TIP:** It's extremely important that every household have an emergency escape plan in case of fire. Each room should have at least two exits (window and door), since one could be blocked by fire. Keep escape routes clear and be sure to practice your plan with spontaneous fire drills.

CREATING A HEALTHY WORK ENVIRONMENT

In this increasingly electronics-dominated age, it's important to be aware that radiation is emitted from many parts of such equipment as computers, video monitors, and microwave ovens. Even televisions and radios can generate electrical fields that may cause headaches. For starters, you should, therefore, use a glare-free screen or radiation filter on your computer monitor.

Laser printers and copy machines can emit ozone, a colorless, odorless gas to which some people are sensitive. Keep such units at a distance from your work area, make sure exhaust ports are directed away from your desk, and take frequent breaks.

Stress from inadequate or poorly designed lighting can produce eyestrain and headaches. Consider using full-spectrum compact fluorescent lights, or bulbs made with neodymium. These bulbs produce a gentle illumination that's more like natural light and they also save energy and cost less to use.

TESTING THE WATERS

As we've all learned, water makes up between 60 and 70 percent of the body's total weight. Besides helping to transport blood, chemicals, food, and wastes, it also lubricates and protects our joints and organs. Water is a necessity of life. In fact, practically every comprehensive fitness/health/beauty program recommends drinking eight twelve-ounce glasses of H_2O each day.

Whether your water supply is derived from a public water system or a well on your property, there are three major threats to its suitability for drinking of which you should be aware:

► Microbes, including viruses, coliform and other bacteria, and even intestinal parasites.

> ☀ **INSIDER'S TIP:** Be sure to use only lead-free materials in all plumbing repairs or installations. Ask the plumber to show you the label from the packaging. It should clearly state that the product is lead-free.

► Chemicals such as lead, benzene, radium, nitrates, and dozens of other harmful contaminants.

► Disinfectant by-products—substances produced by chlorine when it reacts with residues from organic debris, such as decomposing leaves and other plant matter.

PUBLIC WATER SYSTEMS

In general, public water systems are the most worry-free from a mechanical, operating point of view. But that doesn't mean they're completely without concern. The water supply may be plentiful, but what about the quality? For example, the Environmental Protection Agency has estimated that up to 13 percent of the community water services in the United States do not meet the requirements of the Safe Drinking Water Act. We, therefore, must learn how to ensure the safety of our own water supply (see pages 209–11).

WATER WELLS

As anyone who has ever lived in the country knows, the location of a water well can be critical. A well should be located as close to the house as possible, yet as far from any septic disposal system as practical (preferably uphill from it). And well water that once tested safe may not always remain so. Neighbors may install sewage systems at the back or side of your property (most towns do mandate a certain distance between wells and septic systems), or rivers, swamps, and other bodies of water may become polluted and affect your supply.

Well water may also be contaminated through the homeowner's mishandling of the following hazardous household materials:

▶ Automotive products, including brake fluid, antifreeze, and motor oil.

▶ Household cleaners, including bleaches, disinfectants, drain cleaners, and oven cleaners.

▶ Paints and solvents.

▶ Pesticides and herbicides.

Follow the directions on the label concerning the disposal of any of these products and their containers. If you have questions, contact the Environmental

> 💡 **INSIDER'S TIP:** Never flush hazardous products down a toilet or drain. Sewage treatment plants may not be able to break down all the toxic ingredients, and some could enter the groundwater from which your drinking water is drawn. They can also wreak havoc with the biological processes that septic tank systems require to work efficiently. And never dump household toxins in a ditch or in a low area of the backyard.

Protection Agency (EPA) at 401 M Street, S.W., Washington, D.C. 20460, or call their toll-free number, 800–858–7378.

WATER QUALITY

How can you verify the quality of your water? By having it analyzed at a reputable testing laboratory. Signs of trouble include cloudy water; strong tastes and/or odors; or hard-to-clean stains on sinks, bathtubs, and laundry. Contact your local water or health department for the names of qualified independent testing labs.

WATER PURIFYING DEVICES

There are more than 500 manufacturers of water purification systems. The majority of these filtration devices fall into one of the following three categories:

▶ **ACTIVATED CARBON TREATMENT SYSTEMS**—These work by trapping certain contaminants (including many volatile organic chemicals and industrial solvents, as well as lead and certain pesticides) in charcoal filters. There are a wide variety of charcoal filters on the market, ranging from small (practically useless) units that screw on the end of a faucet, to whole-house systems that attach to the water main. The second of these requires periodic maintenance to prevent the breeding of bacteria in dirty filters. Whole-house units cost anywhere from $1,500 to $2,500.

▶ **DISTILLATION SYSTEMS**—Purification devices that fall into this category (which should be installed professionally) operate by heating water into steam and then cooling the steam until it condenses back to water, leaving volatile and non-volatile chemical contaminants behind. These systems also remove heavy metals such as cadmium, chromium, iron, and lead, as well as arsenic, nitrates, and sulfates. Used with a charcoal filter, distillation systems produce the purest water possible. Some units are small enough to fit on a countertop or under the sink, and they range in price from $225 to $1,500.

▶ **REVERSE-OSMOSIS (R-O)**—These devices force water through a membrane that filters out impurities. They are useful in removing arsenic, chlorine, cadmium, chromium, iron, lead, nitrates, radium, and sulfates, as well as certain parasites. Most reverse-osmosis units, however, use 2 to 3 gallons of water for every good gallon produced—the rest goes down the drain. Installed under the sink, these systems run between $250 and $1,000.

All the systems described above benefit distinctly from professional installation.

BYOB

Bottled water sales are increasing at a faster rate than any other beverage in the United States. In fact, one out of every fifteen households now uses it as the primary source of drinking water, according to a recent issue of *Consumer Reports* magazine. While many people buy bottled water because they think it tastes better than tap, many others do so because they are concerned about the safety of what's running out of their faucets.

The reality of the situation, however, is that bottled waters may not be any safer than what's coming out of your tap. And while it's true that standards of quality for bottled waters are at least as stringent as those for tap water, it's also a fact that up to 25 percent of bottled waters are little more than packaged tap water.

If you do opt for bottled water, at least check the label to see that the company packaging it is a member of a trade group known as the International Bottled Water Association (IBWA). Also look for the words "NSF-certified" on the bottle. Most IBWA members undergo a yearly unannounced plant inspection by the National Sanitation Foundation to make sure that certain standards are being met. However, not all IBWA members are NSF-certified.

Finally, here's a quick translation of what the wide variety of bottled water labels actually mean:

▶ **DISTILLED WATER** has been vaporized and recondensed. In the process, it is also demineralized.

▶ **NATURAL WATER** is H_2O that does not originate from a public supply (such as a municipal water system) and has not been modified by the addition or removal of any minerals. It comes from either wells or springs.

▶ **SPRING WATER** flows out of the earth on its own, unlike well water that has to be pumped. It is often labeled "natural spring water" and is unmodified by the addition or removal of minerals.

▶ **MINERAL WATER** is any undistilled water.

▶ **PURIFIED WATER** has been either distilled or processed by reverse-osmosis.

Armed with this information, you can now, confidently, drink to your health!

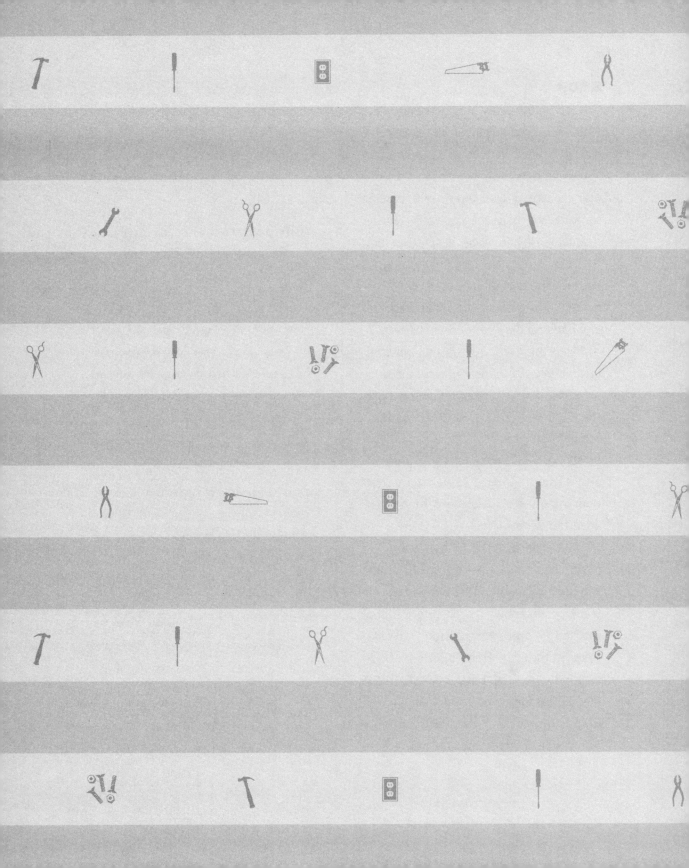

Family Safety

When asked what they hold dearest to their hearts, the vast majority of individuals surveyed would reply, without hesitation, their families. And yet, every year thousands of those who matter most are injured or killed in the "safety" of their own homes. Sadder still is the fact that most of these accidents could have been prevented. The key lies in being aware of the problem areas before tragedy strikes too close to (your) home.

CHILD-PROOFING YOUR HOME

No other class of individuals can be more creative when it comes to accidental injury than babies and young children can. Perhaps it's their natural curiosity, desire to explore, and general unfamiliarity with how things are supposed to work. In any event, make sure your child isn't among the one out of four under the age of three who will suffer an accidental home injury serious enough to require medical attention this year. Here are some particularly threatening areas to concentrate on.

CRIBS

Cribs are minisanctuaries for babies . . . right? After all, what in the world could possibly be safer than a child's crib? Well, for starters, how about teasing a strange pit bull during an August heat wave? Or maybe crossing an eight-lane freeway at rush hour with your eyes closed? In other words, cribs can be extremely dangerous—

even fatal—if not constructed and used properly.

If you assemble a crib yourself, make sure all the nuts and bolts are firmly secured so they can't be loosened by little fingers; then check them periodically. Test the crib by raising and lowering the side rails before putting it into service. If it wobbles or leans one way or the other, either repair what's loose or get another crib.

All of a crib's slats and posts should be solidly attached and spaced no more than 2⅜ inches apart. That also includes the space between the corner post and the sliding rail. If the slats are farther apart, a baby's body can slip through—while the head may not—resulting in possible strangulation. The mattress should fit snugly. If you can fit the width of two of your fingers between the mattress and sides, the mattress is too small or the crib is too big. A baby could slip through the gap and suffocate. And never put any kind of thin plastic material over the mattress. The plastic can cling to a child's face and cause him or her to smother.

OTHER HOUSEHOLD HAZARDS FOR TOTS

Remember, children love to climb and investigate . . . after all, it's a whole new world for them! You must, therefore, inspect your furniture for small or narrow openings. Youngsters have been known to strangle when their head or neck becomes caught in open V-shaped cutouts in pieces of furniture.

> **INSIDER'S TIP:** Keep dishwasher and compactor doors closed and latched at all times.

Wall mirrors should be securely fastened. A child should not be able to twist the fastening tabs so the mirror can fall from the wall. Protective film (available at hardware stores) can be applied over mirrors and windows to prevent splinters of glass from falling and flying through the air in case of breakage. Large paintings, drawings, and similar artwork should likewise be firmly hung on the wall, especially artwork located above couches and chairs that toddlers could climb.

Rocking chairs and recliners can easily pinch or cut a child's fingers. Show them the hazards and train young children to stay away. Screen off hot radiators and install childproof latches on cabinets that hold potentially dangerous items such as bleaches, detergents, disinfectants, or medicines. Keep all poisonous materials off countertops and in locked cabinets. Even in child-resistant containers, hazardous items should be kept out of sight and out of reach.

Remember to protect your electronic equipment. Televisions and VCRs can become popular playthings for toddlers, who find great satisfaction in pushing buttons, changing channels, and turning up the volume. A VCR locking mechanism is available at electronics stores; get one and use it if you have a toddler. You'll be glad you did!

> **INSIDER'S TIP:** Cover unused electrical outlets with plastic safety inserts.

If balusters on stairs and balconies are more than four inches apart, a barrier of some kind should be installed to prevent a child from either falling through or getting stuck. Stairways should have sturdy handrails. (You might consider installing a temporary handrail at a lower level so a toddler learning how to use the stairs can lean on the railing.) Safety gates should be installed at the top and bottom of all stairways.

BATHROOM SAFETY

You've heard the story before. A legendary mountain climber—renowned for scaling vertical heights from the Himalayas to the Alps with hardly a scratch—slips in his bathtub at home and breaks his neck. It's true that per square foot of space, the typical bathroom contains more hazards than any other room in the house. So let's get on with the business of family protection.

If your tub or shower has glass doors, be sure they are made of safety glass. While such material is commonly used now, in older homes it may not have been selected (or even an option) at the time the home was built. That goes for mirrors, too. Safety mirrors are the only kind to use in or near the tub or shower.

Turn off the tub and sink hot water faucets tightly so that children cannot turn them on easily. There are devices available, called "hot stop limits," to restrict how far a handle can be pushed to the hot side. And while we're on the subject, the comfort zone for hot water is between 95 and 105 degrees Fahrenheit. If children are involved, err on the lower side. Faucet spouts in tubs can pose particular dangers to little ones, who can slip and bump against the hard metal. Protective padding is available to prevent injury (and some entries are even cleverly designed as animals!). Again, if children are involved, you

should also consider installing a toilet lock to lock the lid down so a child can't lift it. And on the subject of locks, make sure that children can't lock themselves inside a bathroom. Many bathroom doors have push-button locks. These come with a small predrilled hole on the outside knob so that a piece of wire or a long nail inserted through the knob will unlock the door.

SAFEGUARDS FOR SENIORS AND THE DISABLED

As the huge class of baby boomers matures, increasing longevity will mean that more and more of our population reaches the age of 65 years and older. In fact, by the year 2020, approximately one out of every six individuals living in the United States will be in their late sixties.

That statistic is going to have an effect on home design and construction—especially with regard to kitchens and bathrooms. The government has already stipulated "universal design factors" in public government and other buildings, where wheelchair access is mandatory. That means bathrooms should be spacious enough to maneuver in. Wheelchairs are generally 42 to 45 inches long, and 22½ to 26½ inches wide. They require a 4½- to 5½-foot turning radius. Doorways for wheelchairs should, therefore, be at least 32 inches wide.

Bathrooms may also feature safety rails in the shower, tub, and toilet areas. Various manufacturers offer lines of support rails, grab handles, backrests, and shower seats that can be installed by a professional in existing bathrooms; some models may be raised or lowered, and most can be wall-mounted, free-standing, or floor-mounted. Hanging-ladder grab bars—nylon bars hung on ropes that are suspended from a wall or the ceiling—are designed to make getting out of the tub easier for a handicapped or elderly person.

KITCHEN SAFETY

The very nature of the work performed in kitchens, as well as the amount of time people tend to spend there, creates many opportunities for injury. And if you just think of what's to be found in the typical kitchen—sharp blades, hot cooking surfaces, boiling liquids, spattering cooking oil, wet and greasy surfaces, slippery floors, and a multitude of electrical appliances—it's not hard to see why. So here are the major hazards to watch out for in the room that is very often the center of family activity.

First of all, there are lots of ways to get cut in the kitchen. Among the many sharp kitchen instruments are knives, forks, shears, can openers and sharp can lids, glass containers that can drop and shatter on tile floors, food processor blades, plastic wrap packages, fruit and vegetable peelers, and graters. A classic way to get cut is to reach into a sink full of dirty dishwater and slice a finger on a chef's knife that someone has tossed. Consider washing knives and other sharp implements separately.

When unloading a dishwasher immediately after the washing or drying cycle has ended, avoid reaching down to grab utensils or other items that may have fallen to the bottom of the machine. You could accidently touch the heating element and get burned. Wait until after the heating element cools to retrieve stray objects.

Be especially careful with food processors. Children are naturally inquisitive and have been known to reach into the see-through processing bowls to try to play with the cutting blades. When purchasing microwave ovens, trash compactors, dishwashers, blenders, food processors, or small broiler ovens, opt for models that won't operate unless the doors or tops are fully closed. Trash compactors should be operated only by key, so children cannot just flip a switch and compact anything close at hand. Some compactors have control knobs that are easily removed and stored in a safe place between uses. Garbage disposals operated by a wall switch should have a safety lock for the same reason.

Most instruction booklets included with small appliances say to unplug the appliance when it is not in use. That's because if an appliance is plugged in, there's always the possibility of shock. Thermostat controls on appliances such as irons, electric sauté pans, and electric ovens don't always provide a complete "off" setting. They can be accidentally turned on, too.

A removable thermostat cord that's plugged into an outlet—but not into the appliance—can cause a shock if someone touches the open end. It may also short-circuit if water or another liquid spills on it. When using equipment with detachable electrical cords, plug the

> **INSIDER'S TIP:** The safest garbage disposals use bidirectional vibrators instead of whirring blades. Added safety features include fitted drain covers that keep silverware and other items from falling through. The drain cover can also function as the on-off mechanism for the disposal.

cord into the appliance first, and then into the wall, with dry hands. Keep electrical appliances such as clocks, radios, toasters, and similar units away from sinks, where they could fall into the water or be touched by wet hands.

By following the suggestions outlined in this chapter, your home can be the sanctuary of safety you want it to be for those you love the most.

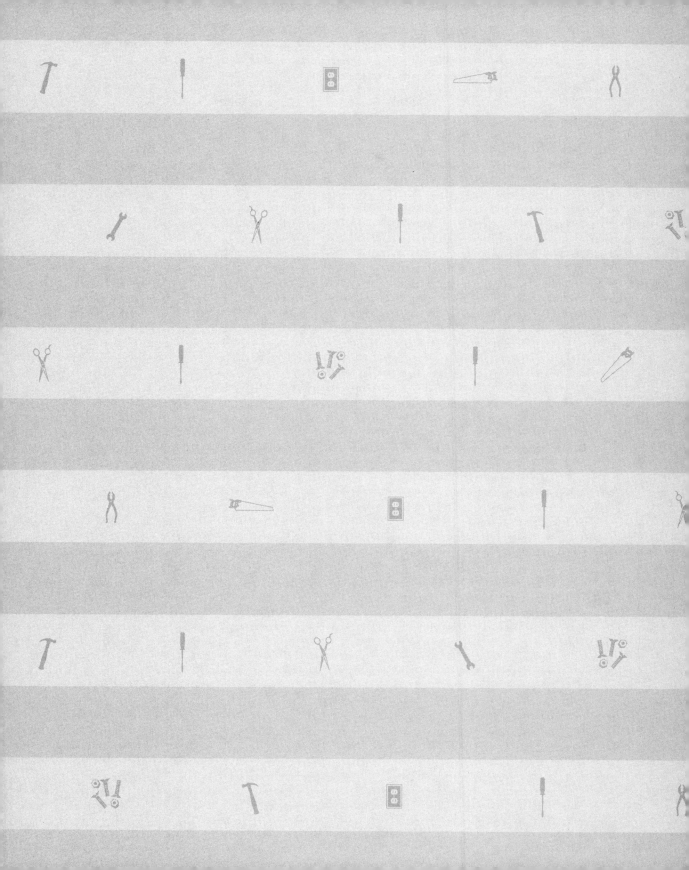

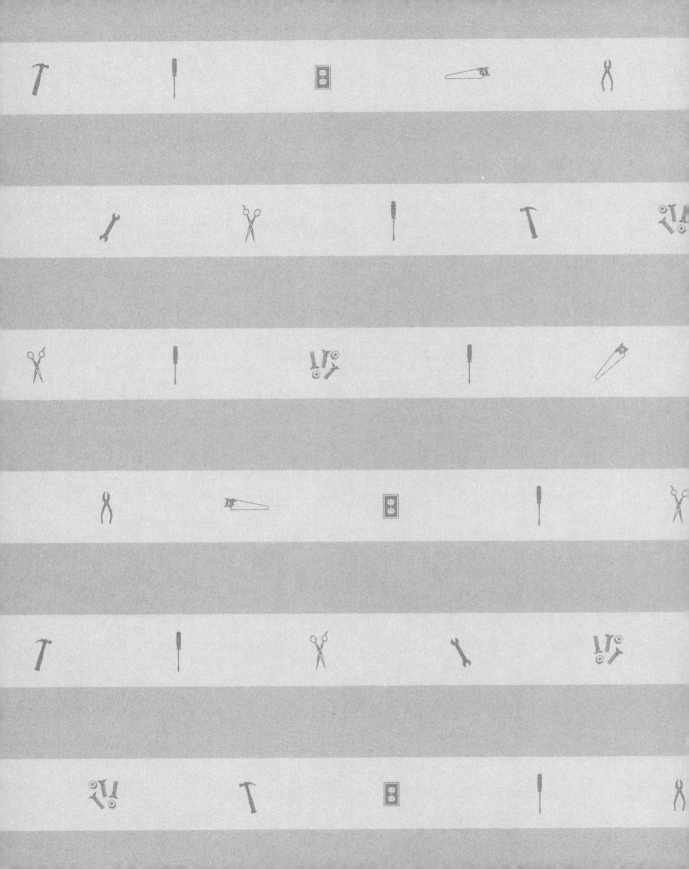

Outdoor Home Security

While we don't want to traumatize our children unnecessarily by hinting that there's a dirty old man hiding behind every tree, or that their room stands a very good chance of being ransacked by an intruder each time they leave the house, we must, nonetheless, instill a healthy regard for personal safety. The fact that crime seems to be on a continual rise is only validated by the steady increase in the number of requests Rent-A-Husband receives to install home security systems. After all, it *is* better to be safe than sorry; and an ounce of prevention is worth . . . well, you get the point.

Unless you live within the walls or fences of a private association or neighborhood, it's likely that the streets, roads, and walks of your neighborhood are open to anyone at any time of day or night. This chapter highlights the wide range of preventative steps that can be taken to discourage individuals who are either opportunists, professional burglars, thieves, or worse.

Common sense and attention to security can certainly tip the scales in your favor. And while no security is completely foolproof, you'll certainly be safer than the typical household by following the suggestions included here.

SAFETY SPECIFICS

▶ Whenever you go out—even if it's just into your own backyard—get into the habit of locking any doors beyond your line of sight.

- When you're away (or even at home) keep your garage doors closed and locked.

- Even though you might be on a first-name basis with the pizza delivery boy, keep *all* strangers (including those bearing fast food) outside your residence whenever possible.

- While no one would ever fault a good Samaritan, respond to someone else's apparent difficulties (such as a flat tire or other car trouble) in a way that guarantees safety to yourself.

- Whenever possible, take all measures necessary to ensure that the entrances to your home and garage are clearly visible from the street and/or from your neighbors' homes.

- Trim all foliage away from your house so it can't be used as a hiding place or to provide access to a second story.

- To give the impression that your residence is occupied (even when you're not actually at home), install a timer so that some lights inside or outdoors will always be turned on.

- If your garage is detached from your home, it is particularly important that the surrounding area be well lit at night.

- Although it seems like common sense to instill in children a sense of caution around swimming pools, ponds, reservoirs, lakes, and the like, the high incidence of children who drown every year indicates that many parents still believe their families will be the exception to the rule. It is, therefore, worth repeating (and taking to heart): *Teach your children to keep away from all bodies of water unless they're accompanied by a responsible adult.*

HOME SECURITY ALARM SYSTEMS

Almost every home can benefit from an alarm system. You just need to decide which one best suits your individual needs. To help you in this regard, it's advisable to call in professionals to analyze your specific security needs. Lock and alarm companies will perform on-site surveys, so be sure to compare their products and services carefully. Find out how many clients they have in your area, how long they've been in business, and whether they're willing to provide demonstrations of how their systems work under actual field conditions. Also, always check the company's references before "signing on the dotted line," and insist on getting both verbal and written instructions on the operation of the system you choose.

It's also wise to talk with local police and contact the National Burglar and Fire Alarm Association for a list of members in your area. Check your Yellow Pages for the listing or write to the national headquarters at 1133 Fifteenth Street, N.W., Washington, D.C. 20005. Or log on to their Website: www.alarm.org

Two basic alarm systems make up the majority of those purchased and installed in residential dwellings: in-house monitoring box systems and central monitoring systems. Here are the specifics of each:

IN-HOUSE MONITORING BOX SYSTEMS— These alarms have a monitoring box in- stalled in an out-of-the-way place within the house. If an intruder attempts to enter, the unit is activated and will set off a loud siren, bell, or horn. As long as there are neighbors who are close enough to respond to the alarm if you're away, this system usually works well. What can happen, however, is that whoever hears the sound will ignore it, assuming that it is a false alarm. Therefore, you should be sure that your neighbors know what the sound means and exactly what to do (call the police and anyone else you've specified), should they hear it.

CENTRAL MONITORING SYSTEMS— For a monthly fee, these home security systems are monitored twenty-four hours a day at a central location outside the home. When an illegal entry is attempted, an alarm is triggered, which alerts the monitoring station. They, in turn, immediately summon police, fire, or medical emergency assistance, as well as notify anyone else the homeowner has designated.

The following is an overview of other home security alarm systems currently on the market:

ANTI-INTRUSION ALARMS—Set up to provide one of two kinds of home protection: perimeter defense or internal space defense.

Establishing a *perimeter defense* means equipping the exterior doors and windows with sensors that will detect any unauthorized entry. An overview of the various types of perimeter protection includes:

▶ Magnetic switches attached to doors, windows, and adjacent frames are wired to signal a control unit when a magnet moves away from its switch.

▶ Thin ribbons of current-conduction foil attached to windows, door panels, and walls monitor any breaking of those surfaces. However, unless the foil is carefully camouflaged, it is very noticeable.

▶ Vibration or shock detectors monitor someone shaking or breaking through walls, doors, or windows.

▶ Special screens containing inconspicuous alarm wires are made to cover windows and other openings. They're installed so an alarm will sound if the entire screen is removed from the opening while the system is on.

▶ Perimeter alarms. Closed-circuit television with a hidden camera captures a picture of any exterior area around the house, which can be viewed on a monitor placed inside the residence. This setup does tend to be confining (what with continually having to monitor the monitor), and is of little use to a homeowner who is asleep or away from the viewing area.

INTERNAL SPACE PROTECTION—Intended to guard specific rooms or hallways, internal space protection is provided by several kinds of motion detectors or other types of sensors that are installed within the home. They include:

▶ Trip wires that, when placed across a room or hall, will sound an alarm when touched.

▶ Photoelectric "eyes" that cast an invisible infrared light beam across rooms, hallways, and other areas.

When the beam is interrupted, an alarm is triggered and sounds.

HALOGEN SOLAR-POWERED ALARMS— Absorb enough energy from the sun during the day to remain on guard throughout the evening hours. These security lights require no wires, so they can be installed almost anywhere with a screwdriver and a few simple fasteners. When motion from a nighttime intruder is detected, the unit floods the area with bright halogen light. During the day, a photoelectric cell keeps the light from activating. The adjustable detector senses movement up to about 75 feet away, turns on the light for 90 seconds, and continues to turn the light on every time that motion is detected.

ENTRY ALERT ALARMS—Used to protect exterior doors. Installed in minutes with no wiring involved, these units react by sounding a powerful 100-decibel alarm if a connected door is opened—by force or with a key. They can only be turned off, however, using a special 4-digit code number. An optional 15-second delay can be programmed into the alarm to allow the homeowner enough time to punch in the code.

WINDOW MINIALARMS—Small but effective units that provide at least 80 decibels of continuous sound when activated by an intruder. Because they are only a few inches long, these alarms, which run on several button-cell batteries, can be installed in a matter of minutes with double-backed tape.

Based upon a professional's advice, your financial situation, and your level of desired comfort, decide which type of alarm system is right for you.

> **INSIDER'S TIP:** Find out whether or not you will receive a discount on your homeowner's insurance with the alarm system you plan to install. If not, inquire as to which alarm system, if any, would result in a lower premium. It's definitely worth investigating, as a lower rate might make a higher-grade system "pay for itself."

And finally, once you have the alarm system, *remember to turn it on!*

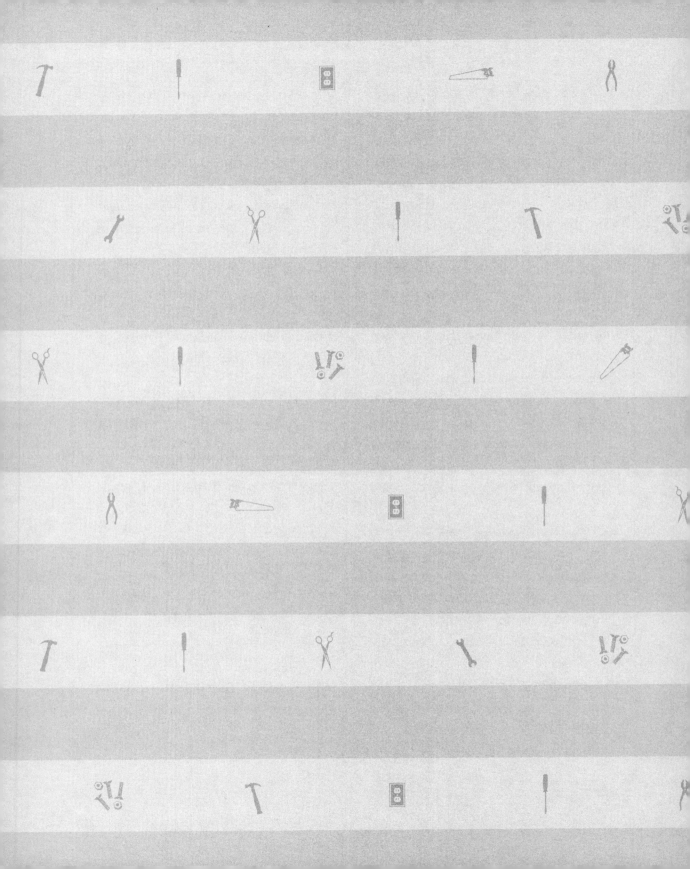

Restoring a House Divided

It seems fitting that this book should end where it all began for Rent-A-Husband: with tried and true advice for finding a peaceful resolution to chronic bickering over household chores. But if the nuggets of wisdom I've gleaned from years in the "trenches" have to be summed up in just a few words, the following are the ones I'd like to leave you with:

▶ **DELEGATE RESPONSIBILITY.** Remember, if you set yourself up as a superwoman (or -man) and continually take care of everything yourself, not only won't there be anything left for the rest of the family to do, they won't even notice that something hasn't been done.

▶ **SET REASONABLE STANDARDS.** Don't expect superhuman behavior from your family, either. We live in an extremely hectic world, and it's important to be realistic when it comes to any given workload.

▶ **FOLLOW THROUGH.** Don't, on the other hand, hesitate to remind other members of the household to do their part. Dividing the work is the only way to truly conquer it. Besides, sharing the load is good for everyone—it keeps you from visiting the "edge" too often, teaches kids responsibility that will serve them well, and allows your significant other to experience life more fully on the homefront.

► **DON'T ASSUME THE WORST.** If a member of the household does neglect a job he or she has agreed to do, resist resigning yourself to the fact that he or she is destined to become a professional slacker. Instead, be generous with *second* chances.

► **IF ALL ELSE FAILS, FLY THE COOP.** You'll be amazed at how fast the newly appreciative chicks will rally round upon your return from a short "vacation"!

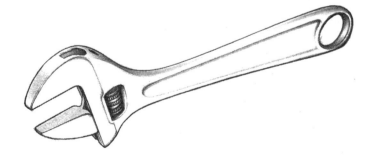

A

abrasives, 10, 11–12
acrylic admix, 121
acrylic latex, 13
acrylic primer-sealers, 84
adhesives, 11, 12–13
alarm systems, home security, 222–25
alkyd paints, 69–70
alkyd primer-sealers, 84
allen wrench, 17
aluminum oxide, 11
amperage, 45, 46
anchors, screw, 8, 150
anchors, wall, 8, 150
anti-intrusion alarms, 224
appliances
    fire hazards from, 202–3, 204
    safety precautions for, 159, 217–18
    shorts caused by, 45
architectural drawings, 133
asbestos, in vinyl squares, 114
awl, 10

B

backsaw, 16
ball peen hammer, 15
basements, 198–99
baskets, for storage, 152, 153, 158, 163, 169
bathrooms
    assessing storage space in, 161–63
    ceramic tiles in, 120
    child-proofing, 215–16
    for elderly and disabled, 216–17
    mildew in, 84
    paint type for, 70
    safety hazards in, 216–17
    storage containers for, 163–64
    storing linens in, 164–65
bedroom(s). See also children's rooms
    armoires and dressers in, 172–73
    assessing storage space in, 171–72
    closets, organizing, 173–74
    wall storage system for, 172
beds
    cribs, 213–14
    storage space under, 152, 172
    types of, 180, 181
benzene, 200
biological contaminants, 196–99
blistering, 73
block plane, 14
booking, 89–91
bottled water, 211
box-end wrenches, 18
box nails, 7
brads, 7
bricklayer's chisel, 14
brushes, paint, 71–72, 74–75
building codes and permits, 135, 137
bullnose tiles, 119
butt chisel, 13
butt seam, 96

C

cabinet screwdriver, 17
cape chisel, 13
carbon monoxide, 201–2
carpenter's level, 8–9
carpeting
    buying, 127
    damp or wet, 198
    laying down, 126
    odors, removing, 127, 129
    stains, removing, 126–29
cartridge faucet leaks, 36–37
casting nails, 7
caulks, 13
ceilings
    paint type for, 70
    storage space in, 152, 173
cement bases, 121
central monitoring systems, 223
ceramic tiles
    in bathrooms, 120
    buying, 119–20
    cracked or broken, repairing, 125–26
    evaluating floor surface for, 120
    grouting, 123–25
    installing, materials for, 120–21
    installing, technique for, 122–25
    professional help for, 120
    quantity needed, calculating, 119–20
    sealers for, 125
    templates for, 122
    types of, 119
chalk lines, drawing, 109, 122
chemical products, 200–201, 215
child-proofing
    cabinets, 215
    cribs, 213–14
    furniture, 214
    kitchens, 214, 215
    stairways, 216
    TVs and VCRs, 215
    wall mirrors and artwork, 214, 215
children's rooms
    adaptable furniture for, 177–78
    baby's storage needs, 178
    children's storage needs, 178–79
    overnight guests in, 179, 180
    paint type for, 70
    shared, 179
    study space in, 181
    teen's storage needs, 179–81

chimes, doorbell, replacing, 61
chisels, 13–14
circuit breakers
    amperage of, 45
    exposed wires around, 43–44
    labeling, 44
    main breaker switch, 43, 44
    purpose of, 42–43
    testing, 48
    tripped, 45, 202
circular saw, 17
claw hammer, 5
closet auger, 24–25
closets
    alternatives to, 180, 184
    bedroom, organizing, 173–74
    linen, for children's toys, 180
    walk-in, for minioffice, 185
clothes, storing, 173–74, 180, 184
combination square, 15
combination wrenches, 18
common nails, 7
compression faucet
    description of, 31
    disassembling, tip for, 33
    drips in, 31–35
    handles, leaks in, 35
contact adhesives, 12
contractors
    final contract with, 135–36
    interviewing, 134
    large upfront payments to, 136
    obtaining bids from, 134
    payment schedule with, 135–38
    punch list for, 138
    references for, calling, 133–34
    reputable, locating, 132–33
    steps prior to hiring, 132
    videos of work by, 137
    who bail out on job, 136
coping saw, 16
cords, electrical shocks from, 218
cords, fire hazards from, 202–3
cords, lamp, replacing, 57–58
countertops, ceramic tiles for, 119
cover-up primers, 69
cracks, in ceramic tile, 125–26
cracks, in walls, 66
cribs, child-proofing, 213–14
crosscut saw, 16
cupboard shelves, labeling, 156

"cutting in," 64, 73
cyanoacrylates, 13

D

diamond-point chisel, 14
dimmer switch, replacing, 52–53
disabled citizens, 216–17
dishwashers, safety around, 214, 217
doorbell, replacing, 58–61
doors
    child-proof locks on, 216
    locking, for security, 221–22
    paints for, 69–70, 71
    wallpapering around, 101–2
double-cut file, 14
double-cutting, 100
drain traps, 22–23
"drain" wire, 47
drills, 6, 14
drop match, 88–89
duct tape, 10
dust mask, 11

E

eggshell paints, 70
elderly citizens, 216–17
electrical outlets
    child-proofing, 215
    fire hazards of, 202
    replacing, 54
    wallpapering around, 102–3
electrical panel
    description of, 42–44
    exposed wires in, 43–44, 47
    labeling, 44
    locating, 43
    safety precautions, 43–44, 47
    shutting off power to, 47
electrical system
    description of, 42–44, 47
    safety precautions, 42, 43–44, 47, 202, 218
electrical wires
    colors of, 47
    "hot," testing, 48
    safety precautions, 47, 202, 218
    sizes of, 46
    types of, 47
electric drill, 6
emery, 11

Enrich bulbs, 58
entry alert alarms, 225
epoxy adhesives, 12
epoxy bases, 121
ergonomics, 155
eye goggles, 11

F

faceplates, wallpapering around, 102–3
faucet(s)
    compression, 31–35
    drips in, 31–37
    handles, leaks in, 35
    spouts, padding for, 216
    washerless, 31, 36–37
feng shui, 185
field tiles, 119
filing cabinets, 152, 189–90
filing tools, 9, 14
finishing nails, 7
fire extinguishers, 206–7
fire hazards
    emergency escape plan for, 207
    fire extinguishers, 206–7
    smoke detectors, 204–5
    sources of, 202–4
fireplaces, 169, 201, 203
flapper tank ball, 28, 29, 30
flat chisel, 13
flat head screwdriver, 6–7
flat-head screws, 7
flat paints, 70
flint, 11
float rod mechanism, 26, 27
float (tool), 121
flocked paper, 78
flooring. See also carpeting; ceramic tiles; sheet
    vinyl; vinyl squares
    indentations in, preventing, 114
    old, removing, 106–8
foil wall coverings, 77–78
food preparation area, organizing, 158–59
food processors, safety around, 217–18
food storage, organizing, 157–58
formaldehyde, 12, 200
freezers, 158
furniture. See also storage
    child-proofing, 214
fuses, electrical
    amperage of, 46

exposed wires around, 43–44
labeling, 44
purpose of, 43
replacing, 45–46
safety precaution, 46
testing, 48
tripped, 45, 202
worn-out, identifying, 45

G

garbage disposals, safety around, 218
garnet, 11
gas stoves, 201
glass, safety, 215
glass shelves, 147
gloss paints, 71
gloves, work, 11
glue. *See* adhesives
goggles, eye, 11
grass cloth, 77
green board, 120
"ground" wire, 47
grouting, 123–25

H

hacksaw, 9
hallways
    furniture in, 184
    lighting in, 184
    office space in, 184
    organizing, 183–84
    paint type for, 70
    storage space in, 152
halogen solar-powered alarms, 225
hammers, 5, 15
hand drill, 14
handle leaks, 35
hand-screened papers, 78
hardware stores, advice from, 5, 133
heating equipment, 203
heavy-duty stapler, 11
hemp, 77
herbicides, 201
high-gloss paints, 71
holes, in subfloor, 108
holes, in walls, 66–68
"holidays," 74
home office
    desk area, 188–89

filing cabinets, 189–90
healthy environment for, 207
infrequently used items in, 190–91
shelving for, 188–89, 190
in walk-in closet, 185
in wide hallway, 184
work zones in, 187–88
home security, indoor, 213–18
home security, outdoor, 221–25
"hot stop limits," 216
"hot" wire, 47
houseplants, 198, 200

I

indoor air pollutants. *See also* fire hazards;
        water quality
    biological contaminants, 196–99
    carbon monoxide, 201–2
    chemical products, 200–201
    home office equipment, 207
    radon, 199–200
in-house monitoring box systems, 223
instant-bonding adhesives, 13
internal space protection, 224–25

J

jigsaw, 17
joint compound, 16

K

keyhole saw, 16
kitchen(s)
    appliances, safety precautions for, 159, 204,
        217–18
    areas and items, categorizing, 156
    child-proofing, 214, 215
    cupboard shelves, labeling, 156
    ergonomics, 155
    fire hazards, 204
    food preparation areas, 158–59
    food storage areas, 157–58
    paint type for, 70
    sink areas, 156–57
knee pads, 11
knife, putty, 11
knife, razor, 107
knife, utility, 9–10

L

lag screws, 7
lamp cords, replacing, 57–58
lamp sockets, replacing, 56–57
lap marks, 74
lap seam, 98
latex-based adhesives, 12
latex paints, 69–70
  brushes for, 71, 74–75
latex primers, 68
lead paint, 64–65
level, carpenter's, 8–9
liens, property, 136
lightbulbs, 58
lights, security, 225
light switches
  defective, identifying, 48–49
  dimmer, replacing, 52–53
  nonfunctioning, 48–50
  three-way, replacing, 50–52
  two-way, replacing, 49–50
linen closets, 180
linens, storing, 164–65
liner paper, 77
living rooms, 167–69
lo-luster paints, 70
longnose pliers, 8

M

main circuit breaker, 43, 44
mallet, 15
mask, dust, 11
masonry nails, 7
mason's hammer, 15
mastics, 12, 121
measuring tools, 8–9, 10, 15
metal file, 9
metal office shelving, 147
meter box, 42
mildew, removing, 65, 84
mirrors, child-proofing, 214, 215
mirrors, to enlarge room, 162
mold, household, 197–98
"Molly bolts," 150
murals, 78
Mylar, 78

N

nails, 7
needle-nose pliers, 8
neon circuit tester, 48
"neutral" wire, 47
notched trowel, 106

O

oil-based paints, 69–70
  brushes for, 71, 74–75
oil-based primers, 68
open-end wrenches, 18
organic bases, 121
O-ring, 32, 35, 36, 37
outlets. *See* electrical outlets
oval-head screws, 7
overflow tube, toilet tank, 25, 26, 27, 29, 30
oxalic acid, 129

P

packing leaks, 35
packing nut, 32, 34, 35
paint
  brushes, 71–72, 74–75
  latex, 69–70
  lead-based, 64–65
  oil-based, 69–70
  paint tray for, 70
  primary color, types of, 69–71
  primer, types of, 68–69
  quantity needed, estimating, 71
  rollers, 72–73, 74–75
  running out of, 74
painting. *See also* paint
  blistering effect, 73
  cleanup procedure, 74–75
  "cutting in," 64, 73
  odors, tip for removing, 71
  painter's tape for, 70, 73
  preparing surfaces for, 64–68
  techniques, 73–74
paper weave, 77
paring chisel, 13
particleboard, 147
paste adhesives, 12
patching materials, 15–16
patching plaster, 16
pattern repeat, 75, 80
payment schedules, contractor, 135–38

peelable wallpaper, 75, 83
perforated rasp, 14
pesticides, 201
Phillips head screwdriver, 6–7
pipe wrench, 18
plane, block, 14
plane, smoothing, 14
plastic adhesives, 12
pliers, 8
plugs, electrical, 55–56, 202–3
plumb bob, 15
plumbing system, description of, 22–24
plumb line, 15
   drawing, 86–88
   hanging strips along, 91–92, 98, 99–101
   on uneven walls, 95
plunger, 23, 24
plywood, 147
plywood subfloor, 120
pocket chisel, 13
polarized plug, 55
polyvinyl resin, 12
pots and pans, storing, 158–59
prepasted wallpaper, 76, 89
primary color paints
   buying, 70
   gloss levels, 70–71
   latex, 69–70
   oil-based, 69–70
   quantity needed, estimating, 71
   testing before buying, 70
primers
   applying, tip for, 69
   types of, 68–69
   when to use, 68
primer-sealer, 84
property liens, 136
pry bar, 107
public water systems, 208
punch list, 138
push drill, 14
putty, wood, 15
putty knife, 11

Q

"quick-connect" replacement plug, 55

R

radiation, from electronics, 207
radon, 199–200
random match, 88, 89
rasp, perforated, 14
razor knife, 107
refrigerators, 158
renovations, 132, 133. *See also* contractors
resorcinol, 12
ripping claw hammer, 15
ripsaw, 16
rollers, paint, 72–73, 74–75
round-head screws, 7
rubber-based adhesives, 12
ruler, steel or straightedge, 15

S

saber saw, 17
safety glass, 215
sandpaper, 10. *See also* abrasives
satin paints, 70
saws, 9, 16–17
scissors, 10
screw anchors, 8, 150
screwdrivers, 6–7, 17
screws, 7, 8
sealants, 13
sealing primers, 69
seat-grinding tool, 33
seat-removing tool, 34
security lights, 225
semigloss paints, 70
senior citizens, 216–17
setscrews, 17
sewer gases, 22–23
sheet vinyl
   buying, 115
   cutting, 116
   damaged, repairing, 118–19
   description of, 106
   installing, 115–18
   quantity needed, calculating, 115
   templates for, 116
   under toilet, 112
shelving
   bathroom, 162
   bedroom, 174
   built-in, 147, 148, 151
   freestanding, 147, 151
   home office, 188–89, 190

installing, 148–51
kitchen, labeling, 156
materials, 147
supports for, 147–49
wall-mounted, 146–47, 148–51
short, electrical, 43, 45
shut-off valve, toilet tank, 30–31
shut-off valves, water, 23–24
silicon carbide, 12
silicone, 13
single-cut file, 14
single slot screwdriver, 6–7
sinks
drain traps under, 22–23
kitchen, 156–57
patching ceramic tiles around, 122
sledgehammer, 15
slip-joint pliers, 8
smoke detectors, 204–5
smoothing plane, 14
socket wrenches, 18
softwood, 147
solid paper wall coverings, 78
space heaters, 201, 203
spacers, for ceramic tiles, 121
spackling compound, 16
spice racks, 159
spring toggle anchor, 150
stairways, 184, 215
stapler, heavy-duty, 11
steel ruler, 15
steel tape measure, 10
steel wool, 12
storage. *See also* shelving
in alcoves, 184, 185
assessing need for, 153
assessing overall spaces for, 143–44
in bathrooms, 161–65
in bedrooms, 171–74
in children's rooms, 177–81
in entrance halls, 183–84
furniture used for, 168–69, 184
in home offices, 187–91
in kitchens, 155–59
in living rooms, 167–69
quick fix ideas for, 152–53
under stairways, 184
units, built-in, 144–45
units, freestanding, 146, 147
units, modular, 145
stoves, gas, 201

stoves, wood, 201, 203
straightedge ruler, 15
straight match, 88, 89
strip, defined, 85
strippable wallpaper, 75, 82–83
stud finder, 148, 149
subcontractors, 136, 138
subfloor, defined, 120
suitcases, for storage, 171

T
tack hammer, 15
tape measure, steel, 10
terminal screws, 50
textile wall coverings, 77
thin-set adhesives, 121
three-payment schedule, 136–38
three-way light switch, 50–52
tile nippers, 122
timers, light, 222
toilet(s). *See also* toilet tank
child-proofing, 216
clogs in, 23, 24–25
inability to flush, 27–29
incomplete flush in, 27
installing vinyl flooring around, 112, 115
patching ceramic tiles around, 122
running water in, 29–31
seats, replacing, 37–38
toilet tank
gallons per flush, reducing, 27
mechanical parts in, 26
overflow mechanism in, 25
water level, lowering, 29–31
water level, raising, 27
toilet tank ball, 26, 27–29
toilet tank float ball, 26, 29–30
tools. *See also specific tools*
buying, 4–5
caring for, 5
expanded kit items, 11–18
starter kit items, 5–11
storing, 4
transformer, doorbell, 58, 59, 60–61
trash compactors, safety around, 214, 218
trichloroethylene, 200
trim tiles, 119, 122
two-prong plug, 55–56

U

universal primers, 68–69
urine odors and stains, 129
utility carts, 158
utility knife, 9–10

V

valve seat, compression, 31
    replacing, 34–35
    resurfacing, 33–34
VCR locking mechanisms, 215
videos, of contractor's work, 137
vinyl latex, 13
vinyl squares
    around toilet, 112
    asbestos in, 114
    cutting, 112
    damaged, replacing, 112–14
    description of, 106
    for heavy traffic areas, 112
    installing, 108–12
    quantity needed, calculating, 108
vinyl wallpapers, 76
volt-ohm meter, 61

W

wall anchors, 8, 150
wall coverings. *See also* wallpaper
    buying, 78–80
    quantity needed, calculating, 78–80
    types of, 75–78
wallpaper
    air bubbles in, 90
    around large openings, 101–2
    around small openings, 102–3
    buying, 78–80
    covering inside corners, 97–98
    covering outside corners, 99–101
    damaged, fixing, 83
    drawing plumb line for, 86–88
    hanging first strip, 91–95
    hanging second strip, 96
    inspecting for flaws, 80, 85
    lumps in, 90
    old, removing, 82–83
    prepasted, soaking, 89
    priming walls for, 84
    problems, anticipating, 85–86
    quantity needed, calculating, 78–80
    scraps, saving, 82
    strips, cutting, 88–89
    strips, defined, 85
    tools for applying, 80–82
    types of, 75–76
    wrinkles in, 102
walls. *See also* shelving; wall coverings;
        wallpaper
    ceramic tiles for, 119
    cracks in, repairing, 66
    holes in, repairing, 66–68
    locating studs in, 148, 149
    mildew on, 65
    organizers hung on, 152, 188
    paint brushes and rollers for, 71–73
    painting, 73–74
    painting, preparing for, 65–68
    paints for, 69–71
    primers for, 68–69
washer, compression, 31–33
washer, defined, 32
washerless faucets, 31, 36–37
water, safety around, 222
water-based paints, 69–70
water heater, 24
water quality
    of bottled water, 211
    contaminants and, 208, 209
    of private wells, 208–9
    of public water systems, 208
    purifying devices for, 210
    testing, 209
water shut-off valves, 23–24
WD-40, 11
windows
    minialarms for, 225
    paints for, 69–70, 71
    wallpapering around, 101–2
wires. *See* electrical wires
wire strippers, 57
wood chisel, 13
wood knots, cutting into, 9
wood putty, 15
wood screws, 7
wood stoves, 201, 203
work gloves, 11
wrenches, 6, 8, 17–18

Propelled by our ongoing commitment to redefine the handyman image in a most positive and trustworthy light, we are currently in the process of expanding Rent-A-Husband's worldwide family of franchises, one solid member at a time. If you would like more information about possibly joining this groundbreaking and dynamic organization as a franchisee, please contact us at our corporate headquarters:

RENT-A-HUSBAND, LLC.
1041 Brighton Ave.
Portland, Maine 04102
(207) 879–7425
FAX (207) 879-7400
www.Rent-A-Husband.com

Be sure to visit our Web site to view the wide array of official Rent-A-Husband® products, all of which reflect the highest possible quality, the standard on which our company is built.